THEY SHALL

THEY SHALL EXPEL DEMONS

DEREK PRINCE

And He went through all Galilee,
preaching in their synagogues
and *expelling the demons.*

MARK 1:39, EMPHASIS ADDED

And signs shall attend those who
believe, even such as those. By making
use of My name they shall *expel demons.*

MARK 16:17, EMPHASIS ADDED

(*The New Testament in Modern Speech*
by Richard Francis Weymouth)

Contents

PART ONE
Fundamentals

NEARLY TWO THOUSAND YEARS AGO JESUS CAME to the help of suffering humanity, working miracles by healing the sick and casting out demons. Throughout the three and a half years of His earthly ministry, this never changed.

In the intervening centuries Christian men and women have been called from time to time with miraculous ministries to the sick and afflicted. Yet, as far as I know, there are few, if any, records of people with a ministry of casting out demons comparable to that of Jesus'. As a result, most victims of demonic oppression have been left to suffer without any offer of practical help from the Church.

The time has come, I believe, to clear away the rubble of religious tradition that has obscured the clear revelation of the New Testament, and to reestablish the Church's ministry on the bedrock of Jesus and the gospels.

ONE

How Did Jesus Do It?

WHEN A MEMBER OF MY CONGREGATION LET OUT a blood-curdling shriek and collapsed just in front of my pulpit, I had to make a split-second decision. I called on some others to help me and, in the name of Jesus, we succeeded in driving out the demon (or evil spirit). That experience in 1963 propelled me into intensive study of the ministry of Jesus. I wanted to be certain my actions were in line with His.

Mark begins his record of the public ministry of Jesus, I discovered, with an incident in which a demon challenged Him as He was teaching in a synagogue in Galilee. This encounter spread His fame immediately throughout the whole of Galilee (see Mark 1:21–28).

From that point on, we see Jesus dealing with demons wherever He encountered them during the three and a half years of His public ministry. Near the end of that time, He sent a message to Herod that He would continue to cast out demons and perform cures until His earthly task was completed (see Luke 13:32).

But the ministry was not to end then! When Jesus commissioned His followers, He transmitted His authority to them. In fact, He never sent anyone out to preach the Gospel without specifically instructing and equipping that person to take action against demons in the same way that He Himself did. I can find no basis anywhere in the New Testament for an evangelistic ministry that does not include the expelling of demons. This is as true today as it was in the time of Jesus.

I soon came to realize that Satan has developed a special opposition to this ministry. He is, by choice, a creature of darkness. He prefers to keep the true nature of his activities concealed. If he can keep humanity unaware of his tactics – or even of his very existence – he can use the twin tools of ignorance and fear to open the way for his destructive purposes. Unfortunately, ignorance and fear are not confined to non-Christians. They are often at work inside the Church. All too often Christians have treated demons with superstitious dread, as if they are in the same category as ghosts or dragons. Corrie ten Boom commented that the fear of demons is from the demons themselves.

For this reason, I chose the verb *expel* (Weymouth) for the title of this book, to describe the action of dealing with demons. *Expel* is a familiar, everyday word that has no special religious overtones. It brings the whole ministry down to the level of everyday life.

Jesus Himself was extremely practical in His dealings with demons. At the same time, He emphasized the unique significance of this ministry of expelling demons when He said, "But if I cast out demons by the Spirit of God, surely the kingdom of God has come upon you" (Matthew 12:28).

Casting out demons demonstrated two important spiritual truths. First, it revealed the existence of two opposing spiritual kingdoms: the Kingdom of God and the kingdom of Satan. Second, it demonstrated the victory of God's Kingdom over Satan's. Obviously, Satan would prefer to keep these two truths hidden!

When Jesus cast out demons, He went beyond the precedents of the Old Testament. From the time of Moses onward, God's prophets had performed many miracles that foreshadowed the ministry of Jesus. They had healed the sick, raised the dead, made miraculous provision for multitudes, and demonstrated God's power to control the forces of nature. But there is no record that any of them had ever cast out a demon. This was reserved for Jesus. It was a unique demonstration that the Kingdom of God had come upon the people of His day.

This makes it all the more remarkable that this ministry has been largely ignored by the contemporary

Church in many parts of the world. Evangelism, especially in the West, has frequently been practiced as if demons did not exist. Let me say, as graciously as possible, that evangelism that does not include the casting out of demons is not New Testament evangelism. I will take this a step further and apply it to the ministry of praying for the sick. It is unscriptural to pray for the sick if one is not prepared also to cast out demons. Jesus did not separate one from the other.

On the other side, there are those today who carry this practice of casting out demons to unscriptural extremes. They give the impression that any kind of problem – physical, emotional or spiritual – should be treated as demonic. But this approach is unbalanced and unscriptural. Sometimes, too, deliverance is carried out in a way that gives more prominence to the minister or to the one receiving deliverance than to the Lord Jesus.

Personally, I see this as further evidence of Satan's special and intense opposition to the ministry of deliverance. If possible, he seeks to exclude it altogether from the Church's program. Failing that, his aim is to discredit it.

For my part, I certainly did not volunteer! As I said, I was confronted by situations in which I was forced to choose between two alternatives: taking action against the demons or backing down and giving way to them. Looking back, I am glad I chose not to back down.

My primary motive in writing this book is to help others in ways that I myself have been helped. I have in mind two specific groups of people.

First, some people are under demonic oppression who do not know how to get free and are enduring the various degrees of torment that demons inflict. In some cases, the mental, emotional and physical torment is as severe as that of people imprisoned and tortured in totalitarian prison camps or gulags. I sincerely believe that it is the purpose of Jesus, through the Gospel, to offer hope and release to such people.

Second, there are those who have been called to the ministry of the Gospel but who are sometimes confronted by people who need desperately to be delivered from demons. Yet nothing in their background or training has equipped them to provide the kind of help that is needed so urgently.

I can identify with people in both of these categories. As a young preacher I was so tormented by uncontrollable bouts of depression that I was actually tempted to give up my ministry altogether. Later, when confronted by people I longed to help, I could not because of my own doctrinal preconceptions and uncertainties. I kept asking myself, *How could it be that so many Christians are oppressed by demons?*

I can now look back over more than thirty years, however, in which scarcely a single month has passed without my being involved in helping someone who needed deliverance from demons. This means that the lessons I share in this book have a solid basis – first on Scripture, then on personal observation and experience.

At times the ministry of deliverance has provoked misunderstanding and criticism from other Christians, but this is far outweighed by the satisfaction of helping desperate people. Recently my wife, Ruth, and I were out walking in Jerusalem when a Jewish woman in her fifties came up to me and asked, "Are you Derek Prince?" When I nodded, she said, "I owe my life to you," her eyes filling with tears. "Twenty years ago, I was so demonized that there was no hope for me. Then I met Jesus and somebody gave me your tapes on deliverance. Now I'm free! The people who knew me said I was like somebody who got up out of a wheelchair."

Testimonies like that make me glad I did not back down before criticism and opposition.

My experience over these years has also greatly reinforced my confidence in the accuracy of Scripture. Liberal theologians often suggest that the descriptions of demonic activity in the New Testament are not to be taken literally, but are simply a concession to the superstitious ignorance of the people in Jesus' time. To the contrary, I must affirm that, time and time again, I have witnessed demonic manifestations that are exactly in line with the descriptions of the New Testament. In this as well as other respects, the record of the New

Testament is totally accurate. It provides the one, all-sufficient basis for our ministry today.

In this book I seek, first, to lay a solid, scriptural foundation, and then to build on it a practical explanation of what is involved in dealing with demons. The foundation, as I have indicated, is the ministry of Jesus Himself. But before we can build on this foundation, we must clear away some misunderstandings due to misleading or inaccurate terminology that has been traditionally used in English versions of the New Testament. This will be the theme of the following chapter.

Since it was my own personal experience that led me into this ministry, I describe this in some detail in Part 2. Then, in Part 3, I respond to the seven questions I have encountered most frequently in my ministry. Finally, in Part 4, I give practical systematic teaching on how to recognize and expel demons and walk in victory.

Questions for This Study

1. How was the ministry of casting out demons to continue after Jesus ascended to heaven?
2. What are Satan's two main tools in opposing the ministry of casting out demons?
3. Name two important truths the ministry of expelling demons demonstrates.
4. According to the New Testament, is it scriptural to evangelize or pray for the sick without being prepared to deal with demons?
5. What are the two foundations presented from the teachings in this book?

Life Application

1. Before you were a believer, what was your perception of "casting out demons"?
2. What is your present understanding of this ministry? What experiences have led to this present understanding?
3. Does approaching this subject cause fear or dread to rise in you? If so, why?

Memory Verse

"But if I cast out demons by the Spirit of God, surely the kingdom of God has come upon you." Matthew 12:28

Faith Response

Lord, remove any resistance I may have to this ministry or to helping others receive the ministry of expelling demons.

Answers are on page 407

TWO
Terminology

THE NEW TESTAMENT WRITERS GIVE A CLEAR PIC-
ture of the nature and activity of demons, but the key
to understanding these areas is an accurate explanation
of the terminology they used. Unfortunately, there are
weaknesses in the way different English versions have
translated certain expressions from the original Greek
text, which have obscured the meaning for English
readers. It is necessary, therefore, to begin by examining
the main words used in the Greek.

Three expressions are used to describe the evil spirit
beings who are some of Satan's main agents in his warfare against humanity. First, *demon* (Greek, *daimonion*).
This is the neuter singular of the adjective *daimonios*,
which is derived from the noun *daimon*. Thus, the
adjective *daimonios* indicates some connection with
a *daimon*. Although *daimonion* is adjectival in form, it
is used regularly as a noun. It is, in fact, an adjective

that has become a noun. We can illustrate this from a contemporary example in English. *Green* is another adjective that has become a noun, describing a person concerned about protecting the environment. Hence, we now talk of the "greens."

In English the important distinction between *daimon* and *daimonion* is obliterated by the fact that both words are normally translated by one and the same English word: *demon*. Throughout this book, however, wherever it is necessary to preserve the distinction, we will continue to use the Greek words transliterated into English and italicized – that is, *daimon* and *daimonion*. We will form the plural in English simply by adding *s*, although this is not the correct way to form the plural in Greek.

The reference to the original Greek indicates that there are two distinct entities: *daimon*, which is primary, and *daimonion*, which is derivative. (This has an important bearing on the nature of demons, to which we will return in chapter 11, "What Are Demons?") The derivative form, *daimonion*, occurs about sixty times in the gospels, Acts and Revelation. In other words, it represents an important New Testament concept. In the best texts, *daimon* occurs only once – in Matthew 8:31, where it is apparently used with the same meaning as *daimonion*. But this is not a normal use.

The second expression used in the New Testament

to describe an evil spirit is *unclean spirit*, used about twenty times in Luke, Acts and Revelation.

The third expression, *evil spirit*, is used six times in Luke and Acts.

In Luke 4:33 two of these expressions are combined as the writer speaks of "a spirit of an unclean demon" (*daimonion*).

Altogether it seems that all three expressions are used interchangeably. "Demons" are "unclean spirits" and also "evil spirits."

The original King James Version regularly translates *daimonion* as "devil." This has led to endless confusion. The English word *devil* is actually derived from the Greek word *diabolos*, which has no direct relationship with *daimonion*. *Diabolos* means "slanderer." In all but three occurrences in the New Testament, it is a title of Satan himself. In this sense it is used only in the singular form. There are many demons but only one devil.

Satan is given this title because his primary activity is to slander – that is, to defame a person's character. First and foremost, Satan defames the character of God Himself. He did this in the Garden of Eden, when he suggested to Adam and Eve that God was not treating them fairly by withholding from them the knowledge of good and evil. Second, Satan defames the character of all those who in any way represent God. This is his primary weapon against the servants of God. All the main translations subsequent to the KJV have observed the distinction between *diabolos* and *daimonion*, and have translated *diabolos* as "devil" and *daimonion* as "demon."

Unfortunately, there is another area of confusion that has not been cleared up in some of the modern translations. The Greek noun *daimon* gives rise to a verb *daimonizo*, which occurs about twelve times in the New Testament. The obvious English equivalent of this verb is *demonize*, which the *Collins English Dictionary* defines as "to subject to demonic influence." In the New Testament this verb occurs only in the passive form: "to be demonized." In the original KJV, it is translated regularly as "to be possessed of [or with] a devil or devils." Most modern versions have correctly changed *devil* to *demon*, but incorrectly retain the form *to be possessed*.

The problem with this form is that, to English ears, the word *possess* immediately suggests ownership. To be "possessed" – by a devil or demon – implies that a person is "owned" by a devil or demon. But there is no basis for this in the Greek word *daimonizo*, which conveys no suggestion of ownership, but means merely "to subject to demonic influence."

Obviously, the form of words we use is of vital importance. It is one thing to say to a person, "You are subject to demonic influence." It is quite another to say, "You are possessed by a demon," or, worse still, to say, "You are possessed by the devil."

Let me say emphatically that there is nothing in the verb *daimonizo* to imply possession. Personally, I believe that every born-again Christian sincerely seeking to live for Christ belongs to Christ and is owned by Him. It is monstrous to suggest that such a person belongs to the devil or is owned by the devil.

On the other hand, I know on the basis of my own experience, and of ministering to thousands of others, that a born-again Christian can be subject to demonic influences. Such a Christian undoubtedly belongs to Christ, yet there are areas of his or her personality that have not yet come under the control of the Holy Spirit. It is these areas that may still be subject to demonic influence.

Throughout the rest of this book, then, I will for the most part speak of such people as those who are "demonized."

The Greek verb that usually describes the action of getting rid of a demon is *ekballo,* normally translated "to drive out," but in the KJV regularly translated "to cast out." As I said before, I chose Weymouth's translation *expel* because it describes a familiar action of everyday life. Throughout this book I will use these expressions more or less interchangeably: *cast out, drive out, expel.*

Another Greek verb used in this connection is *exorkizo,* normally translated "to exorcise." The KJV translates it "to adjure." In contemporary English, to exorcise is defined as "to expel evil spirits from a person or a place by prayers, adjurations and religious rites." The word is used frequently in the rituals of liturgical churches but occurs only once in the New Testament.

Questions for This Study

1. In the New Testament, what are the three expressions used to describe the evil spirit beings Satan uses in his warfare against humanity?

2. Confusion has been caused by the original King James Version of the Bible because it regularly translates the Greek word *daimonion* as

   _____.

3. What is the meaning of the Greek word *diabolos*, which is properly translated as "devil"?

4. Does the Greek word for "to be demonized" mean that an individual is "possessed" or owned by a demon or demons?

5. What is a more accurate description of a person who is demonized?

6. What are some areas of an individual's life that can be open to demonic influence?

Life Application

Describe some behaviors, or attitudes, that you believe might open an individual to demonic influence.

Memory Verse

And as you go, preach, saying, "The Kingdom of heaven is at hand." Heal the sick, raise the dead, cleanse the lepers, cast out demons. Freely you received, freely give. Matthew 10:7–8

Faith response

Lord, I will diligently trust You to lead me into a greater understanding of the spiritual world.

Answers are on page 407

THREE

The Pattern and Mission of Jesus

WHEN I WAS CONFRONTED PUBLICLY BY THE OPEN defiance of a demon in a Sunday morning worship service (as I explained in chapter 1), I was impelled to study the New Testament accounts of how Jesus dealt with such things. He is the one and only foundation and pattern for all Christian ministry. In this chapter, therefore, I will examine in some detail how Jesus Himself dealt with demons.

One of the earliest scenes in His public ministry, in a synagogue in Capernaum, is described vividly in Mark 1:21–26:

> *Then they went into Capernaum, and immediately on the Sabbath He entered the synagogue and taught. And they were astonished at His teaching, for He taught them as one having authority, and*

not as the scribes. Now there was a man in their synagogue with an unclean spirit. And he cried out, saying, "Let us alone! What have we to do with You, Jesus of Nazareth? Did You come to destroy us? I know who You are – the Holy One of God!" But Jesus rebuked him, saying, "Be quiet, and come out of him!" And when the unclean spirit had convulsed him and cried out with a loud voice, he came out of him.

The reaction of the people is described in verses 27 [margin translation of NU-manuscript] and 28:

Then they were all amazed, so that they questioned among themselves, saying, "What is this? A new doctrine with authority. He commands even the unclean spirits, and they obey Him." And immediately His fame spread throughout all the region around Galilee.

In verse 23, when the NKJV says *with an unclean spirit,* the Greek actually says *in an unclean spirit.* Perhaps the nearest English equivalent would be *under the influence of an unclean spirit.*

It is noteworthy that the New International Version translates this phrase *possessed by an evil spirit.* This exemplifies how translations can mislead us regarding the activity of evil spirits (or demons). Nothing in the original Greek justifies the use of the word *possessed,* with its suggestion of ownership. This translation is an accommodation to traditional religious terminology that obscures the meaning of the original text.

Jesus had been preaching in Galilee, "The time is fulfilled, and the kingdom of God is at hand" (Mark 1:15). Now He had to demonstrate the superiority of His Kingdom over the kingdom of Satan. There are six important points to notice.

First, Jesus dealt with the demon, not with the man. The demon spoke out of the man, and Jesus spoke to the demon. Literally translated, what Jesus said to the demon was, "Be muzzled!"

Second, Jesus expelled the demon from the man, not the man from the synagogue.

Third, Jesus was in no way embarrassed by the interruption or disturbance. Dealing with the demon was part of His total ministry.

Fourth, the demon spoke in both singular and plural forms: "Did You come to destroy us? I know who You are..." (verse 24). This response is characteristic of a demon speaking for itself and on behalf of others. The demon in the man in Gadara used the same form of speech: "My name is Legion; for we are many" (Mark 5:9).

Fifth, it is reasonable to assume that the man was a regular member of the synagogue, but apparently no one knew he needed deliverance from a demon. Perhaps even the man himself did not know. The anointing of the Holy Spirit on Jesus forced the demon out into the open.

Sixth, it was this dramatic confrontation with a demon in the synagogue that launched Jesus into His public ministry. He became known to His fellow Jews first and foremost as the Man with unique authority over demons.

How Jesus Dealt with Demons

On the evening of the same day, when the people's movements were no longer restricted by the Sabbath regulations, we might say that Jesus held His first "healing service":

> *At evening, when the sun had set, they brought to Him all who were sick and those who were demon-possessed* [demonized]. *And the whole city was gathered together at the door. Then He healed many who were sick with various diseases, and cast out many demons; and He did not allow the demons to speak, because they knew Him.*
>
> Mark 1:32–34

The same events are described in Luke 4:40–41:

> *When the sun was setting, all those who had anyone sick with various diseases brought them to Him; and He laid His hands on every one of them and healed them. And demons also came out of many,*

*crying out and saying, "You are the Christ, the Son
of God!" And He, rebuking them, did not allow
them to speak, for they knew that He was the Christ.*

For a clear picture of how Jesus dealt with demons,
we need to combine the two accounts of Mark and Luke.
Mark says, "He did not allow the demons to speak," but
Luke says, "And demons also came out of many, crying
out and saying, 'You are the ... Son of God!'" As in the
incident in the synagogue, the demons declared their
recognition of Jesus publicly as the Holy One of God,
or the Son of God, but after that He allowed them to
say nothing more.

It is noteworthy that people came to Jesus seeking
healing for their sicknesses, but many of them had
demons cast out of them. Apparently, the people did
not realize that some of their sicknesses were caused by
demons. One remarkable characteristic of Jesus' ministry, from beginning to end, is that He never made a hard
and fast distinction between healing people's sicknesses
and delivering them from demons.

The same applies to His ongoing ministry of preaching, as described in Mark 1:39: "And He was preaching
in their synagogues throughout all Galilee, and casting
out demons." Expelling demons was as normal a part
of Jesus' ministry as preaching. Delivering people from
demons was both the confirmation and the practical

application of the message He was preaching, which was: "The kingdom of God is at hand" (Mark 1:15).

To what kind of people, we might ask, was Jesus ministering in this way? Primarily observant Jews who met every Sabbath in the synagogue and spent the rest of the week caring for their families, tending their fields, fishing the sea, and minding their shops. The people who received help from Jesus were mainly "normal," respectable, religious people. Yet they were demonized. A demon had gained access to some area or areas of their personalities, and as a result they themselves were not in full control.

We need to remember that the moral and ethical code of Jewish people in Jesus' time was based on the Ten Commandments and the Law of Moses. This meant that most of them were probably living better lives than the majority of people in our contemporary Western society.

Undoubtedly there are many similar people to be found in the Christian community today – good, respectable, religious people who attend church and use all the right religious language, yet are like the observant Jews of Jesus' day. Some areas in their personalities have been invaded by demons and, as a result, they are not in full control. Surely, they need deliverance just as much as the people to whom Jesus ministered!

In Luke 13:32 Jesus made it clear that His practical ministry to the sick and demonized was to continue unchanged to the end: "Behold, I cast out demons and perform cures today and tomorrow, and the third day I shall be perfected." "Today, tomorrow and the third day" is a Hebraism that could be paraphrased, "From now on until the job is finished." The practical ministry of Jesus began, continued and concluded with two activities: healing the sick and expelling demons. The way He began was the right way, and He never needed to improve on it.

Further, when the time came for Jesus to commission and send out disciples, He instructed them to continue in exactly the same pattern of ministry that He Himself had demonstrated. To the first twelve apostles He imparted a twofold authority: first, to expel demons; and second, to heal every kind of sickness and disease (see Matthew 10:1). Then He gave them explicit instructions as to how to use this authority: "And as you go, preach, saying, 'The kingdom of heaven is at hand.' Heal the sick, cleanse the lepers, raise the dead, cast out demons" (Matthew 10:7–8).

Mark gives a brief description of how the disciples carried out their task: "And they cast out many demons, and anointed with oil many who were sick, and healed them" (Mark 6:13). Casting out demons, then, was not an optional "extra"!

Later Jesus sent out seventy more disciples, in pairs, to prepare the way before Him in every place He intended to go. We do not have a detailed account of His instructions, but clearly it included casting out demons, for on the disciples' return they reported with joy, "Lord, even the demons are subject to us in Your name" (Luke 10:17).

After His death and resurrection, Jesus again commissioned His disciples, but He now extended their ministry to the whole world. The message of those who went forth in faith and obedience, He promised, would be attested by five supernatural signs. The first two were these: "In My name they will cast out demons; they will speak with new tongues" (Mark 16:17).

Since the beginning of the twentieth century, a great deal has been preached, taught and written about the second sign: speaking with new tongues. But the sign Jesus put first, casting out demons, has not received the same positive attention. It is sad that the contemporary Western Church has been unwilling to come to grips with the issue of demons.

A further account of Jesus' final commission to His disciples is given in Matthew 28:19–20:

> *"Go therefore and make disciples of all the nations, baptizing them in the name of the Father and of the Son and of the Holy Spirit, teaching them to observe all things that I have commanded you; and lo, I am with you always, even to the end of the age."*

This commission was simple and practical: to make disciples and then to teach them to obey all that Jesus had commanded the first disciples. Then these new disciples would in turn make further disciples, and teach them all that Jesus had taught. So it would go from one generation to another – "even to the end of the age." Jesus started His disciples off with the right "program" and never made any provision for it to be changed. Unfortunately, through the centuries the Church has made many unauthorized changes, none of them for the better!

The Pattern of New Testament Evangelism

The New Testament provides one clear example of a disciple who patterned himself on the ministry of Jesus: Philip. He is the only person in the New Testament specifically described as an "evangelist" (see Acts 21:8), and his ministry, described in Acts 8:5–13 and 26–40, is the pattern for New Testament evangelism.

Philip's message was refreshingly simple. In Samaria it was "Christ." To the Ethiopian eunuch it was "Jesus." Philip needed no organizing committee, no trained choir, no rented auditorium. The crowds gathered to hear him for one reason only: the dramatic demonstration of God's supernatural power:

And the multitudes with one accord heeded the things spoken by Philip, hearing and seeing the miracles which he did. For unclean spirits, crying with a loud voice, came out of many who were possessed [demonized]; *and many who were paralyzed and lame were healed.*

Acts 8:6–7

This is New Testament evangelism: The Gospel is preached and the multitudes hear; they see the miracles and casting out of demons and they believe; they are baptized and the Church is established. A central element is the expelling of demons, which is often accompanied by noisy and disorderly manifestations. Other features of evangelism vary, but this element is central to evangelism as practiced in the New Testament, first by Jesus, then by His disciples.

The pattern of evangelism was not confined to the disciples who had been eyewitnesses of the ministry of Jesus. It was conspicuous in the ministry of the apostle Paul. At one point, in fact, Paul's success in dealing with demons had an impact on the entire city of Ephesus:

God did extraordinary miracles through Paul, so that even handkerchiefs and aprons that had touched him were taken to the sick, and their illnesses were cured and the evil spirits left them.

Some Jews who went around driving out evil spirits tried to invoke the name of the Lord Jesus over those who were demon-possessed [demonized]. *They would say, "In the name of Jesus, whom Paul preaches, I command you to come out." Seven sons of Sceva, a Jewish chief priest, were doing this.*

One day the evil spirit answered them, "Jesus I know, and I know about Paul, but who are you?" Then the man who had the evil spirit jumped on them and overpowered them all. He gave them such a beating that they ran out of the house naked and bleeding.

When this became known to the Jews and Greeks living in Ephesus, they were all seized with fear, and the name of the Lord Jesus was held in high honor. Acts 19:11–17, NIV

Since these sons of Sceva were deliberately imitating Paul, they provide us with a "shadow" from which we can form a picture of how Paul dealt with demons. Apparently, he spoke directly to them and commanded them in the name of Jesus to come out of their victims. In other words, Paul followed the pattern of Jesus Himself.

The ignominious failure of the sons of Sceva is also clear proof that success in casting out demons does not depend merely on using the right "formula." The person using the formula must be a sincere and yielded channel for the supernatural Person of the Holy Spirit.

These events in Ephesus provide a further New Testament example of how the ministry of deliverance can affect an entire community. The spectacle of the sons of Sceva fleeing in disarray before a demonized man had an impact on the whole city of Ephesus, but especially on the Christians living there. It served to draw a clear dividing line between the disciples of Jesus and the unbelievers.

> *Many of those who believed now came and openly confessed their evil deeds. A number who had practiced sorcery brought their scrolls together and burned them publicly. When they calculated the value of the scrolls, the total came to fifty thousand drachmas.*   Acts 19:18–19, NIV

Up to that time many of these believers had apparently been trying to live with one foot in the Kingdom of God and one in the kingdom of Satan. They had made a profession of faith in Christ but had retained in their possession scrolls containing the secret formulas they had used in their occult practices. Apparently, these scrolls were very valuable, which may have been one reason the Christians were reluctant to part with them. But once their eyes were opened to the real spiritual issues, they were willing to watch their scrolls burn.

A drachma was one day's wage. If we were to calculate the value of these scrolls in our own currency, basing it on forty dollars a day, the approximate minimum wage in the U.S., the equivalent would be more than two million dollars. Obviously, there is money to be made in the occult!

The result of this dramatic confrontation between the two kingdoms is summed up in a closing verse:

"So the word of the Lord grew mightily and prevailed" (Acts 19:20).

If evangelism is seldom conducted with these results in the Western world, we need to ask who has changed. Is it Jesus? Or the demons? Or the Church?

Questions for This Study

1. The practical ministry of Jesus began, continued and concluded with what two activities?
2. True or false? Most of Jesus' ministry of casting out demons was to the worst sinners and/or immoral people in the Jewish population.
3. When the man cried out in the synagogue in Capernaum, did Jesus deal with the man or the demon?
4. What twofold authority did Jesus impart to His disciples?
5. What happened to the seven sons of Sceva who tried to cast out demons using a formula rather than in the authority and power of the Holy Spirit?
6. According to the New Testament pattern, what is a central element in true Christian evangelism?

Life Application

1. Have you ever personally witnessed the ministry of expelling demons? If so, what was your reaction?
2. Do you believe you have been given the same authority and power to expel demons that the early disciples had? Why or why not?

Memory Verse

He has delivered us from the power of darkness and conveyed us into the kingdom of the Son of His love, in whom we have redemption through His blood, the forgiveness of sins Colossians 1:13–14

THE PATTERN AND MISSION OF JESUS

Faith Response

Lord, please remove all fear and unbelief when I am encountering any aspects of supernatural ministry.

Answers are on page 408

PART TWO
In the School of Experience

PERSONAL EXPERIENCE BY ITSELF IS NEVER A SUF-
ficient basis for establishing biblical doctrine. At times,
however, it can have the effect of illuminating a doctrine
that previously one did not know how to apply.

This was true in my personal confrontation with
demons. I had read the New Testament accounts of
Jesus and His disciples dealing with demons, and
accepted them as part of the revelation of Scripture.
But they had never come alive to me.

I had often had the joy of leading a sinner to Christ.
I had also seen people healed physically in answer to
prayer. But I had no conscious experience of confronting and dealing with demons, with the outward manifestations described so vividly in the New Testament.

Then God in His sovereignty began to give me direct personal experience in recognizing and dealing with demons. First of all, I myself received release from persistent, crippling bouts of depression when I recognized the source behind them and called out to God for deliverance. Later I encountered demons manifesting in other people, and proved in my own experience the truth of Jesus' promise to His disciples in Mark 16:17: "In My name they will cast out demons." This added an important new dimension to my ministry.

Looking back, I realize God had enrolled me in His "school of experience," guiding me sovereignly from one demonic encounter to the next. In the end, dealing with demons became a regular part of my Christian ministry.

In the chapters that follow, I share some of the most important lessons God taught me on the path by which He led me.

FOUR

My Struggle with Depression

MY MIND GOES BACK TO THE YEARS AFTER WORLD War II. I had served four and a half years with the British forces in the Middle East. Then, at the time of my discharge, I married Lydia Christensen, a Danish schoolteacher who was head of a small children's home in Jerusalem. Through my marriage to Lydia, I became father of a ready-made family of eight girls, of whom six were Jewish, one was a Palestinian Arab and the youngest was English.

Together as a family we witnessed the rebirth of the State of Israel in 1948, and then moved to London. We found a city still struggling wearily to rebuild its life from the shattering impact of the war. Night after night the Nazi bombers had rained down terror and destruction on a population that had no way to retaliate.

Long after the bombs had ceased to fall, the raw scars were still visible throughout the city.

Many of the streets reminded me of a person trying to smile with two or three front teeth knocked out. In the midst of the rows of houses that remained standing, vacant, weed-filled lots served as a wordless memorial to whole families that had perished with their homes. Uglier still were vacant shells of houses that remained standing but with blackened, crumbling walls and boarded windows. The eye searched in vain for any remnant of elegance or beauty.

The external scars of the city were matched by the emotional scars the people bore within themselves. The prevailing mood was one of weary cynicism. Britain had emerged victorious from the war, but the fruits of victory were bitter. All but the most basic forms of food were scarce. Such commodities as sugar, butter, tea and tobacco, which might have made life just a little easier to enjoy – or at least to endure – were still strictly rationed. Queues were long, tempers frayed.

The level of spiritual life in Britain was lower than it had been for at least two hundred years. Fewer than five percent of the population regularly attended any place of worship. Many churches had been either boarded up or converted into furniture storehouses. Of the churches that remained open, few presented any positive message of hope that could serve as an antidote to the prevailing depression.

Shortly after we settled in London, I began pastoring a small Pentecostal congregation near the center of the city.

My prevailing impression of that time is one of grayness. The streets were gray, the houses were gray, the people were gray. Most of the time the skies, too, were gray. The fuel being used for heating at the time blocked at least 25 percent of the sunlight that would have helped to relieve the grayness. In winter the city was shrouded from time to time by fog so dense you could not see your own hand stretched out in front of you.

Yet there was another kind of grayness that was even more depressing. It was the strange, indefinable grayness inside my own soul. By the spiritual standards of the time, I was a relatively successful minister. Each week a person would come to the Lord or I would witness a miracle of healing or some other demonstration of the supernatural power of the Holy Spirit. Yet I had a continuous inner sense of frustration. An inaudible voice seemed to whisper, *Others may succeed, but you won't.*

My experience up to this time had been a series of successes. Elected as a King's Scholar at Eton at age thirteen, I had gone on to King's College, Cambridge, as the senior scholar of my year. After graduating with first-class honors in both parts of the Classical Tripos (the official course of study in the Latin and Greek languages, culture and history), I had then been selected as the senior research student of the university for two

41

years. Finally, at age 24, I had been elected to a coveted position as a Fellow of King's College, Cambridge. During the war my service with the Medical Corps in a noncombatant role had barred me from promotion to officer rank. Nevertheless, I had emerged with the highest character qualification that the British Army had to bestow: *exemplary*.

During my military service I experienced a supernatural encounter with Jesus Christ that revolutionized my goals in life. Since my discharge I could see how God had led me step by step to my present ministry as a pastor. This was the irony I could not resolve. While I had been making my own way through life, ignoring God, I had an unbroken record of success. Yet now, as I was sincerely seeking to follow God's plan for my life, I was oppressed by the continuing sense that I could never expect to succeed.

In all of this I never doubted the reality of my salvation. It was too deep and too permanent. Yet at times depression descended on me like a gray mist that shrouded my head and shoulders. Breaking out of this mist was like attempting to break out of a prison. I felt isolated and lonely, shut off from meaningful communication, even with those closest to me – my wife and daughters. I did not know any mature minister to whom I could turn for help.

I tried every spiritual means I knew to throw off this depression. I read my Bible faithfully at least twice a day.

I fasted one day each week. At times I devoted several days or a week to intensive prayer and fasting. At such times the depression lifted for a while, but inevitably it returned. Each time it did, my hopelessness grew deeper.

I was familiar with Romans 6:11, which instructs us to "reckon [ourselves] to be dead indeed unto sin" (KJV). Day after day I reckoned myself dead to sin and to any consequence of depression that it had brought on me. But I could not seem to experience the latter half of the verse: being "alive unto God through Jesus Christ" (KJV).

Overcoming My Enemy

Finally, in 1953, when I had exhausted all my own resources, God came to my help in a way I had never contemplated. I was reading the opening verses of Isaiah 61, which describe the supernatural work of the Holy Spirit in bearing testimony to the message of the Gospel – verses Jesus applied to Himself in the synagogue in Nazareth (see Luke 4:16–21). As I came to the words in verse 3, "the garment of praise for *the spirit of heaviness*" (KJV, emphasis added) – also called "a spirit of despair" (NIV) and "a spirit of fainting" (NASB) – I could read no further. It was as though the phrase *the spirit of heaviness* was underlined by some invisible hand.

I repeated the phrase to myself: *the spirit of heaviness.* Was this God's diagnosis of my condition? Could it mean that the force I was struggling with was not part of myself, but an alien person – an evil spirit being that somehow occupied an area of my mind?

I recalled a term I had once heard but did not understand: *familiar spirit*. Did it possibly refer to some kind of evil power that attached itself to the members of a family, moving down from generation to generation?

I thought about an aspect of my father's character that had always puzzled me. He was a good, moral man and a successful officer who had retired from the Army with the rank of colonel. For 98 percent of the time, he behaved like the English gentleman he was. But during the fractional two percent of the time, I had seen something in him quite alien to his own personality. Some apparently trivial incident would upset him and, for as long as 24 hours, he would lapse into rigid, stony silence. He would shut himself off from my mother and would not open his mouth even to say thank you for a cup of tea. Then, with no apparent reason, he would return to his normal, well-mannered self.

With this new insight, I saw that a similar "dark spirit" had followed me through my life, from childhood onward. Apparently, it had studied my temperament and was familiar with my weaknesses and my reactions. It knew just when I would be most vulnerable to its pressures. It now had one main objective: to prevent me from serving Christ effectively.

This was a decisive moment in my life. I had always

regarded my depression and negative attitude as an expression of my own character – something I had been born with. I had felt guilty that I was not a "better" Christian. Now it became clear to me that my struggle was not against part of my own personality at all.

Immediately, the Holy Spirit brought to my mind the promise of Joel 2:32: "And it shall come to pass, that whosoever shall call on the name of the LORD shall be delivered" (KJV). From my study of Hebrew, I knew this verb also means "to save, to rescue." I determined to apply this promise and to act on it. I said a simple prayer that went something like this: "Lord, You have shown me that I have been oppressed by a spirit of heaviness, but You have promised in Your Word that if I call on Your name, I shall be delivered. So, I'm calling on You now to deliver me, in the name of Jesus!"

The response was immediate. Something like a huge, heavenly vacuum cleaner came down over me and sucked away the gray mist that shrouded my head and shoulders. At the same time a pressure in the area of my chest was forcibly released, and I gave a little gasp.

God had answered my prayer. Suddenly everything around me seemed brighter. I felt as if a heavy burden had been lifted from my shoulders. I was free! All my life I had been under that oppression. It felt strange to be free. But I discovered quickly that freedom was normal and that oppression was abnormal.

My old enemy did not give up on me; I still had to

Exercize ✓

struggle against depression. But the great difference now was that its attacks came from without, not from within. I gradually learned how to withstand it.

The main thrust of the attacks was to induce in me reactions or attitudes of pessimism. When everything seemed to be going wrong, I would begin to entertain negative thoughts about what I could expect to happen. Quite soon I would feel the all-too-familiar gray mist beginning to settle down over my head and shoulders.

At this point God taught me another important lesson: He would do for me what I could not do for myself, but He would not do for me what He required me to do for myself. God had responded to my cry and delivered me from the spirit of heaviness, but after that He held me responsible to exercise scriptural discipline over my own thoughts.

Clearly, I needed something to protect my mind. As I meditated on Paul's list of spiritual armor in Ephesians 6:13–18, I concluded that what Paul calls "the helmet of salvation" was provided for the protection of my mind. This left me wondering, *Do I already have the helmet of salvation? I know I'm saved. Does that mean I have the helmet automatically?*

Then I saw that Paul was writing to Christians who were already saved, but he still instructed them to "take" the helmet of salvation. This placed the responsibility on me. I had to "take" the helmet for myself. But what was the helmet?

THE HELMET OF SALVATION ✓

Fortunately, I was using a Bible with cross references. The cross reference to Ephesians 6:17 was 1 Thessalonians 5:8: "Putting on ... for an helmet, the hope of salvation" (KJV). So, the helmet God had provided to protect my mind was hope!

This appealed to my logical mind. My problem was pessimism, but the opposite of pessimism is optimism – hoping continually for the best. Hope, therefore, was my protection.

From 1 Thessalonians 5:8 I was led to Hebrews 6:18–20:

> That ... we might have a strong consolation, who have fled for refuge to lay hold upon the hope set before us: which hope we have as an anchor of the soul, both sure and steadfast, and which entereth into that within the veil; whither the forerunner is for us entered, even Jesus. ... (KJV)

I found here two further pictures of hope. First, hope is compared to the horns of the altar. Under the old covenant, when a man was being pursued by an enemy seeking to kill him, he could find asylum by clinging to the horns of the altar, where his enemy could not reach him. For me the altar spoke of the sacrifice Jesus made for me on the cross. Its horns represented my hope, which was based on His sacrifice. As long as I clung tenaciously to this hope, my enemy could not approach to destroy me.

What about the second picture of hope, as an anchor? This provoked a brief dialogue in my mind.

What needs an anchor?

A ship.

Why does a ship need an anchor?

Because it floats in water – an unstable element that provides nothing for it to hold onto. It passes its anchor through that unstable element, therefore, and fastens it onto something firm and immovable, such as a rock.

I saw that hope could be like that in my life – an anchor passing through the turmoil and instability of this life and fastened forever onto the eternal Rock of Ages – Jesus.

As I meditated on this, however, I realized there is a difference between hope and wishful thinking. Reading on in Hebrews, I saw that "faith is the substance of things hoped for" (Hebrews 11:1, KJV). The kind of hope I needed as an anchor had to be based on a solid foundation of faith in the statements and promises of God's Word. Without this biblical foundation, hope could prove to be nothing but wishful thinking.

Gradually I worked out a simple, practical way to apply these truths in my daily life. I learned to distinguish between thoughts that proceeded from my own mind and those insinuated by the demon. Every time my enemy approached me and sought to induce negative and pessimistic thoughts, I disciplined myself to counter with a positive word from Scripture.

Atmosphere ✓

If the demon suggested that things were going wrong, I would counter with Romans 8:28: "All things work together for good to those who love God, to those who are the called according to His purpose." *I love God*, I would answer my invisible enemy, *and I am called according to His purpose. Therefore, all these things are working together for my good.*

From time to time the demon would resort to the tactic it had often used successfully in the past: *You'll never succeed.* I would counter this with Philippians 4:13: "I can do all things through Christ who strengthens me."

Complete victory did not come immediately. But over the course of time, my mental reflexes were built up to the point that it was almost automatic to counter any negative suggestion from the demon with some opposite, positive word from Scripture. As a result, that particular demon seldom wastes much time now in attacking me.

God also began to teach me the importance of thanking and praising Him continually. This would surround me, I discovered, with an atmosphere that repelled demons. I was impressed by the words of David in Psalm 34:1: "I will bless the LORD at all times; His praise shall continually be in my mouth."

The introduction to this psalm indicates that at this point in David's life he was a fugitive from King Saul, who was seeking to kill him. He had escaped to the court of a Gentile king (Abimelech or Achish), who did not give him a warm welcome. To save his life David "feigned madness in their hands, scratched on the doors of the gate, and let his saliva fall down on his beard" (1 Samuel 21:13).

If David could continue blessing God in that situation, I reasoned, *there is no situation in which I should not be doing the same.*

Lessons

Out of all these struggles, I learned three lessons that have ever since proven invaluable: first, the reality of demonic activity as described in the New Testament; second, the supernatural provision God has made for deliverance; and third, the need to maintain deliverance by the disciplined application of Scripture.

Christians often tend to be one-sided in their approach to the issue of deliverance. Some place all their emphasis on the actual process of expelling a demon. Others reject the supernatural element in deliverance and stress only the need for Christian discipline.

The truth is that neither is a substitute for the other. Deliverance cannot take the place of discipline, and discipline cannot take the place of deliverance. Both are needed.

Looking back over the years, I have asked myself from time to time, *What course would my life have taken if God had not come to my help with His supernatural power and delivered me from that evil "spirit of heaviness"?* I have no doubt that sooner or later I would have given way to despair and been forced out of the ministry. How wonderful, therefore, to look back on the more than forty years of fruitful ministry that have followed my deliverance!

I realize, however, that my struggle with demons was not a strange or unique experience. On the contrary, those called into Christian ministry are, I believe, among Satan's prime targets. He subjects them to relentless demonic pressure and torment, aiming to force them out of their ministry. All too often he is successful!

There is only one sure protection: learning how to recognize demonic activity and deal with it according to the pattern established by Jesus.

That is one main reason I feel constrained to write this book.

Questions for This Study

1. Derek experienced oppression when he sincerely started to follow God's plan for his life. What form did this oppression take?

2. What spiritual disciplines did Derek apply in trying to lift these oppressions? Were they effective?

3. God revealed to Derek that this oppression stemmed from a _____.

4. What was the main objective of this spirit upon Derek's life?

5. One way this spirit tried to regain influence was by prompting reactions or attitudes of _____.

6. How did Derek counter these attacks?

7. What three important lessons did Derek learn from his struggle with depression?

Life Application

1. List any areas in your own life where you have struggled to experience lasting freedom.

2. What steps can you use from this study to find freedom in these areas?

3. Find one or two promises from God's Word to assist you in gaining freedom from this oppression.

Memory Verse

And it will come about that whoever calls on the name of the Lord will be delivered.   Joel 2:32 NASB

Faith Response

Lord, help me to determine what You must do for me that I cannot do for myself, and what I am required to do for myself through faith and discipline.

Answers are on page 408

FIVE

People I Failed to Help

IT WOULD BE NATURAL TO ASSUME THAT, AFTER my wonderful deliverance from depression, I began immediately to share these exciting truths with my congregation. Unfortunately, this was not so. There were two main reasons.

The first, quite simply, was *pride*. I felt it was my duty as a pastor to live on a higher spiritual level than the members of my congregation. I was supposed to be the person with the answer to their problems, the one to whom they came for help. What would happen if I were suddenly to announce publicly that I had been delivered from a demon? Many of my members would have shuddered at the mere mention of the word *demon*. Perhaps they would no longer respect me as a pastor. Perhaps they would no longer come and listen to my sermons. I would be left without a congregation.

Deliverance from a demon, I decided, was a "personal" matter. It was not appropriate for a pastor to share such things with his congregation.

But there was another reason for my reticence. I had been identified since my conversion with the Pentecostal movement and had given assent to their main doctrinal positions. One such widely held position was that a person who had been saved, baptized in the Holy Spirit and had spoken in tongues could never afterward need deliverance from a demon. In fact, it would have been considered irreverent even to make such a suggestion.

I had never heard or read a reasoned, scriptural presentation of this doctrinal position. Most Christians seemed to consider it so obvious that it did not need support from Scripture. From time to time, however, someone quoted the words of Jesus in John 8:36: "Therefore if the Son makes you free, you shall be free indeed," as if that settled everything.

Just a few verses previously, however, Jesus says:

> *"If you abide in My word, you are My disciples indeed. And you shall know the truth, and the truth shall make you free."* John 8:31–32

According to this earlier passage, being "free indeed" is not automatic, but conditional on knowing the truth of God's Word and walking in obedience to it.

This left me with some difficult questions. Suppose that at any time I was not as obedient as I ought to be.

Would I need further deliverance? How could I know, in personal experience, that I really was "free indeed"?

I concluded that I was not in a position to answer these questions immediately. I also recognized that religious tradition is one of the most powerful influences molding the life of a minister. To break away from tradition requires real strength and conviction. It was one thing, I reasoned, for me to have received my own personal experience of deliverance. It would be quite another for me to come out and teach others that a Spirit-baptized Christian might need deliverance from a demon. Many of my fellow Pentecostals – and doubtless other sections of the Church, too – would immediately classify me as a heretic.

Actually, I was not quite sure myself that what had happened to me could be taken as a pattern for others. Perhaps my case was unique. If so, even to suggest to my congregation that they might need deliverance from a demon could undermine their faith and destabilize them.

In the end, I shared my experience of deliverance only with my wife, and said nothing about it in public. Even though Christians came to me struggling with problems they could not resolve, I never suggested that their problems might be due to demons from which they needed to be delivered. I am ashamed to say that I shut out this possibility from my own thinking.

This unscriptural decision set limits to the effectiveness of my ministry. Some of the people I sought to help came through to real freedom and victory. But others progressed a certain distance and then came up against what seemed to be an invisible barrier. They never attained their full potential as Christians.

Marcus and Roger

Today I realize that I failed in my pastoral responsibility. I grieve that I did not give them the help they needed. Two particular cases stand out in my mind.

The first was Marcus, a Jew from Germany. He and his older brother were the only two members of a large family who did not die in Hitler's gas chambers. Then, in England, Marcus had a powerful personal encounter with Jesus of Nazareth and was baptized in the Holy Spirit. Many times, when praying with him, I heard him speak clearly and fluently in an unknown tongue. (I am familiar with German and know that was not the language he was speaking.) All the time I knew Marcus, he was a bold and faithful witness to Jesus as his Savior and Messiah. Yet he never seemed to enter the deep, inner peace that Jesus promises to those who believe in Him.

Apart from the trauma of the Holocaust, Marcus had another emotional problem in his background. When he was born, his mother had wanted a daughter and would not accept the fact that he was a boy. Throughout his childhood, she dressed him as a girl and treated him in every way as if he were female.

From time to time, Marcus enjoyed periods of real peace and victory, but then he relapsed into moods of black despair. He was tormented by a sense of guilt that he could neither explain nor resolve. At times, to punish himself, he would put his fingers in the door and then close the door on them. He was even driven to drink his own urine.

After these episodes he would come to me for help. "Can't you get this 'devil' out of me?" he would cry. But I closed my mind to the possibility that he could really need deliverance from a demon. After all, I had heard him speak in tongues!

After I gave up my pastorate in London, I gradually lost direct contact with Marcus. But through a mutual friend I learned that he had undergone a prefrontal lobotomy – the surgical severing of one or more nerve tracts in the frontal lobe of the brain in order to treat intractable mental disorders. Apparently, this treatment was of no permanent benefit to Marcus, however, and some years later he died prematurely.

Looking back now, I feel I should have been able to help Marcus if I had been willing to acknowledge the demonic element in his problem.

The other case was Roger, a young man who came to the Lord in a street meeting at which I was preaching. He had a powerful conversion, was baptized in the Holy Spirit and became an eager, dedicated witness and worker for the Lord. In fact, he put some of our other members to shame by his zeal and dedication.

Nevertheless, Roger had one besetting sin – a very embarrassing one that no one talked about in those days. It was masturbation. He hated it and struggled against it, but could never get permanent victory.

Roger would come to Lydia and me and say, "Pray for me." One time we prayed for him from ten at night until about two in the morning. By that time Roger was saying, "It's leaving me, it's leaving me! Don't stop praying; I can feel it. It's in my fingers; it's going!" Victory seemed within our grasp – but somehow it always eluded us.

In all the years that I knew Roger, he never got victory over his problem.

The Probe and the Forceps

Marcus and Roger are but two examples of people I failed to help because I did not deal with their problems as demonic. It was like an incident that occurred during World War II while I was serving as a medical orderly with the British forces in North Africa.

A British soldier had come into our reception station with a shrapnel wound caused by a bomb exploding near him. He took off his shirt, exposing a small puncture wound in one shoulder. The edge of the wound was slightly black.

Thinking of the ready-to-use sterile dressing that was part of our medical equipment, I said to the medical officer, "Shall I get a first field dressing, sir?"

"No, that's not what's needed," the doctor replied. "Bring me a probe."

The doctor had the man sit down on a chair. Then he stuck the little silver stick into the man's wound and wiggled it around gingerly for a few moments. Suddenly the man let out a yelp and went up in the air.

"Now fetch me the forceps," the doctor said.

I gave him the forceps, which he inserted into the wound in the area where the probe had located a foreign body. Cautiously he extracted a little piece of black metal. After cleaning the wound, he finally said to me, "Now you can bring the dressing."

Afterward he explained, "You see, the piece of shrapnel that caused the puncture was still in there. If you just cover that shrapnel up with a dressing without removing it, it will be a continuing source of infection and will cause further complications."

As I look back over my period of ministry in London, I realize that at times I made the same kind of mistake as I did in the reception station during the war. In helping some of the people who came to me, I tried to apply a first field dressing to a wound that still contained a demonic source of "infection." Before I could really help such people, I needed two essential items of spiritual equipment: the "probe" of discernment and the "forceps" of deliverance.

In the chapters that follow, I will describe how God moved in my life to provide me with these two essential tools of ministry.

Questions for This Study

1. What were the two main reasons Derek did not share his deliverance experience with members of his congregation?
2. If Derek had begun to teach that Spirit-baptized Christians could have a demon, many would have classified him as a _____.
3. From his experiences as a medical orderly, Derek compared a shrapnel wound to what situation?
4. Why was it necessary to remove the shrapnel?
5. To what spiritual tools did he compare the probe and the forceps?

Life Application

1. Have you tried to heal certain areas of your life with a "surface dressing" of Christian discipline? If so, what areas are they? Is this method working for you?
2. Are you open to allowing the Lord to show you more effective ways to heal these areas?

Memory Verse

"If you abide in my word, you are my disciples indeed. And you shall know the truth, and the truth shall make you free"
John 8:31–32

Faith Response

Lord, grant me the discernment to understand my spiritual condition and to apply Your remedies.

Answers are on page 409

SIX

Confrontation with Demons

IN 1957 I LEFT MY PASTORATE IN LONDON, AND Lydia and I went out to Kenya as educational missionaries. We became friends with a team of African evangelists who used to describe to us their personal encounters with demons.

On one occasion they were ministering to an uneducated African woman who spoke only her own tribal dialect. But the demon spoke out of the woman in English: "You can't cast us out; you don't have enough education." To which my friends replied, "We're not casting you out because we have education, but because we're servants of the Lord Jesus Christ!"

I knew my friends well enough to be convinced that they were not exaggerating or fantasizing. Their accounts of their dealings with demons reminded me of incidents recorded in the New Testament. But I did not know what to do with this information. Busy with my work as principal of a teacher training college, I put it in my "pending" file.

After serving for five years, Lydia and I left Kenya and traveled and ministered for two years in Europe, Britain, Canada and the United States. Then, in 1963, I accepted a position as pastor of a small Pentecostal congregation in Seattle.

One Saturday I received a phone call at home from Eric Watson, a charismatic Baptist pastor I knew slightly.

"I have a woman here," he said, "who's been baptized in the Holy Spirit. But she needs deliverance from evil spirits."

I had never heard a Baptist pastor talk like that before. What followed was even more unexpected.

"The Lord has shown me that you and your wife are to be the instruments of her deliverance," he continued. "And it's to happen today."

I was somewhat taken aback. I was certainly not prepared to let another person make such a decision for me. So I breathed a quick prayer: *Lord, is this from You? Do You really want me to do what he says?*

To my surprise I sensed the Lord respond, *Yes, this is from Me.*

"All right," I said to the pastor. "Bring the woman over."

The First Battle

While Lydia and I were waiting for Pastor Watson and the woman, we received a surprise visit from John and Sherry Faulkner, a Presbyterian couple who had recently been baptized in the Holy Spirit. We told them about the visitors we were expecting and invited them to stay and pray.

Then Eric Watson arrived with a fair-haired, blue-eyed woman he introduced as Mrs. Esther Henderson. I scanned her closely, looking for some outward evidence of her strange spiritual condition – a wild look in her eye, perhaps, or a metallic ring in her voice. But she seemed to be a perfectly ordinary, middle-class American housewife, somewhere in her middle thirties, I judged. She did not seem nervous or frightened.

Pastor Watson got down to business immediately. He sat Esther down in a chair and explained, "She's been delivered from a demon of nicotine, but there are others."

Listening to what he had to say, I decided to remain neutral until the Lord gave me some clarity or direction.

Pastor Watson stood in front of Esther and said in a loud voice, "You evil spirits, I command you to come out of Esther!"

When there was no obvious response, his voice grew louder and he repeated the same words: "I command you to come out!"

Still nothing happened.

"I know you are there," the pastor continued, "and I command you to come out, in the name of Jesus!"

The moment he mentioned the name of Jesus, there was a definite reaction from Esther. As I watched closely, her countenance changed. It was as though another personality was coming to the surface. A yellow, sulfurous glow appeared in the center of each eyeball. I knew there was another power inside this ordinary-looking Baptist housewife.

Eric Watson continued to stand and shout at whatever it was. Apparently, he felt that shouting gave him more authority. But after a while, seeming to realize he was making no progress, he looked questioningly toward me.

I had been thinking it over, recalling especially the methods of Jesus. So, I took my stand in front of Esther and said something like this: "Now, you evil spirit that's in this woman, I'm talking to you and not to the woman. What is your name? In the name of the Lord Jesus Christ, I command you to answer me."

The answer came immediately – just one syllable, uttered with incredible venom: "Hate!"

Everything in the woman's face registered pure, undiluted hatred. Never in all my life had I seen such hatred in anybody's eyes.

The promptness of the demon's answer took me by surprise. I did not know what to do next. But I decided to follow the instructions Jesus had given His disciples.

"In the name of the Lord Jesus Christ," I commanded, "you spirit of hate, come out of this woman."

An insolent voice, not in the least like Esther's, replied, "This is my house. I've lived here 35 years. And I'm not coming out."

Unbidden, there came to my mind the Bible passage in which the unclean spirit that goes out of a man says, "I will return to my house from which I came" (Matthew 12:44). So, the demon's reference to Esther as "my house" was in line with Scripture.

With this in mind, I said to the demon, "In the name of the Lord Jesus Christ, you are coming out."

The demon continued to defy me while I continued to say, "In the name of the Lord Jesus, you are coming out!"

It was a real conflict of wills. It seemed that I had to beat the demon down stage by stage. Each stage took quite a while. But the more I quoted Scripture and used the name of Jesus, the more I gained ascendancy over my enemy. Eventually the demon began to bargain with me. "If I come out," it said, "I'll come back." I said, "No, you'll come out and you'll stay out."

Then it said, "Well, even if I come out, my brothers are here and they'll kill her." I said, "No, you'll come out first and your brothers will come out after you." At the same time, I realized I had picked up a useful piece of information. Apparently, there was more than one demon there.

Then the demon said, "Even if we come out of her, we've still got her daughter." I said, "No, you'll come out of Esther first and then you'll come out of her daughter." I had not known that Esther had a daughter, but I was following a simple principle: Whatever the demon said, I said the opposite.

At this point the demon changed its tactics. Without any warning Esther's arms rose up and crossed over her throat, and she began to throttle herself with her own hands. Her face turned purple and her eyes began to protrude out of her head. John Faulkner, the Presbyterian, who was taller and heavier than I, joined me, and with our united strength we finally succeeded in pulling Esther's hands away from her throat. Her strength was supernatural.

Then I returned to my battle with the demon. I began to feel a tremendous pressure inside my belly, like an inflated balloon, that seemed to be pushing against the demon in Esther. Suddenly a hissing sound came out of Esther's mouth. Her head fell forward limply and her body relaxed. At the same time, the "balloon" inside me was deflated. I knew the demon had gone out.

Soon, however, Esther stiffened up again and the "balloon" inside me was reinflated. I realized I was in contact with one of what the demon had called its "brothers."

I went through the same procedure with the next demon, which named itself as fear. After another battle, it, too, came out. Once again Esther relaxed and the "balloon" inside me was deflated. Becoming tired, I stepped back and one of the other people took over, following more or less the same procedure that I had established.

By the time the struggle ended, nearly everyone present had participated. In all, the session lasted about five hours.

After fear, the next demons that named themselves and came out were pride, jealousy and self-pity. *So self-pity can be a demon!* I said to myself. I was beginning to understand why some people could never seem to keep a positive, scriptural attitude during difficult circumstances. In fact, this whole process was opening up a new window through which I would henceforth view people's behavior and the forces that motivated them.

The next demon that named itself and came out was infidelity. I understood this as a spiritual force that sought to drive a married woman – and perhaps a married man also – to sexual immorality.

The next demon that named itself was death. At first, I was skeptical. I had always regarded death as a purely physical condition. Then I recalled the horse in Revelation 6 whose rider was named Death. So, death could be a person! Did that mean it could be a demon, too?

Intrigued, I said to this spirit of death, "When did you enter this woman?"

"About three and a half years ago," it replied, "when she nearly died on the operating table."

When the spirit of death finally came out, Esther was stretched on her back on the floor. Her skin was waxy and cold, her face like a death mask. There was no hint of color anywhere in it. Anyone walking into the living room at that moment would have concluded that there was a dead woman on the floor.

I recalled the incident after Jesus had delivered a boy from a deaf and dumb spirit, and the boy "became as one dead, so that many said, 'He is dead.' But Jesus took him by the hand and lifted him up, and he arose" (Mark 9:26–27).

Esther lay there for about ten minutes, then raised her hands and began to praise the Lord and speak in tongues. Finally, her strength beginning to return, she stood up. After about half an hour, we handed her over to Pastor Watson, who put her into his car and drove her home.

Lydia and I went back into our house where the Faulkners were waiting. We all looked at one another in amazement. Then someone said, "Let's have a cup of tea!"

As we talked it over, we were all excited. For the first time we had seen a dramatic, objective, supernatural demonstration of the authority Jesus had given us over demons.

Another Captive Set Free

About halfway through the following week, Esther Henderson phoned my wife and said, "I think they're trying to come back. Could you come out and help me?"

We drove out to Esther's home to counsel and pray with her. It seemed that the demons were oppressing her with fear, seeking to use that as a door of reentry. We encouraged her to take her stand on the words of James 4:7: "Submit to God. Resist the devil and he will flee from you."

While we were there, Esther's youngest child, a little girl of six, lingered in the background. Rose was a thin, unhappy, withdrawn child. Each time I looked her in the face, she averted her eyes and bent her head down. She was, I learned, considered retarded.

Eventually I said to Esther, "I know the devil can't be trusted to speak the truth, but when those demons said they had your daughter, I believe they must have been speaking the truth."

"Would you pray for her?" Esther replied.

So, Lydia and I made an appointment for her to bring Rose to our home for prayer the following Saturday. Then we invited the Faulkners to come and support us in prayer.

That Saturday, before we began to pray in our living room, I asked Esther how much she remembered of what had happened to her the previous Saturday. She remembered nothing, she said, from the time the demon of hate took over until she found herself lying on her back on the floor, praising God. The demons had completely submerged her personality and used her voice and features as channels through which they could express themselves. Esther also confirmed, when we asked her, that she had undergone a serious operation three and a half years previously and had nearly died on the operating table.

Now, when we began to pray for Rose, we followed much the same procedure as we had with Esther. Demons manifested themselves once again and took control of Rose's countenance and features. They also spoke through the child's lips.

I turned to Esther at one point and said, "Is that your daughter's voice?"

Bewildered, she replied, "It isn't even like my daughter's voice. I never expected anything like this."

Some of the demons in Rose had the same names as those in her mother, but there were not so many. As with Esther, the first one to manifest itself was hate, and the last was death. When death came out, Rose was stretched out on the floor looking like a corpse, just as her mother had been.

Once Esther and Rose were fully delivered, it

seemed right to commit them to Pastor Eric Watson for ongoing spiritual oversight. I did maintain contact with Esther, however, for the next two years. During that time, she apparently made good spiritual progress, although from time to time she still had to fight off demonic attacks.

As for Rose, she was transformed into a normal, happy little girl who was no longer considered retarded. The demons, it seemed, had been suppressing her natural personality and intelligence.

These experiences with Esther and Rose caused me to look at my congregation in a new light. I saw traits and forces at work in them that I had never understood. Could it be that they, too, had demons at work within them? If it was true of a "good" Baptist like Esther, could it also apply to "good" Pentecostals?

Questions for This Study

1. True or false? The woman, Esther (who was brought to Derek and Lydia for deliverance) appeared unkempt, disheveled and had a wild look in her eye.
2. Name some of the demonic spirits that came out of Esther.
3. How did Derek gain dominion over these demonic powers?
4. List some of the arguments the demons used for remaining in Esther.
5. When had the demon of death entered Esther?

Life Application

1. Take a moment and ask the Holy Spirit to reveal any time in your life when you were unknowingly in direct conflict with spiritual powers of darkness. Now describe what you believe He has shown you.
2. Do you believe you would be able to confront demonic powers in the manner described in this account? Why or why not?

Memory Verse

Therefore submit to God. Resist the devil and he will flee from you.   James 4:7

Faith Response

Lord, I open myself up to whatever You have planned for my growth and maturity as Your servant.

Answers are on page 409

SEVEN

Challenged in My Own Pulpit

MY CONGREGATION WERE GOOD PENTECOSTALS and I loved them. They sometimes testified, as Pentecostals are trained to do, of the peace and joy they enjoyed as Christians. I did not doubt their sincerity. But I also knew that at times their claims to peace and joy were a religious façade. Behind it were unrelieved tensions and pressures, which they did their best to suppress or conceal but which they never really overcame.

I began to preach about deliverance in a roundabout way. I suggested that perhaps some personal problems that were never fully resolved might be due to demonic activity. But my hints had little effect. My people sat back with indulgent smiles. "Our pastor's got a bee in his bonnet," they seemed to be saying, "but he'll get over it."

Left to myself, I do not know how I would have resolved this issue. But I was not left to myself. One Sunday morning, about a month after we ministered to Esther and Rose Henderson, both God and Satan intervened unexpectedly and shattered the superficial calm.

That morning I had chosen as my text part of Isaiah 59:19: "When the enemy comes in like a flood, the Spirit of the LORD will lift up a standard against him." Although I was not aware of it at the time, I discovered later that one of my members had been recording the service on a reel-to-reel recorder. Listening to the tape later, I was able to evaluate objectively the content of my message, as well as the events that followed.

After I had been speaking for about fifteen minutes, the Holy Spirit took control of me, and I started saying things I had not planned to say. Even the pitch of my voice changed. I became unusually bold.

The theme of my message was: No matter what the devil does, God always has the last word. God began to bring examples to my mind.

"Egypt had their magicians," I said, "but God had His Moses. Baal had his prophets, but God had His Elijah."

Then the thought came to me that when God wanted to show Abraham what his descendants would be like, He took him out on a dark night, showed him the stars of heaven and said, "So shall thy seed be" (Genesis 15:5, KJV).

"We are the seed of Abraham by faith in Jesus Christ," I said, "and we're like the stars. When all the other lights are shining, you don't see the stars. But when every other light has gone out, then the stars shine brighter than they have ever shone before. That's how it is going to be at the close of this age. When every other light has gone out, we who are the seed of Abraham – through faith in Jesus Christ – are going to shine like the stars."

When I spoke these words, a young woman seated alone on the front pew let out a prolonged, blood-curdling shriek, threw her arms into the air and slumped to the floor in a very unladylike posture. She lay there writhing and moaning right in front of my pulpit.

This was Satan's challenge to my declaration that no matter what the devil does, God has the last word – a demonic manifestation directly in front of my pulpit! I had to either prove what I was preaching or stop preaching it.

At that moment I decided I would not back down before Satan. On the other hand, I felt I needed some support, so I called my wife, Lydia, forward. I knew I could count on her. Feeling I needed more reinforcement, I scanned the faces of my good, Pentecostal church members. They were all in a state of shock. Then, at the back, I saw our Presbyterian friends, the Faulkners, and called them forward.

The four of us gathered around the woman, whom I did not immediately recognize, as she lay writhing and moaning on the floor. Sherry Faulkner did not wait for a word from me. She was like a terrier after a rat.

"You spirit that's in this woman," she said, "what is your name?"

From the young woman's throat came a harsh, gruff, masculine voice that said, "My name is...." But it would go no further.

Again Sherry asked her question, and the demon said, "My name is..." and stopped.

Each time she asked, she got the same response. So, I stepped in and addressed the demon with the same formula I had used with Esther: "You spirit that's in this woman, in the name of the Lord Jesus Christ, I'm speaking to you and not to the woman. What is your name?"

The demon responded again, "My name is..."

Each time I repeated the question, the response was the same. I found myself in the same, intense, person-to-person conflict I had experienced while ministering to Esther. But this time I had my congregation as an attentive audience!

I recalled that the disciples had reported to Jesus, "Lord, even the demons are subject to us in Your name" (Luke 10:17). So, I said to the demon, "In the name of Jesus, you are subject to me. What is your name?"

Still the same answer: "My name is..." and no more. I saw that I had to beat the demon down with Scripture and the name of Jesus, and began to do so.

Suddenly the demon gave in. It shouted loudly, "My name is ... *lies!*"

Everyone in the congregation went up into the air and came down on their seats with a bump!

I did a quick mental check with Scripture. In 1 Kings 22, I recalled, there was a lying spirit in the mouths of the prophets of Ahab. So the reply I had received was scriptural. And I got the impression somehow that this woman had been listening to lies rather than telling them.

I said to the demon, "You lying spirit, come out of this woman!"

The demon defied me; it refused to come out. But by this time, I was confident that if I persisted in using the name of Jesus, it would have to obey me. Finally, after about ten minutes, the demon came out with a loud, sustained roar, like an express train going past. No human lungs could have sustained that volume of sound for so long. As the demon came out, the woman's tongue protruded out of her mouth, bluish in color and twisting like a snake. Then, as the roar subsided, she collapsed on the floor like an empty sack.

Standing there at the front of the sanctuary, I thanked the Lord quietly for my previous experience with demons in the privacy of my own home!

More to Follow!

It was evident that one demon had gone out of this young woman, but the pressure within me warned me that there were others still to be dealt with. Without this warning I could easily have said, "Praise the Lord, our sister has been delivered!" – and done no more. Sooner or later, however, her conduct would have revealed that she was not fully free, and the ministry of deliverance would have been discredited.

At the same time, I felt it would not be appropriate to continue the public ministry in the Sunday morning worship service. So, I said to John Faulkner and the church treasurer, who was standing nearby, "If you will take this lady into my office, I'll continue with my sermon."

The two of them, along with Lydia, marched her off into my office while I returned to the pulpit. I found myself preaching to round eyes and open mouths. The morning's demonstration had convinced them of the reality of demons far more effectively than any sermon!

After a little while, I heard dull thuds coming from the direction of my office. Then Lydia put her head around the corner.

"You'd better come in here quickly," she said.

I knew she was not given to panic, so I said to the people, "I'll close my sermon now, and you can either stay in the church and pray, or go home – whatever you feel like."

Just as I left the platform, a member of the congregation, a godly woman who was the mother of the church pianist, walked up to me and said, "Mr. Prince, was that our daughter?"

I stopped in surprise. Sharon, our pianist, always sat in the front row. She was a solid Pentecostal, saved and baptized in the Holy Spirit since childhood. Her father was a Pentecostal pastor, her husband a Pentecostal Bible student and her brother-in-law a Pentecostal minister. She was a quiet young woman whose ministry was to play the piano, not in the least like the woman on the floor. I did not know how to answer.

Finally, I said, "I think it must have been Sharon. There was no one else on that pew."

"May I come with you to the office?"

"By all means."

Sharon's husband and father joined us, too, and we made our way together to the office. It was a scene such as I had never imagined. John Faulkner and the church treasurer each held one of Sharon's arms, but whenever she could get a hand free, she was tearing off her clothes.

This is where preachers get into trouble! I thought to myself.

Aloud I said to Sharon's husband and parents, "If you'd like to take Sharon to a psychiatrist, that's perfectly all right with me. I will do nothing more unless you all assure me you want me to continue to handle this case."

"We'd like you to handle it," they all replied.

John Faulkner asked to be excused and left, followed by the treasurer, as Sharon's husband and father took charge of holding her. As she came under their authority, the manifestations subsided.

Then Sharon's mother drew me aside and began to tell me that she had been seeking an appointment for me to counsel with Sharon and her husband. This mother, a trained nurse, used discreet, professional language to describe what was happening between the young couple. In that decade Christians did not use the term *oral sex*, but I understood that was what she wanted to communicate.

I recalled the strange contortions of Sharon's tongue as the lying spirit came out of her. Was that perhaps a manifestation of the demon's activity?

As I began to talk to the family, another element came to light. Sharon had developed a strange infatuation with her brother-in-law – her husband's brother – who was a minister. The two of them were exchanging letters that seemed harmless, yet could have sexual overtones. Sharon actually had one such letter, addressed to her brother-in-law, in her purse at that moment.

"That is a sinful relationship," I said immediately, "and unless you repent and give it up, I cannot pray for you. You cannot expect Jesus to deliver you if you continue in this sin. But if you are willing to renounce it, then give me the letter that's in your purse, and I'll tear it up in front of you."

It took ten minutes to convince Sharon. Finally, she handed me the letter, and I tore it up and dropped it into the wastebasket.

As I put my hand on Sharon to pray for her, she slumped to the floor in a sitting posture, and I slipped down beside her. I felt the Lord showing me that there was only one position in which Sharon could receive deliverance: with her body pressed forward and her head between her knees. It was as if the Lord Himself was gently directing my movements. I put my hand on the small of Sharon's back and pressed her body forward. Then I began to command the demons to come out.

For the next hour or more, they came out one by one, naming themselves as they did. Nearly all the names had a sexual connotation. One named itself as flirtation and another as petting. Some of the names were obscene.

Surprisingly, my hand on Sharon's back served as some kind of electronic instrument. As each demon came out, I felt a gentle impact against the palm of my hand as if it were "registering" its departure.

When it seemed that the last demon had gone out, Sharon collapsed limply on her back on the floor and lay there for about ten minutes. Then she raised her arms in the air and began to praise God for her deliverance. As far as I could perceive, Sharon was fully delivered.

Yet the final outcome was sad. Sharon never came back to our church. She was too ashamed to be seen by the people who had witnessed her conduct that Sunday morning. To me, that seemed an indictment of our church. We were so "respectable" that people who were really in trouble would not come to us.

This led me to search my own soul. What was I pastoring? A middle-class social club that met on Sunday mornings? Or a place where people with real needs could come for help?

The decision I made determined my future. I could not in good conscience give the rest of my life to pastoring a middle-class social club. I decided I must devote the abilities God had given me to helping the people who most needed my help, even if it meant departing from accepted norms of religious behavior.

But I had no idea what direction this decision would take me.

The Splash and the Ripples

The events of that Sunday morning were like a rock tossed into the middle of a pond. First there was a large splash, but then ripples moved out until they reached the margin of the pond. The splash took place when the demon cast Sharon to the floor in front of my pulpit. Within the next week, Lydia and I began to feel the effect of the ripples. People came to us from everywhere, most of whom we had never seen before. They came mostly to our home, not to the church. I have no idea how they found us, but week after week we counseled and prayed with people in our home for deliverance from demons. We seldom got to bed before two or three in the morning.

After a while my physical strength began to break down. I learned a serious lesson: If I do not care for my own physical and spiritual condition, I will not be in a state to help others get delivered. In fact, I might need help myself. I realized that a person who is worn down physically or spiritually is vulnerable to demonic attack.

I soon discovered, too, that proper instruction out of Scripture is essential for effective deliverance. (I will provide such instruction in chapters 21 and 22.) Before praying with people, I had to give them a sound biblical basis for what I was doing. In this way I built up faith in them to appropriate what Jesus had provided for them through His sacrificial death. Then, through our mutual faith, victory would be assured.

All this demanded many long hours. I realized I was in danger of neglecting my other pastoral duties. Was the time coming for me to resign my pastorate?

Meanwhile, God was leading me step by step from one new situation to another. Each successive situation revealed new aspects of the ministry – aspects I had to come to grips with. Then He led me on to the next situation – but only after I had "graduated" from the previous one. Evaluating all that had been happening, I realized God was not using the classroom method of a theological seminary to instruct me in the ministry of deliverance. He had me enrolled in a less prestigious school: the school of experience.

Questions for This Study

1. What tool did Derek use in the deliverance process?
2. How did Derek assist the young woman in renouncing her sinful relationship to her brother-in-law?
3. What kind of church did Derek decide he wanted to pastor?
4. A person needs to receive biblical _____ before they receive _____ .
5. God enrolled Derek in the school of _____ to teach him about deliverance.

Life Application

1. If someone in your church began screaming as Derek described, how do you think most of the congregation would respond?
2. If asked to assist in an individual's deliverance, would you be able to help? Explain your answer to this question.

Memory Verse

When the enemy comes in like a flood, the Spirit of the Lord will lift up a standard against him.   Isaiah 59:19

Faith Response

Father, open my faith to comprehend and exercise the authority that has been given to me in the name of Jesus.

Answers are on page 410

EIGHT

Beneath the Surface

THESE DRAMATIC ENCOUNTERS WITH DEMONS HAD opened a window onto a strange, new spiritual realm. Passages in the gospels describing demonic manifestations were no longer records from an alien culture or the remote past. They had suddenly come alive. I had seen in my own experience that these accounts were just as relevant in twentieth-century United States as in first-century Israel.

Years later, while on vacation, I had an experience that brought back memories of these first confrontations with demons. When I went snorkeling for the first time and looked under the surface of the water, I was confronted with a new world. Unfamiliar creatures in dazzling colors moved to and fro against a background of plants and coral unlike anything I had ever seen on dry land. *Just imagine,* I said to myself. *This other world has been close to me nearly all my life and I was scarcely aware of its existence!* Yet all I had to do was put on a snorkel and look down into the water!

It seems to me that we in our "advanced" Western civilization have been like swimmers without snorkels. Our humanistic, anti-supernatural view of the universe has kept us from recognizing the reality of a demonic realm that has never been far from us. In parts of the world like Africa or Asia, people have always been conscious of demons and can describe many tangible demonstrations of their intrusion into human affairs.

In the West, too, demons exercise a continuous and powerful influence on our lives, but our humanistic prejudice has blinded us to the evidence. In fact, our refusal to acknowledge the evidence makes it easier for demons to operate undetected. We tend to cloak their activity with high-sounding psychological or psychiatric terminology – yet the "cures" we claim are often disappointing.

The "snorkel" we need is a return to the spiritual perspective of the New Testament. Jesus and His apostles openly recognized the reality of demons and demonstrated how to deal with them. The cures they achieved were often dramatic and always effective.

Now, as I studied the gospel accounts in the light of my new experiences, my previous ministry began to seem superficial. I took to heart the Lord's assessment of the prophets of Israel in Jeremiah's day: "They have also healed the hurt of My people slightly, saying, 'Peace, peace!' when there is no peace" (Jeremiah 6:14).

Frequently I had failed to discern the demonic nature of the problems in people I had counseled. I had dealt with only superficial behavioral manifestations. As a result, some of the apparent victories were incomplete or short-lived. All too often there was no real spiritual progress. We had been like Israel at Mount Sinai, going around the same mountain again and again instead of setting out on the road toward our God-given destination.

The apostle Paul said of his ministry, "I do not fight like a man beating the air" (1 Corinthians 9:26, NIV). I saw that I had at times been an unskillful boxer, lashing out with my fists but not landing blows on my opponent's body. My preaching and prayers had failed to come to grips with the demons tormenting and crippling those to whom I ministered.

But now that began to change. In a few, brief weeks, God moved my ministry into a new dimension. As desperate people came to me almost every day, I tried to follow the pattern of Jesus, and I evaluated my progress against the record of the New Testament.

When Jesus dealt with demons, for instance, they apparently asked him not to do certain things, such as sending them "out into the abyss" (Luke 8:31), but there is no record that they ever defied or refused to obey

Him. In my first encounters, on the other hand, some of the demons had, for a time, openly defied me. In the case of Esther, I believe they were hoping to frighten me, so I would not press my attack against them.

I recognized that my authority over them was derived from Jesus, but manifestly it was not on the same level as His. I learned, however, that when I quoted Scripture persistently, declaring His victory and invoking His name, the demons were brought into subjection.

One particular theological question arose from my experiences with Esther, Rose and Sharon: How far is it wise, or right, to exchange words with demons? The clearest pattern in the ministry of Jesus is recorded in Luke 8:27–33:

> When Jesus stepped ashore, he was met by a demon-possessed [demonized] man from the town. For a long time this man had not worn clothes or lived in a house, but had lived in the tombs. When he saw Jesus, he cried out and fell at his feet, shouting at the top of his voice, "What do you want with me, Jesus, Son of the Most High God? I beg you, don't torture me!" For Jesus had commanded the evil spirit to come out of the man. Many times, it had seized him, and though he was chained hand and foot and kept under guard, he had broken his chains and had been driven by the demon into solitary places.

> *Jesus asked him, "What is your name?"*
>
> *"Legion," he replied, because many demons had gone into him. And they begged him repeatedly not to order them to go into the Abyss.*
>
> *A large herd of pigs was feeding there on the hillside. The demons begged Jesus to let them go into them, and he gave them permission. When the demons came out of the man, they went into the pigs, and the herd rushed down the steep bank into the lake and was drowned.* (NIV)

Luke's record makes certain points clear.

Jesus began by commanding the demon to come out of the man. Then the man – or the demon in the man – not only spoke but shouted at Jesus (see verse 28).

Jesus then asked the demon, "What is your name?" (verse 30). The demon answered, "Legion." A legion normally numbered between 4,200 and 6,000 soldiers. Clearly there were many demons in the man.

Then the demons "begged him repeatedly" not to order them into the Abyss (verse 31). Probably many different demons were speaking out of the man and had a lot to say! Jesus apparently made no attempt to prevent them speaking.

Eventually the demons sought to strike a bargain – "If we have to go out, please let us go into the pigs" – and Jesus gave them permission (see verse 32).

When the demons entered the pigs, all two thousand of them (see Mark 5:13) stampeded into the lake and were drowned (see verse 33). Isn't it amazing that one man could contain enough demons to send two thousand pigs to their death in the lake?

Meditating on this account, I arrived at two conclusions. First, it is scriptural – and sometimes necessary – to ask a demon, "What is your name?" Second, if demons answer back, it is necessary to deal with their answers, until they are forced to acknowledge the authority of Christ and to come out of their victim.

Since then, I have learned that getting to know the name of a demon provides a "handle" to bring it into subjection. We might compare it to getting to know the name of a dog threatening to attack us. Calling the dog by its name in an authoritative tone of voice can be the first step in bringing it into subjection.

I wondered why Jesus allowed those demons to go into the pigs. Perhaps because it was an alternative they were willing to accept. If they had been forced to go out of the man without being allowed to enter alternative victims, they might have put up such a struggle that the man would not have been able to survive the pressure.

It is important to bear in mind that all Jesus said and did was directed toward one practical end: to get the demons out of the man. This incident cannot be used to justify conversing with demons for any other purpose.

In particular, I came to understand that it is altogether wrong and extremely dangerous to seek any kind of special revelation from demons. God has given us His Holy Spirit as our all-sufficient Teacher and Revelator. The Holy Spirit is the Spirit of truth, whereas Satan is the father of lies. To seek revelation from some satanic source, therefore, is to dishonor the Holy Spirit and to expose ourselves to deception.[1]

In those first few weeks God gave me deep compassion for those who are bound by demons. I began to look below the surface of problems that appeared purely physical or psychological, and to identify the underlying demonic forces at work. It was exciting to be able to help people whose needs I could never previously have understood. God began to put within me a burning indignation that so many of His people are still in bondage to demons.

After Jesus released a woman who had been bent double for eighteen years with a spirit of infirmity, the religious leaders challenged Him because He was not following their rules for observing the Sabbath. He responded indignantly, "Ought not this woman, being

---

1. In the 1970s a group of ministers who had experience dealing with demons began to hold lengthy conversations with them, seeking to obtain special understanding about things in the spiritual realm. In the end this proved disastrous. The group went into serious doctrinal error and some of them died prematurely.

a daughter of Abraham, whom Satan has bound – think of it – for eighteen years, be loosed from this bond on the Sabbath?" (Luke 13:16).

"Amen, Lord!" I reply. "She ought to be loosed! And so ought thousands of others of Your people who are bound and tormented by demons."

Questions for This Study

1. As Derek states, our Western society's _____ and _____ mindsets keep us from recognizing the reality of demonic activity.
2. In refusing to acknowledge the influence of demons in our lives, what have we allowed them to do?
3. How do we in the Western world tend to cloak demon activity?
4. Scripturally, in what circumstances would it be permissible to converse with a demon?
5. What kind of information is off-limits when speaking with a demon?
6. Give two reasons why this is wrong and extremely dangerous.

Life Application

List some demonic behaviors you have personally observed or seen through the media. Even though they are demonic in their source, describe how they are explained away in psychological or medical terminology.

Memory Verse

Finally, my brethren, be strong in the Lord and in the power of His might. Put on the whole armor of God, that you may be able to stand against the wiles of the devil. For we do not wrestle against flesh and blood, but against principalities,

against powers, against the rulers of the darkness of this age, against spiritual hosts of wickedness in the heavenly places.
Ephesians 6:10–12

Faith Response

Lord, remove any humanistic thinking in me that would blind me to the reality of evil spiritual beings.

Answers are on page 410

NINE

Lessons from an Expanding Ministry

WHILE LYDIA AND I WERE BUSY MINISTERING TO people in our home, our congregation was busy, too, discussing what had happened to Sharon, our pianist. Some of our people were jubilant over the victory that had been won. Others were fearful and confused. So, I announced that I would give some systematic teaching on this topic at our midweek Bible study.

About one hundred people gathered. I led them objectively through the New Testament references to demons, taking care to point out how to recognize and deal with them. But as I prepared to close the Bible study with a standard pastoral prayer of dismissal, the people began to protest.

"You can't stop now!" they said. "We need help."

"How many people need help?" I asked. "Put up your hands."

When about fifty people raised their hands, I was faced with a crisis. I remembered my intense struggles in ministering to one individual at a time. How could I possibly cope with fifty?

At that moment I received a flash of inspiration. I recalled occasions when I had preached a message of salvation and ten or twenty people had come forward to repent. Never for a moment had I imagined that it was my responsibility to save them. As I had led them in a prayer, each one made personal contact with the only One who could save him or her – Jesus Christ, the Savior. Over the years I had seen hundreds of people receive salvation by this simple procedure.

The same Christ who is the only Savior, I reasoned, is the only Deliverer. Only Jesus can break the power of demonic bondage in people's lives and set them free. So, I should be able to introduce them to the Deliverer in just the same way.

I asked those who had raised their hands to come to the front, telling the others to stay and pray quietly in their seats. Then I explained to those wanting deliverance that they needed to make direct personal contact with Christ, and I outlined four simple conditions they needed to meet:

1. Be sure you have repented – that is, turned away from every form of sin.
2. Look only to Jesus; He alone is the Deliverer.

3. Base your appeal solely on what Jesus did for you through His death on the cross, not on any "good works" of your own.

4. Be sure that, by an act of your will, you have forgiven every person who ever harmed or wronged you.

Finally, I reminded them of the promise through which I myself had received deliverance from the demon of depression: "Whoever calls on the name of the Lord shall be saved" (Joel 2:32). I also quoted the words of Jesus: "In my name you shall expel demons" (Mark 16:17, Weymouth). And I added, "In the name of Jesus you have the authority to expel them from yourselves."

I led them in a simple, step-by-step prayer covering the conditions they needed to meet, and closed with, "And now, Lord Jesus, I renounce any evil spirit that has gained any control over me, and I claim Your promise of deliverance. In Your name, Lord Jesus." Then I prayed a collective prayer for all of them, as they began to receive deliverance.

The next fifteen minutes were lively – screaming, sobbing, coughing, shaking. Some fell to the floor, while others gave no outward indication that anything was taking place inside them.

When things quieted down, I asked how many of them felt they had received the deliverance they had prayed for. About 75 percent raised their hands. The

THEY SHALL EXPEL DEMONS

remaining 25 percent needed further, individual ministry. I dismissed the people whose needs had been met, and Lydia and I did our best to help those who remained behind. In most cases we simply stood with them, encouraging them to press through to deliverance for themselves and to use the name of Jesus against their enemy. We also gave them appropriate Scriptures to quote.

In some cases, it became clear that they had not fulfilled all the conditions I had outlined. The hindrance we needed to emphasize most, as it turned out, was failure to forgive those who had harmed or wronged them.

Out of this experience I learned one vitally important principle: The most important issue was not whether I had the necessary authority, but whether the people seeking deliverance had met God's conditions for receiving it. The promise of Jesus to His disciples has never varied: "Behold, I give you the authority... over all the power of the enemy, and nothing shall by any means hurt you" (Luke 10:19). The variable factor in each situation is the response of those to whom we minister. When people meet the scriptural requirements, deliverance follows.

Full deliverance, however, may not be immediate but progressive, as people come to understand the various areas of their lives that have been affected by demonic influence. Often there looms in the background the dark shadow of a generational curse or a curse from occult sources. (I deal with this in my book *Blessing or Curse: You Can Choose!* and will say more about it in chapter 21.)

Controversy

From that first experience I came to see that the ministry of deliverance is not primarily a test of my personal authority. It is a means of helping people in desperate need. Since then, I have continually placed my main emphasis on explaining God's conditions and urging people to make the right response.

That midweek Bible study was a turning point in my ministry. When I discovered that the majority of people could receive their deliverance collectively, after proper instruction, I was no longer restricted to one-on-one deliverance. In fact, I found that the combined faith of one hundred people all gathered for the same purpose is usually greater than the faith of a single individual.

Once I grasped this principle, the Lord began to open the way for me to apply it on a much wider scale. In 1964 I finally resigned my pastorate and moved out in faith as an itinerant Bible teacher, combining the ministries of teaching and deliverance.

The Lord made it clear to me at the outset that He did not want me to become a "specialist" in deliverance. I understood that delivering people from demons is an integral part of the message of the Gospel, not some unusual extra reserved for "experts." My example was Jesus, who "traveled throughout Galilee, preaching in their synagogues and driving out demons" (Mark 1:39, NIV). Apparently, Jesus was always ready to drive out demons when He preached. If He had not done so, He would have failed to meet the needs of some of the people, and His ministry would have been incomplete.

As the Lord began to open one door after another before me, my name became known to various sectors of the Body of Christ in the U.S. Some people objected vehemently to the manifestations that frequently accompanied the ministry of deliverance, but others sent urgent messages asking for my help. The cries for help outnumbered the criticisms.

One early experience stands out in my memory. In 1965 I was asked to be the Bible teacher at a large, international Full Gospel convention in the Conrad Hilton Hotel in Chicago. One day I gave a Bible study to about six hundred people on deliverance from demons. When I asked at the end how many felt they might need deliverance, at least two hundred people put up their hands. Looking at them, I breathed a prayer of thanks to God for teaching me the principles of collective prayer for deliverance!

When the people came forward, I gave them the same basic instruction on meeting God's conditions that had proved effective with smaller groups. Then I led them in a step-by-step prayer, just as in other such meetings. Finally, I told them to cry out to the Lord individually for deliverance, while I prayed a collective prayer for them all.

The scene that followed was somewhat chaotic. Two or three fell to the floor and lay writhing and struggling as the demons came out. Some women were screaming as demons came out of them. Still others rushed out in a panic and went up to their hotel rooms, declaring they would not come back so long as I was preaching.

This meeting provoked a good deal of adverse criticism. Yet in subsequent years I often met people from all over the U.S. who told me, "I got delivered in that service in the Conrad Hilton Hotel in 1965."

Some people opposed my ministry of deliverance on the basis that I did not do it as effectively as Jesus. They would quote Matthew 8:16: "He cast out the spirits with a word, and healed all who were sick" – implying there were no noisy or disorderly disturbances when Jesus ministered. But, as I said in chapter 3, that is not correct. Other passages in that gospel describe incidents that were both noisy and disorderly.

Furthermore, Matthew records that Jesus not only expelled demons but also "healed all who were sick." Like many other preachers, I had prayed for the sick and had not seen them all healed. Yet I did not recall anyone ever attacking me for not ministering to the sick as effectively as Jesus did. Why, then, should people focus only on the area of dealing with demons?

Again, I knew that I did not teach as well as Jesus, yet no one had ever criticized me for this or suggested it as a reason I should stop teaching. Furthermore, some of the very people who criticized my deliverance meetings were themselves Bible teachers. I was sure they, too, would acknowledge that they did not teach as well as Jesus. Yet it did not seem to occur to them that they should give up teaching. So, again, why was criticism focused on this ministry of deliverance?

I suggest two main reasons. First, because Satan jealously guards the secrets of his demonic kingdom. Over the centuries he has built up in the minds of Christians a barrier of fear and superstitious ignorance keeping us from acknowledging either the truths of Scripture or the facts of experience.

The second reason is that the professing Christian Church has established a pattern of behavior considered "appropriate" for the house of God. Too often this leaves no room for the messy facts of human sin and demonic oppression. Some churchgoers are offended by the noisy and disorderly manifestations that sometimes accompany the driving out of demons. Dignity takes precedence over deliverance.

I looked again at the ministry of Jesus and discovered various instances in which a demon or demons screamed and shouted at Him; interrupted His preaching; convulsed people when they came out, leaving them apparently dead; caused a person to wallow on the ground foaming at the mouth; and stampeded a herd of two thousand pigs into a lake. Yet Jesus was never disturbed, nor did He suppress these manifestations. He simply dealt with them as part of His total ministry to suffering humanity.

Gradually I came to see that there are three possible sources of such manifestations: the Holy Spirit, evil spirits or unruly human flesh. To each we need to respond appropriately. If certain manifestations are from the Holy Spirit, we need to acknowledge Him and flow with Him. If they issue from an evil spirit, we need to take a stand against it and expel it. If they come from unruly human flesh, we need to exercise discipline and bring it under control.

The scriptural solution, however, is not to exercise such rigid control over every meeting that no disorderly manifestations are ever permitted. This would go far beyond the pattern set by Jesus. Furthermore, it overlooks the fact that in the ministry of Jesus it was the anointing of the Holy Spirit that forced the demons to manifest themselves. A similar anointing today will produce similar results.

If demons never manifest themselves, then there is no opportunity to expel them. They remain below the surface in people's lives, free to continue their harmful and destructive activities. Given their choice, no doubt demons would rather be "controlled" than expelled. At the same time, I recognize that I was slow sometimes to identify the source of certain manifestations. I tolerated fleshly demonstrations, attributing these to a spiritual source and not dealing appropriately with them. (Over the years, I trust, I have become more sensitive to these issues.)

But not all the criticisms I received were hostile. Some of my friends said to me, "Derek, it's all right to cast out demons, but you don't have to do it in public where it disturbs people." This seemed reasonable to me, but I felt that before changing my methods, I ought to further study the ministry of Jesus and see whether He normally dealt with demons in private.

To my surprise, I found in the gospels that there was nothing Jesus did more regularly and consistently in public than drive out demons. I could not find a single instance in which He took a person aside in private for this purpose. This aspect of His ministry excited more public attention than any other. Apparently, He was not concerned that those who needed deliverance might be deterred by embarrassment. I decided I would not try to improve on the methods of Jesus!

Other Lessons I Learned

The deepest and most enduring effect in my own life was the new light deliverance cast upon the cross. I discovered in experience that our authority over demons is derived *solely* from the victory Jesus won for us by

His shed blood, His death and His victorious resurrection.

Satan's primary weapon against the whole human race is *guilt*. This is why he is "the accuser of [the] brethren" (Revelation 12:10). He reminds God continually that we are all guilty of transgressing God's righteous law. Hence, he contends that we have no claim on God's mercy but are justly subject to God's judgment.

But Jesus, by His atoning death on our behalf, "wiped out the handwriting of [legal] requirements that was against us" and "disarmed [the satanic] principalities and powers" (Colossians 2:14–15) by taking from them their primary weapon against us: *guilt*. As a result, we are now "justified" and "have peace with God" (Romans 5:1). To be justified means to be made righteous with Christ's righteousness, which retains no record of sin, nothing of which to be guilty. In effect, each of us has been on trial in the court of heaven, and the verdict has been handed down: *not guilty!* On this basis – and this basis only – we have the right to exercise the authority Jesus has given us over demons.

Through many personal encounters with demons, I have learned that they are not impressed by religious terminology. They scorn denominational labels or ecclesiastical status. But when we use the name of Jesus and boldly affirm the words of Scripture that declare His victory won on the cross – and the unchallengeable

righteousness we have received from Him by faith –
then their arrogance and viciousness melt away. They
begin to act like the contemptible creatures they truly
are, and we witness a fulfillment of Revelation 12:11:
"[The believers] overcame him [Satan] by the blood of
the Lamb and by the word of their testimony."

On several occasions I have seen a demon manifest
fear in the trembling of the body of its victim. This is
why James said that "the demons believe – and tremble!"
(James 2:19). At other times a demon forces its victim
to cover his ears with his hands to avoid hearing the
bold proclamation of Jesus' victory on the cross, which
is the only and all-sufficient basis of deliverance, but is
torment to demons.

Early in this ministry God impressed me with
another truth: the importance of *repentance*. People
who have been taken over by a demon and who then
commit some sinful act may say, "I'm not responsible.
A demon made me do it! I couldn't help myself." By this
they imply that they are not guilty and do not therefore
need to repent.

But in Acts 17:30 Paul told the men of Athens,
"God … commands all men everywhere to repent." The
phrase *all men everywhere* leaves out no person and no
place. Every human being without exception is required
by God to repent.

The universal reason we all need to repent is that we
have all yielded to the rebellious nature we have each

inherited from Adam. We are rebels at war with God. We cannot make peace with Him until we lay down our rebellion – that is, until we repent. That is the true nature of repentance: to lay down our rebellion. This is not primarily an emotion; it is an act of the will.

But beyond our universal responsibility for rebellion, each one of us has added our own individual acts of sin and self-will. Sometimes a series of such wrong choices and acts actually brings people to the point that they are no longer able to resist demonic pressure to commit certain sinful acts. They are literally *compelled*. Nevertheless, they are still responsible for all the wrong things that brought them to that state of powerlessness in the face of evil. Therefore, they still need to repent.

There are, I discovered, two main barriers to deliverance: failure to repent and failure to forgive others and lay down resentment. Once people met these two requirements, I discovered that I had the authority, delegated by Jesus, to drive the demons out of them. But I had to determine the boundaries of my authority.

I had heard, for example, about people who, after they drove demons out, "cast them into the pit." Was this scriptural? I could find no incident in the New Testament where Jesus cast demons into the pit. In dealing with the man from Gadara (see Matthew 8:28–32), Jesus did accede to the demons' plea and allow them to go into the herd of pigs. But He did not go beyond that. Previously the demons had asked Jesus, "Have You come here to torment us before the time?" (verse 29). Apparently, the demons already knew there was a set time in God's eternal program for them to undergo their final punishment, but until that time, they would be permitted to continue their present activities. Accordingly, Jesus stayed within the boundaries set by His Father.

International Ministry

As I declared the truths God was teaching me about deliverance, tape recordings of my teachings began to circulate in the U.S. and in other nations. In 1967 I received an invitation to New Zealand, where I conducted my first public deliverance service outside the U.S. In subsequent visits to New Zealand, I have met Christians still talking about that service, and even some who received deliverance there. Since then, I have conducted public deliverance services in more than twenty other nations.

One of the most memorable was in 1984 in a remote, rural area in the northwest corner of Zambia in Central Africa. About seven thousand African men and women gathered for a teaching convention at which I was the main speaker. The "auditorium" was a large, natural amphitheater about the size of an American football field, sloping gently downward toward the speaker's platform. The underbrush had been cleared away, but trees had been left standing to provide shade. It was like an open-air cathedral with the sunlight streaming through the branches. The people all sat on the ground – men, women, old, young, mothers with babies and small children – completely filling the area.

I had been asked to teach for five days. I saw this as a wonderful opportunity to take the people stage by stage through the redemptive plan of God – out of the slavery of sin and Satan "into the glorious liberty of the children of God" (Romans 8:21).

My first message was on the one, all-sufficient sacrifice that meets the need of all ages and all races: the cross. When I called for those who needed to repent, many responded and received salvation.

Then I taught them how to pass from curse to blessing. I explained that, on the cross, Jesus "[became] a curse for us" so that we might inherit "the blessing of Abraham," whom God blessed in all things (Galatians 3:13–14). Then I led these Africans – who are very conscious of the reality of curses and fear them greatly – in a prayer of release, in which nearly all participated. (Again, I will say more about this in chapter 21.)

At the end of my message, a well-dressed man came up to me, threw himself on the ground and rolled in the dust at my feet. "Thank you, thank you, thank you!" he said. "All my life I have never known a day without pain. Today, for the first time, I am free from all pain."

On the third day I taught them how to recognize the

activity of demons and to be delivered from them. At the end I led them in a collective prayer of deliverance.

The scene that followed was, to say the least, dramatic. The Africans in that area, keen hunters of animals, had been taught by witch doctors that, in order to be successful, they must open themselves up to the "spirit" of the particular animal (such as a lion, elephant or boar) that they intended to hunt. Unfortunately, often their wives were also taken over by similar spirits.

When we prayed the collective prayer for deliverance, these animal spirits began to manifest themselves. There was a cacophony of jungle sounds. Near the front, a man with a lion spirit attempted to charge me, but another man tripped him and he fell to the ground without reaching me. Several other people, both men and women, dug in the ground with their noses like boars. A number of women slithered on their bellies on the ground like snakes. One man rolled like a log all the way up the incline to the entrance.

I was reminded of the word *pandemonium*, describing a situation in which many demons are let loose simultaneously. It was remarkable that there was no violence. The name of Jesus was continually on the lips of the workers who were assisting. After about an hour the uproar subsided. The supernatural peace that followed led me to believe that most of the people had been set free.

On the fourth day of the conference my theme was

the baptism in the Holy Spirit and how to receive it. After I led the people in a prayer, several thousand began to speak in tongues simultaneously. It was awe-inspiring! Then on the final day I taught the people how to exercise the vocal gifts of the Holy Spirit, and led them into the personal exercise of these gifts. The result was a confirmation of the words of Paul in 1 Corinthians 14:31: "For you can all prophesy one by one, that all may learn and all may be encouraged."

The conference in Zambia was in many ways the culmination of what God had been teaching me. Deliverance is not an end in itself, but one vital stage without which some Christians will never enter into the fullness Jesus intended for them. Since that time in Zambia, I have conducted similar teaching conferences in several other nations, including Russia, Kazakhstan, Turkey and Poland. In each place I have taught people how to recognize and expel demons – and this has always led to a glorious experience of the power and gifts of the Holy Spirit.

Because of the pressure of these public conferences, and also because the Lord has led me to place greater emphasis on my writing ministry, I rarely counsel individuals today. Through the printed word I am able to help many more people than by on-one-one counseling.

In the next chapter, I will share some important personal lessons that I learned from ministering to others.

Questions for This Study

1. Only Jesus can break the power of _____ in people's lives and set them _____.

2. What are the four simple conditions people must meet to receive deliverance?

3. Satan is called "the accuser of [the] brethren" in Revelation 13:10, because he uses _____ as his _____ against the human race.

4. What are the two main barriers to deliverance?

5. List three possible sources for unusual manifestations and how we should respond in each case.

6. Authority over demons is derived solely from what source?

Life Application

1. Ask the Holy Spirit to show you anyone regarding whom you have unforgiveness, a grudge, resentment or bitterness. Then take appropriate steps to resolve your issue with them.

2. Ask the Holy Spirit to help you remove any habitual sin or disobedience by doing the following: confess this sin, submit to the Lord and ask Him for help to obey.

Memory Verse

"Behold, I give you the authority to trample on serpents and scorpions, and over all the power of the enemy, and nothing shall by any means hurt you." Luke 10:19

Faith Response

Lord, as You grant me grace, I will walk in forgiveness toward anyone who has wronged or hurt me.

Answers are on page 411

TEN

Ongoing Personal Conflicts

IN CHAPTERS 4 AND 5 I RELATED MY AGONIZING
struggle with depression, and the pride that made me
reluctant to acknowledge to my congregation that I had
actually needed deliverance from a demon.

Also, I had always assumed that a person must be
demon-free in order to minister deliverance to others.
Yet I knew that someone who has been saved through
faith in Christ does not have to become a perfect Christian before he or she can testify about salvation or lead
others into it. In fact, the enthusiastic testimony of a
new convert is often more effective than a sophisticated
presentation by a mature believer.

The same can be true, I discovered, in the ministry of
deliverance. People who have themselves experienced
deliverance from demons are often the most successful
in ministering deliverance to others, because they know

from personal experience the power of the name of Jesus and the Word of God. They can also empathize with them in their struggles. Theological knowledge, on the other hand, can be more of a hindrance than a help. Deliverance is a ministry in which a person must be willing to "get his hands dirty," dealing directly with representatives of Satan's evil kingdom.

The basic requirement for ministering deliverance is stated by Jesus in Mark 16:17: "And these signs will follow those who believe: In My name they will cast out demons...." Jesus required only one thing: simple faith in His name and His Word. This is true whether one is casting demons out of others or expelling them from oneself.

Diagnosing the problems of others and helping them to be set free assisted me, paradoxically, in discerning and dealing with problems of my own. I soon learned two important principles. First, many – perhaps most – problems with demons begin in childhood. Second, if a person has persistent or intractable problems with demons, there is almost always some root in the occult. In that case, full deliverance will probably not come until this root has been exposed and dealt with.

Both of these principles applied in my own case. I was born to British parents, nominal Christians, in India, where I spent the first five years of my life. In accordance with the established custom among the British upper classes, my mother soon handed me over to a nanny, in my case a Hindu *ayah*, who undoubtedly became the strongest spiritual influence in my early life. I do not remember just what she did, but later, as a young boy, I often had the impression that some evil power was dogging my footsteps.

This dark influence followed me through all my early years. In my teens I formed glamorous images of India as a source of esoteric wisdom on a higher level than the materialistic culture of the West. In my student years at Cambridge, I studied yoga and even conceived an ambition to become a yogi. Had global travel been as easy then as it is now, I would doubtless have beaten a path to the door of some Indian guru.

My field of study at Cambridge was Greek philosophy, and particularly the philosophy of Plato. My two heroes at this time were Socrates and Plato. Then in World War II I had a supernatural encounter with Jesus Christ (as I mentioned in chapter 4), and this completely changed the course of my life. From then on, I became an ardent student of the Bible. But much of my thinking was still influenced by Plato, and I kept some of his writings as works of reference.

As I gained further insight into the way people become exposed to demons, I saw that my admiration for Socrates and Plato kept open a door in my personality that made me vulnerable to demonic influence. Socrates himself acknowledged the influence of a demon in his life. As he was dying of the hemlock that he had been sentenced to drink, his last words to one of his associates were, "We owe a cock to Aesculapius." He was ordering that a cock be sacrificed on his behalf to Aesculapius, the heathen god of healing.

Even though Socrates enjoys great prestige in the intellectual world, his behavior fell into the same category as that of a man sacrificing a cock in a voodoo ceremony. Idolatry is still idolatry, even when described in elegant, classical Greek.

I realized, too, that a similar occult influence pervaded the writings of Plato, my other hero. In his last major dialogue, the *Timaeus*, he actually acknowledged, "We have no word from God." So, he turned to the occult literature of Egypt for revelation concerning the mysteries of the universe.

Again and again, as I sought to help those needing deliverance, I observed the close association between occult involvement and serious problems of depression. It became clear to me that this had probably contributed to my own struggles against depression when I was a young pastor.

One day in 1970 I was meditating on Deuteronomy 7:26: "Nor shall you bring an abomination into your house, lest you be doomed to destruction like it; but you shall utterly detest it and utterly abhor it, for it is an accursed thing." I walked around my home and realized I had a number of "abominations." So, I made a decision that I believe had an important bearing on the future course of my life and ministry: I determined not to keep in my possession anything that in any way dishonored Jesus Christ or that opened the door to demonic influence.

I rid myself of a succession of items I had inherited from my family: four antique, beautifully embroidered Chinese imperial dragons and a whole assortment of Chinese antiques, all carrying the emblem of the dragon. I also disposed of items containing elegant Arabic calligraphy, some of which undoubtedly gave glory to Mohammed and the Muslim god, Allah. I also cleared out my library, especially Plato's books, and everything that in any way glorified the occult. Then I threw away a series of poems I had written in the days when I was still enamored of India.

This dramatically changed the spiritual atmosphere around me. It was like passing out of twilight into the clear light of day.

I have real concern for the many Christians slow to recognize God's intense hatred of every form of the occult. Tolerating any kind of continuing occult influence in our lives exposes us to forces that threaten our own spiritual well-being.

I remember when the TV series *Bewitched* brought the occult into our homes in a way that seemed amusing and harmless. Recognizing its seductiveness, I warned other Christians of the danger of permitting such influences to enter their minds and spirits. Thirty years later occult programs are proliferating on the TV screen and, in many cases, having a subtle, destructive effect on families. This is no less true of the Internet and, on a much wider scale, of movies, videos, toys and other forms of entertainment for children.

Struggling with Fear

My release from demons has been progressive, perhaps because of my occult background and heritage. At times I have still had to seek the Lord for deliverance for myself. One of the enemies that has assailed me persistently is a spirit of fear that began in my childhood. In certain circumstances I would be gripped by fear. My stomach would tighten up, my body would grow tense and sometimes my face would turn pale, even though, by the exercise of my will, I could usually maintain outward control, so that people were not aware of the struggle going on inside me.

I remember vividly when I first experienced this kind of fear. I was nine years old, sitting on the back seat of a car going too fast down a steep incline. My whole body became tense, and suddenly I felt a tingling sensation in my feet that worked its way up my legs and seemed to settle in the pit of my stomach. We did not have an accident, but a spirit of fear entered me.

After I was saved and baptized in the Holy Spirit, these attacks of fear diminished but did not altogether cease. Once I came into deliverance, I knew what to do. I would call on the Lord and He would set me free. Yet somehow, I did not immediately succeed in keeping my deliverance. In moments of physical or emotional weakness, when my spiritual defenses were weak, the spirit of fear would come on me unawares. As soon as I recognized its presence, I would once again claim and receive deliverance.

At first, I could not understand why I should have this continuing struggle, but then I saw from the Scriptures that many of God's strongest servants experienced an ongoing battle with fear. I thought of David, the mighty man of valor, captain of the armies of Israel. He had a close and intimate relationship with the Lord, yet he had many fears. In Psalm 34:4, for example, David says, "I sought the LORD, and He heard me, and delivered me from all my fears."

I pondered on that phrase *all my fears*. Then I began to consider many different kinds of fear: fear of the dark, fear of heights, fear of man, fear of failure, fear of sickness, fear of death, fear of confined places (claustrophobia), fear of open or public places (agoraphobia), fear of the unknown. . . . A complete list would be very long. Every one of these fears is agonizingly real to the one suffering from it.

I recalled, too, Paul's description of the troubles he encountered in Macedonia. He was attacked not only from without but also from within: "We were troubled on every side. Outside were conflicts, inside were fears" (2 Corinthians 7:5).

I would not dare to compare myself with David and Paul, two of the Lord's most valiant servants. Nevertheless, since they struggled with fears, I did not necessarily have to write myself off as a failure because I, too, experienced such struggles.

In time I learned how to deal with this particular attack. Today, whenever I recognize the familiar symptoms of fear coming on me, I quote 2 Timothy 1:7, applying it personally: "God has not given [me] a spirit of fear, but of power and of love and of a sound mind [self-discipline]." Then I take my stand against the spirit of fear. When I do this, I am victorious. The spirit of fear can attack me from without, but it cannot enter me.

Essential Spiritual Conflict

This experience and others led me to rethink my concept of the Christian life. I shall always be grateful to the Christians through whom I came to the Lord in 1941. I respected their uncompromising acceptance of Scripture as the inspired, authoritative Word of God. But as I studied the Bible and encountered the problems Christians face, I realized that some of their doctrinal positions were based on human tradition, not Scripture. For instance, they often presented a simplistic picture of the Christian life: You get saved and born again, baptized in water, baptized in the Holy Spirit with the evidence of tongues – and then you have no more problems. Although not presented explicitly as a doctrine, this was the assumption behind much of their thinking.

Unfortunately, it does not correspond to the realities of the Christian life. As I have walked with the Lord, I can testify, like many others, that we never really know what spiritual problems are until we are baptized in the Holy Spirit. Only then do we begin to understand the full meaning of words such as *temptation* or *oppression* or *spiritual conflict*. This is no reason, however, to become discouraged. We need only look at the pattern of Jesus Himself. After the Holy Spirit came upon Him and He entered His ministry as Messiah, the Anointed One, His next experience was forty days of intense, person-to-person conflict with Satan in the wilderness.

He entered this conflict *"filled with the Holy Spirit"* (Luke 4:1), but He came out of it victorious over Satan, and began His public ministry *"in the power of the Spirit"* (verse 14). The full power of the Holy Spirit was not released even in Jesus until He had met and defeated Satan in a direct, person-to-person encounter.

The pattern Jesus set is one that each of us must follow. God releases the power of the Holy Spirit through us only in the measure that we are victorious in our spiritual conflict with Satan. It took Jesus forty days to gain His victory, but at the end it was total. We must follow the same pattern, although our victories will never be on the same level as His. We cannot bypass the conflict with Satan if we desire to see the power of the Holy Spirit released in our lives. Spiritual conflict of this kind is not the evidence of failure. Rather, it is an essential condition for fruitful ministry.

Meditating on this, I thought about my first wife, Lydia, who is now with the Lord. When I came to know her in the 1940s in what was then Palestine, she was one of the boldest and most committed Christians I had ever met. She had been a successful schoolteacher from a well-to-do family in Denmark. She left all that and came to Jerusalem in obedience to God, not knowing what He had in store for her. In 1928 she took a little dying baby girl and nursed her to health. (This story is told in my book *Appointment in Jerusalem*.)

For the next twenty years Lydia maintained a home for girls without parents, as a woman on her own in a culture where women are generally considered inferior. During those years she had faced riots, bandits, economic privation, primitive living conditions and opposition from Jews and Muslims, but she had never wavered. She continued that life of victory – whether in the pressures of post-war London, on a mission station in East Africa or traveling with me in ministry – right up to her death in 1975.

Yet one episode in her life surprised me. In the 1970s she and I ministered to hundreds of people needing deliverance, and we saw many glorious victories. One time after a particularly powerful session, we were returning to the apartment the church had made available to us, but Lydia refused to take the elevator. Instead, she chose to walk up four flights of stairs. When I questioned her about this, she replied, "I don't feel comfortable in an elevator."

We talked a little more, and she recalled an incident in Denmark when she was five. She had been playing in a cupboard under the stairs in her aunt's house, and the aunt, seeing the door open, closed and latched it. Finding herself a prisoner in the dark, Lydia became hysterical. She began to scream and pound on the door. The aunt came to her rescue quickly, but in those few moments a demon of claustrophobia – a fear of confined spaces – had apparently entered Lydia.

As soon as Lydia's problem was brought out into the open and identified as a spirit of fear, we prayed together and she was completely delivered. She never again had a problem with elevators.

We were both astonished that Lydia herself could need deliverance after helping set so many others free. But it taught me that we need to be ready to respond to the Holy Spirit's prompting even if it does not suit our theology! If Lydia and I had not prayed that evening, she would never have come to full victory in that area.

So I am no longer taken aback by demonic conflict even in mature Christians. I have learned, for example,

133

to look for demonic activity in some physical infirmities. At times I have had a sore throat, cold or sinus congestion and prayed for healing with no obvious change. I would endure a week or two of frustrating infirmity before the conditions cleared up. One day, however, I was reading about the time Jesus entered the house of Simon Peter and found Peter's mother-in-law sick with a high fever. "So, He stood over her and *rebuked* the fever, and it left her. And immediately she arose and served them" (Luke 4:39, emphasis added). Why would Jesus *rebuke* a fever? Clearly, He saw in that fever something more than a mere physical condition.

Common
COLD

The next time I was fighting a feverish cold, I decided to follow the example of Jesus. I took my stand against it as a demon and received a powerful deliverance. The condition, instead of lasting a week or two, cleared up within 24 hours.

Now, when I experience pain or sickness of any kind, I consider the possibility that there is a demon behind it. If this diagnosis proves correct, complete deliverance usually follows quickly. If the problem is due to a natural physical condition, on the other hand, I pray for healing and wait on God to respond. I am also grateful for the help of doctors and medications when God leads in that way.

It would be absurd to suggest that all sicknesses are caused by demons. Some are, some are not. This makes it important to cultivate discernment, so that we can

Discernment

Senses exercized

recognize which sicknesses have demonic causes and which do not. The writer of Hebrews provides a key to developing this kind of discernment: "But solid food belongs to those who are of full age, that is, those who by reason of use [*practice*] have their senses exercised to discern both good and evil" (Hebrews 5:14).

There are two requirements, then. First, we need to *feed* on solid food – that is, the full revelation God has given us through the complete Bible. A thorough knowledge of Scripture is essential. Second, we must *practice* discerning. This is not something that will come to us only by Bible knowledge or theory. Nor does it apply only to recognizing the activity of demons. It requires the consistent exercise of our spiritual senses in every situation we encounter.

The Moment of God's Choosing *spirit of stiffness*

In 1994 I had a strange, unexpected experience. I was with a group of Christian intercessors, waiting on the Lord. Suddenly, without any act of my will, my hands went up into the air and my body went through a series of convulsive jerks. For a moment I felt embarrassed, wondering what the other people would think. Then I asked myself, *Which is more important – what people think or what God wants to do?*

I decided to yield without reservation to what God was doing. (Actually, most of the others were too pre-occupied with God to notice what was happening to me.) The convulsive jerks lasted for a few minutes; then I relaxed and my body went limp. I knew I had received deliverance from a spirit, and the word *stiffness* came to my mind. Then God showed me when and how that spirit had gained access.

When I was born in India in 1915, the local medical facilities were relatively primitive. When I was eighteen months old, the doctor detected that my legs were unequal in length. He put one leg in a splint for several months and instructed my mother to keep me on my back. As a result, I developed a stiffness in some parts of my body and an inability to make certain normal physical movements.

In the intervening nearly eighty years, I had experienced a whole series of blessings from God: salvation, the baptism in the Holy Spirit, miraculous healing, the exercise of various spiritual gifts. Yet that spirit of stiffness did not leave me until the moment God sovereignly intervened to expose it and drive it out. Now, since my deliverance, I have begun to experience new freedom of movement.

Like Lydia, my second wife, Ruth, has been an active participant with me in helping set many people free from demons. But her life, too, has not been free from demonic conflict. We have learned that God, in His sovereignty, uncovers demonic activity at times of His own choosing.

One morning about ten years ago, we had been

Spirit of humanism

sitting up in bed reading our Bibles, as we regularly do, when Ruth began to speak of some of the influences to which she had been exposed as a practicing Jew. She related how powerfully her thinking had been affected by the humanistic element in Jewish culture. Suddenly she said, "I wonder if humanism could be a spirit."

When Ruth renounced that spirit and commanded it to leave her, she began to shake violently. In fact, if I had not held onto her, it would have thrown her out of bed. As soon as the spirit was cast out, Ruth regained control of her body and began to praise and worship God.

What surprised us both was that something that seemed so abstract and intellectual could produce such a powerful physical reaction. As I meditated on this, I realized that humanism has its roots in Greek philosophy. It is one of the major satanic forces at work in the world today, I believe, and will ultimately open the way for the rise of the Antichrist.

From this and other experiences in the demonic realm, I have come to see that we are in a war. The more battles we win, the more we learn to recognize Satan's tactics, and thus come closer to the full victory Jesus won for us on the cross.

I can sum up the lessons I have learned in the words of Paul in Philippians 3:12: "Not that I have already attained, or am already perfected; but I press on, that I may lay hold of that for which Christ Jesus has also laid hold of me."

Questions for This Study

1. Give two reasons why people who have received deliverance are sometimes more effective in ministering to others.

2. What was Jesus' one requirement for those who minister deliverance?

3. For most people, many problems with demons begin in _____.

4. When someone has a consistent problem with demons, most often the root is occultic in nature. How can this person receive full deliverance?

5. Spiritual conflict in one's life is not always evidence of _____, it may be an essential condition for a _____ ministry.

6. What are the two requirements needed for developing discernment?

Life Application

1. Ask the Holy Spirit to show you any past experiences with the occult which may be influencing you today. These experiences may be from you or one of your ancestors.

2. Repent of each of these activities (naming each one). Renounce them, asking the Lord for forgiveness. Please remember that even if this act was done by an ancestor, you must repent as if you had been the one involved.

Memory Verse

Not that I have already attained, or am already perfected; but I press on, that I may lay hold of that for which Christ Jesus has also laid hold of me.

Philippians 3:12

Faith Response

Lord, make me aware of places and situations in which I may practice learning to discern spirits.

Answers are on page 411

PART THREE
Seven Questions

THE SUBJECT OF DEMONS, AS I POINTED OUT IN the introduction to this book, has often been surrounded with superstitious dread. Christians have sometimes had the attitude that "if I leave demons alone, they will leave me alone." Regrettably, that is not true. Demons will not leave you alone. The fact that you are a Christian does not in itself protect you. On the contrary, demons view Christians as their primary target for attack.

Your best protection, therefore, is to discover what Scripture reveals about the nature and activity of demons. Then you will be able to avail yourself of the protection God has provided for you through faith in Christ.

I have found there are certain questions concerning the realm of the demonic that people frequently ask. In this section I consider seven such questions:

1. What are demons?
2. Flesh or demons?
3. How do demons come in?
4. What is the occult?
5. Is witchcraft still at work today?
6. Do Christians ever need deliverance from demons?
7. Will the Holy Spirit indwell an unclean vessel?

To each question I offer an answer based on Scripture and on my personal observation and experience over many years. These will help clear up many common misunderstandings and will prepare you for Part 4, in which you will actually come to grips with demons. At the end of chapters 14, 16 and 17, you will find personal testimonies of Christians who relate their experiences with demons.

ELEVEN

What Are Demons?

WHEN PEOPLE BECOME AWARE OF THE REALITY OF demons, two questions naturally arise: What kind of creatures are they? And what is their origin?

What Kind of Creatures?

I describe demons as disembodied spirit beings that have an intense craving to occupy physical bodies. Apparently their first choice is a human body; but rather than remain in a disembodied condition, they are willing to enter even the body of an animal (see Luke 8:32–33).

It is hard for us to entertain the idea of a person without a body. Nevertheless, even though demons have no bodies, they have all the normally accepted marks of personality:

1. Will
2. Emotion

3. Intellect
4. Self-awareness
5. Ability to speak

1. Will

The demon who has gone out of a man says, "I will return to my house from which I came" (Matthew 12:44). The demon here exercises its will to make a decision, and then follows it up with the corresponding action.

2. Emotion

"You believe that there is one God. You do well. Even the demons believe – and tremble!" (James 2:19). Trembling is an outward mark of strong emotion. As I have said, I have at times seen a demonized person, when confronted with the authority of Christ, begin to tremble violently. This may be an outward manifestation of the fear of the demon inside.

3. Intellect

Demons have knowledge not derived from natural sources. The first time Jesus confronted a demonized man in the synagogue in Capernaum, the demon spoke out of the man and said, "I know who You are – the Holy One of God!" (Mark 1:24). It was more than a year before Jesus' own disciples began to realize what this demon had discerned immediately.

4. Self-Awareness

When Jesus asked the demonized man in the country of the Gadarenes, "What is your name?" a demon answered on behalf of itself and the other demons, "My name is Legion; for we are many" (Mark 5:9). The demon was aware of both its own identity and that of the other demons occupying this man.

5. Ability to Speak

In the first three gospels and also in Acts, we see several examples of demons able to speak through the vocal organs of the persons they were occupying. They could answer questions and carry on a conversation. Normally we regard the ability to speak as a distinctive mark of personality.

Now to the second question.

What Is Their Origin?

I have heard two main theories concerning the origin of demons.

1. They are some of the fallen angels associated with Satan in his rebellion against God.
2. They are disembodied spirits of a pre-Adamic race that perished under some judgment of God not recorded in detail in Scripture.

I do not believe that Scripture provides us with sufficient evidence to say with certainty which, if either, of these theories is correct. I must say, however, that on the basis of my experience, I find it hard to believe that demons are fallen angels. It seems clear to me that even fallen angels still maintain their dwelling place somewhere in "the heavenly places" (Ephesians 6:12) – although not "in the third heaven" where God dwells (2 Corinthians 12:2–4). It is not scriptural, therefore, to represent angels as operating continually on the plane of earth.

Demons, on the other hand, appear to be earth-bound creatures.

Demons, as I have encountered them, display a wide range of character traits. Some are vicious, violent, supernaturally strong. Others are weak, cowering, even ridiculous – characteristics one would not expect to find in angels, even when they are fallen.

Let me illustrate from a particular case. A woman had asked me to cast the demons out of her husband. After I had prayed with him for a while, he showed signs of becoming violent. At this point his wife drew me aside and said, "At home he throws chairs at me."

Why didn't she tell me that before she asked me to pray for him? I said to myself, resolving not to get myself in such a situation again!

After a while, as I continued to pray for the man, what seemed to be the last demon spoke out from the man and said, "I'm unclean."

Not wishing to ask questions and embarrass the

man in front of his wife, I said simply, "You demon of unclean thoughts, come out of this man!" The rather vague phrase "unclean thoughts," I felt, would not be too embarrassing.

The demon, however, responded, "That's not my name."

"Whether that's your name or not, I don't care," I said. "I command you to come out in the name of Jesus!"

Eventually the demon came out of the man, but protesting to the last, "That's not my name."

My subjective opinion is that no angelic being, even a fallen angel, would behave that way.

Classical Greek literature may offer us some light on the nature of demons. The philosopher Socrates, for instance, acknowledged that he had a *daimonion* influencing some of his actions. This *daimonion* would never tell him positively what he should do, but would warn him negatively that he should not do certain things. One time, for example, a group of men were waiting for Socrates in the marketplace, planning to attack him. His *daimonion* warned him not to go to the marketplace that day.

In our terminology, we would probably classify that as the work of a divining spirit. It would be out of line with Greek thought, however, to suggest that Socrates had a fallen angel directing him.

I find it hard to believe that any angel would have the intense desire – which is characteristic of demons – to

It is likely that demons were once human and therefore desire human bodies.

occupy a human body or, failing that, the body of an animal such as a pig. Surely, for an angel, that would be a place of confinement, not one through which such a being could express itself.

It is true that for the specific purpose of tempting Adam and Eve into rebellion, Satan did temporarily come to them in the form of a serpent. But subsequent passages of Scripture make it clear that he did not continue to occupy the body of a serpent.

Again in Luke 22:3–4 the writer records, "Then Satan entered Judas.... So he went his way and conferred with the chief priests and captains, how he might betray [Jesus] to them." This does not necessarily indicate that Satan entered Judas in person.

Earlier the writer describes how Jesus healed a woman of a crippling back condition by casting "a spirit of infirmity" out of her (Luke 13:11). In commenting on this, Jesus described the woman as "a daughter of Abraham, whom Satan has bound...for eighteen years" (verse 16). The actual, immediate cause of the woman's condition was "a spirit of infirmity." But since this spirit was directed and controlled by Satan, its activity was attributed to Satan himself. Jesus said that Satan had "bound" her.

Similarly, in bringing about the betrayal of Jesus, Satan may have acted through some demon that he caused to enter Judas. (It might have been a spirit of covetousness, since Judas was apparently motivated by the love of money.) Alternatively, if Satan did enter Judas in person, it would have been similar to his temptation of Adam and Eve. His appearance to them as a serpent was a special action that lasted only a short while.

The fact remains that up to this present time, Satan's headquarters and permanent residence are still in "the heavenlies."

From the Heavenlies or Earthbound?

In chapter 2 I pointed out that the Greek word for *demon* (*daimonion*) is derived from a primary word, *daimon*. What, then, is a *daimon*?

Greek mythology, which is at best a fractured mirror, depicts two main orders of "gods" who dwell in the "heavenlies." The higher is called *theos* (plural *theoi*). The lower order is called *daimon*.

One special function of the *daimons* was apparently to assign to each human being the destiny appointed for him by the *theoi* – the gods on the highest level. On a lower, earthly level are the *daimonions* (demons). They are dominated and directed by the "gods" on the higher level. Possibly the *theoi* direct the *daimons*, who in turn direct the *daimonions*.

It can be difficult for those who think only in English to form a clear picture of these three orders of spiritual beings, because English lacks the needed vocabulary. A *theos* is easily translated as a "god" and a *daimonion* as a "demon," but there is no obvious English word for the intermediate category, a *daimon*. In this book I have chosen to use the transliterated form *daimon*.

It is possible that the two categories of *theoi* and *daimons* correspond to what Paul in Ephesians 6:12 calls "principalities and powers" ["rulers and authorities," NIV]. Both are apparently resident in "the heavenlies."

On the other hand, the New Testament seems to picture *daimonions* (demons) as earthbound. There is no suggestion of their ever descending from, or ascending to, the heavenly regions.

In Matthew 12:43–44 Jesus gives a picture of the activity of a demon:

> *"Now when the unclean spirit goes out of a man, it passes through waterless places, seeking rest, and does not find it. Then it says, 'I will return to my house from which I came'; and when it comes, it finds it unoccupied, swept and put in order."*
>
> (NASB)

There is no suggestion that the demon either descends from, or ascends to, the heavenly regions. The Greek verb translated "passes through" is apparently used only of movement on the plane of earth.

Theoi, daimons and *daimonions* are united in a ceaseless war against the human race. Under Satan's domination they work together to inflict on humanity every possible form of harm, deception and torment.

Let us suppose for a moment that *daimonions* are spirits that once occupied the bodies of members of some pre-Adamic race who led ungodly and sinful lives. In their present condition, however, they have no way to give expression to the various lusts and passions and emotions they developed in their former bodies. It is conceivable that they could find some kind of vicarious release by acting out their lusts or passions or emotions through human bodies. This would explain one dominant characteristic of demons: their intense craving to inhabit and work through human flesh.

We need to remember that the Bible records only the history of the race descended from Adam. In this connection it uses the phrase *sons* (or *descendants*) *of Adam*. It was to redeem the members of this race that Jesus came as "the last Adam" (1 Corinthians 15:45). If other races existed before Adam, the Bible makes no explicit reference to them. In his book *Earth's Earliest Ages* (1876, reprinted by Kregel in 1975), G.H. Pember deals at length with this question.

I consider this theory of the origin of demons to be one possible hypothesis, but I am content not to pursue it further. There are some things God keeps secret (see Deuteronomy 29:29), and it is foolish to try to pry His secrets from Him.

It may be that neither of the two theories about demons is correct – that they are neither fallen angels nor disembodied spirits from an earlier race of beings.

Our concept of demons, however, has a practical bearing on how we deal with them. I have confronted many demons of different kinds, but have never had the impression that I was dealing with angelic beings.

On the other hand, I have had a certain amount of contact with satanic angels through intercessory prayer and spiritual warfare, which could best be described in the words of Paul in Ephesians 6:12: "For we do not wrestle against flesh and blood, but against...the rulers of the darkness of this age, against spiritual hosts of wickedness in the heavenly places."

The New Testament does not depict Jesus or His apostles as "wrestling" with demons. Rather, they confronted demons (as I said in chapter 3) and exercised the authority needed to expel them.

Demons in Scripture

Demons manifest themselves through humanity under many different names. The following is a list of specific names actually applied to demons in Scripture. Since translations vary in their use of names, I have given the name used in three translations, in the following order: the New King James Version, the New American Standard Bible and the New International Version. In each case the Scripture reference follows.

In the Old Testament

Jealousy/jealousy/feelings of jealousy	Numbers 5:14, 30
Ill will/evil/evil	Judges 9:23
Distressing/evil/evil	1 Samuel 16:14–23; 18:10; 19:9
Lying/deceiving/lying	1 Kings 22:22; 2 Chronicles 18:20–22
Perverse/distortion/dizziness	Isaiah 19:14
Deep sleep/deep sleep/deep sleep	Isaiah 29:10
Heaviness/fainting/despair	Isaiah 61:3
Harlotry/harlotry/prostitution	Hosea 4:12; 5:4
Unclean/unclean/impurity	Zechariah 13:2

In the New Testament

Mute/mute/robbed of speech	Mark 9:17
Deaf and dumb/deaf and dumb/deaf and mute	Mark 9:25

THEY SHALL EXPEL DEMONS

Infirmity/causing sickness/ crippling	Luke 13:11
Divination/divination/ predicting the future	Acts 16:16
Deceiving/deceitful/ deceiving	1 Timothy 4:1
Fear/timidity/timidity	2 Timothy 1:7
Error/error/falsehood	1 John 4:6

Other Demons

In addition to the names taken from Scripture and listed above, I will add some other names of demons that I have encountered personally.

In the Area of Physical Infirmity

Arthritis	Asthma
Cancer	Crippling
Epilepsy	Head pain
Migraine	Sinusitis
Thrombosis	

In Other, More General Areas

Adultery	Claustrophobia
Criticism	Disappointment

Envy	Fantasy
Gossip	Hatred
Hopelessness	Masturbation
Murder	Perversion
Rebellion	Rejection
Religion	Self-pity
Violence	Witchcraft

The lists given above are by no means exhaustive, but indicate the diversity of demonic activity. Satan apparently has at his disposal vast numbers of demons with which to assail and torment humanity.

Questions for This Study

1. How does Derek describe demons?
2. List the five normally accepted marks of a personality that demons exhibit.
3. What are two common theories about the origin of demons?
4. Give a reason why demons cannot be fallen angels.
5. The New Testament pictures demons as being _____. There is no suggestion of them _____ from or _____ to heavenly regions.
6. Instead of "wrestling" with demons, how did Jesus and his apostles deal with them?

Life Application

Read the lists of demons in this chapter. Ask the Holy Spirit to reveal to you any unnatural influence in your life that could be the result of a demon. Make a note of anything He shows you.

Memory Verse

For though we walk in the flesh, we do not war according to the flesh. For the weapons of our warfare are not carnal but mighty in God for pulling down strongholds, casting down arguments and every high thing that exalts itself against the knowledge of God, bringing every thought into captivity to the obedience of Christ. 2 Corinthians 10:3–6

Faith Response

Lord, I receive from You the discernment to know whether the battles I fight within myself are my flesh or demonic influence.

Answers are on page 412

TWELVE
Flesh or Demons?

FROM THE BEGINNING, EVER SINCE MAN TURNED from God in rebellion, he has been subjected to two main spiritual evils: sin and demons.

The effect of sin is universal and total: "All have sinned and fall short of the glory of God" (Romans 3:23). Sin has defiled the human race as a whole and every area of each personality individually.

The personality thus corrupted by sin is called in the New Testament "our old man" (Romans 6:6) or "the flesh" (Galatians 5:24). *The old man* describes the rebellious nature each of us has inherited from our first parent, Adam. Adam did not beget any children until he was in a state of rebellion against God. Therefore, in every descendant of Adam there is the nature of a rebel.

The term *the flesh* does not refer, in this context, to our physical bodies, but to the corrupt nature that is part of the inheritance each of us received at birth. Two different adjectives are used in English translations to describe this corrupt nature: *fleshly* or *carnal*. These are merely two different ways of translating the same Greek word.

For practical purposes, these two expressions – *the old man* and *the flesh* – may be used interchangeably. Each describes our corrupt, fallen, sinful nature.

The NIV, however, has moved away from the original language. It replaces both expressions by *our old self* and *the sinful nature*. It could be said that in this respect the NIV is more of an *explanation* than a translation.

With due allowance made, however, for these differences in translation, the truths unfolded in this book apply equally to *the old man, the flesh* and *the sinful nature*.

Although the problem of sin is universal, the problem with demons is not. Many members of our fallen human race have come under the power of demons, but not all. There is a close connection, however, between sin and demons. If mankind had never sinned, we would never have been vulnerable to demons.

A biochemist once explained to me, "A human body is attacked regularly by cancerous cells. When that body is healthy, its immune system identifies and attacks the cancerous cells, and they are unable to harm the body. But when the body has been weakened by illness or some kind of emotional shock, the immune system is unable to do its job effectively, and some form of cancer can develop somewhere in the body."

Immediately I said to myself, *That's just how it is with demons!*

Demons continually seek to invade a person, but when the person is healthy spiritually, the spiritual "immune system" within the person identifies and attacks the demons, and they are not able to move in and take control. Any kind of unhealthiness or emotional weakness, on the other hand, makes a person vulnerable to demonic attack.

The Remedy for Each

In the spiritual realm, as in the physical, correct diagnosis is essential. So it is important to know, in confronting our own problems or those of other people, what we are dealing with. Is it the flesh? Or is it demons? The question is of vital importance because the remedies are quite different.

The remedy for the flesh is crucifixion. By Jesus' sacrificial death on the cross, He canceled the claim sin has on our fleshly nature. Paul states this as historical fact: "Our old man was crucified with [Jesus]" (Romans 6:6).

But each of us must make a personal application of the cross to our fleshly nature. Paul says, therefore, in Galatians 5:24, "And those who are Christ's have crucified the flesh with its passions and desires." Once we have made this personal application of the cross, we can echo Paul's words in Galatians 2:20: "I have been crucified with Christ; it is no longer I who live, but Christ lives in me...." Crucifixion, then, is the remedy for our fleshly nature. It is a remedy each of us needs to apply personally.

The remedy for demons, on the other hand – as often demonstrated in the ministry of Jesus – is to cast them out.

These two remedies are not interchangeable. It is not possible to cast out the flesh, and it is not possible to crucify a demon.

Looking back over my own struggle with depression, described in chapter 4, I realized that was precisely the mistake I was making. I was trying to apply crucifixion – the remedy for the flesh – while I was actually dealing with a demon, and the remedy was to expel it. As soon as I understood my problem and applied the right remedy, I was delivered.

I have also confronted the problem in reverse when a person tries to apply to the flesh the remedy appropriate only for demons.

A man came to me once and said, "Brother Prince, I want you to cast a demon out of me."

"How does the demon affect you?" I asked.

"I just can't get on with my wife," he replied. "There's no harmony between us."

I listened carefully as he described how the disharmony between them affected both their lives. Eventually I said, "I don't believe you have a demon that needs to be cast out. What you need is to apply the cross to your fleshly nature."

It was obvious, however, that he was not satisfied. He had viewed deliverance from a demon as a "quick fix" that would substitute for the painful task of crucifying his own flesh.

Crucifixion is the distinguishing mark of those who truly belong to Christ. God is not interested in our church membership or denominational labels. He looks to see if our old, fleshly way of life has come to an end at the foot of the cross. Crucifixion is always painful, but it is the gateway to new life.

The Old Man and the New

Even after the life-transforming application of the cross in our lives, we still have to maintain personal discipline to keep the "old man" in subjection. In Colossians 3:3 Paul says to believers, "For you died, and your life is hidden with Christ in God." But in verse 5 he says, "Therefore, put to death your members which are on the earth: fornication, uncleanness, passion, evil desire, and covetousness, which is idolatry." We each have the continuing responsibility to keep the "old man" dead.

But even the death of the "old man" is not the final stage in the process. After that occurs, we must "put on the new man which was created according to God, in righteousness and true holiness" (Ephesians 4:24). The sacrifice of Jesus on the cross made possible an exchange. Our "old man" was crucified in Him so that the "new man" might come to life in us.

Just as a completely healthy human body is immune to cancerous cells, so the "new man" in Christ is immune to demonic activity. Most Christians, however, have not yet arrived at this state of complete spiritual health. In my limited personal experience, I have to say I have encountered comparatively few Christians who did not seem vulnerable to demonic activity.

Once again, we may borrow an example from the diagnosis and treatment of cancer. Since most people are not in the state of physical health in which they are immune to cancerous cells, it is necessary for scientists to do research and for doctors to acquire all the information available. This enables them to diagnose the presence of cancer and to prescribe appropriate treatment.

Likewise, there is an urgent need for Christians to learn all we can about the nature and activity of demons. This knowledge is important for all believers, since none of us can claim immunity from the attacks of demons. It is especially important, however, for pastors, evangelists and other Christian workers to whom people look for help. Without this knowledge, as I said in chapter 5, we will often be unable to make a correct diagnosis or to apply the appropriate remedy, and therefore we will not really help people.

Without the probe of discernment, we cannot effectively use the forceps of deliverance. (As I said before, I will offer practical instructions in Part 4 for diagnosing and dealing with demonic activity.)

Questions for This Study

1. By turning away from God, man subjected himself to what two main spiritual evils?
2. In the New Testament, man's corrupted personality is called _____ (Romans 6:6) or _____ (Galatians 5:24).
3. People can become vulnerable to a demonic attack when they are experiencing what two situations?
4. How is the remedy for problems caused by the flesh different from the remedy for problems caused by demons?
5. What is the best defense against demonic attack?

Life Application

Read Galatians 5:19–21. Consider the following areas of your life: Your physical appetite, your emotions and your thoughts. List anything from these three areas that requires the work of the cross to be applied.

Memory Verse

For you died, and your life is hidden with Christ in God. When Christ who is our life appears, then you also will appear with Him in glory. Therefore put to death your members which are on the earth: fornication, uncleanness, passion, evil desire, and covetousness, which is idolatry.

Colossians 3:3–5

Faith Response

By faith I commit myself to the work of the cross, to put to death the areas I have listed above in the Life Application.

Answers are on page 412

THIRTEEN

How Do Demons Come In?

FOR SOME TIME IN THE 1950S, I WORKED WITH A Christian medical specialist in London who had unusual insight into various areas of spiritual experience. He made one comment that has always stayed with me. "Remember," he said, "the devil chooses the weakest moment and the weakest place." I will apply this principle in seeking to answer the third question regarding the realm of the demonic: How do demons come in?

To attempt a comprehensive explanation of all the possible ways is far beyond the scope of this book. I will simply describe seven examples of moments or places of weakness through which demons habitually gain access to human personalities:

1. A family background in the occult or false religions
2. Other negative prenatal influences
3. Pressures in early childhood
4. Emotional shock or sustained emotional pressure

5. Sinful acts or habits
6. Laying on of hands
7. Idle words

Let us look at each of these areas of vulnerability.

1. A Family Background in the Occult or False Religions

In Exodus 20:3–5 the Lord warns of the evil consequences when people become involved in idolatry or false religion:

> *"You shall have no other gods before* [or beside] *Me.*
> *"You shall not make for yourself any carved image, or any likeness of anything that is in heaven above, or that is in the earth beneath, or that is in the water under the earth; you shall not bow down to them nor serve them. For I, the LORD your God, am a jealous God, visiting the iniquity of the fathers on the children to the third and fourth generations of those who hate Me."*

God warns against all forms of idolatry or other involvement with false "gods." The evil consequences of these particular sins can extend to four generations. Counting backward for four generations gives us four levels of ancestors:

Parents:	2
Grandparents:	4

Great-grandparents: 8
Great-great-grandparents: 16
Total: 30

Any or all of these thirty persons could be a channel through whom we may have been exposed to satanic influence. I doubt if any of us can guarantee that none of our thirty immediate ancestors was ever involved in any form of the occult or false religion.

This occult influence can begin while we are still in the womb. After all, what is weaker or more helpless than an unborn baby? It is entirely dependent on its parents for protection. Righteous, God-fearing parents provide that protection, but parents with an occult background expose their babies to the same spiritual influences that are at work in their own lives.

I have discovered that such babies are often demonized before they emerge from the womb. This is particularly true of people with backgrounds in Eastern religions such as Hinduism or Buddhism, or other false religions such as Freemasonry or Mormonism. In the next chapter I will deal more fully with the whole area of the occult.

2. Other Negative Prenatal Influences

Other negative forces may also affect an unborn child and expose it to demonic influence. A mother may resent or even hate the baby in her womb. Perhaps the mother is not married, or the father is unfaithful and irresponsible, or the mother may simply not want a child.

One thing a baby longs for, both before and after it is born, is love. When it does not feel love, it will probably begin to feel unwanted. This will in turn expose it to a deeper wound: *rejection*. Many babies are born with a spirit of rejection already in them.

At one time in the U.S. I encountered an unusually large number of people in a certain age group who suffered from rejection. When I checked their birth dates, I discovered that these fell between 1929 and 1934 – a time all older Americans remember as the Great Depression. I realized that mothers who were already having a hard time making ends meet resented the prospect of yet another mouth to feed. They may or may not have verbalized their resentment, but the sensitive little personalities in the womb felt it and came forth already carrying a spirit of rejection. This is just one of various demons that may affect an unborn child.

My own wife, Ruth, is a typical case. She was born in 1930, the eighth child in her family. Her parents were farmers who were struggling financially because of the Depression and the drought which caused that region of the U.S. to be labeled "the Dustbowl." At age forty Ruth was saved and baptized in the Holy Spirit and in water. She was already in the Lord's service when we married in 1978, yet she had an ongoing battle with rejection until the demon was identified and driven out. Even today she must be on her guard lest it assault her in a moment of weakness.

3. Pressures in Early Childhood

In James 3:16 we are warned, "Where envy and self-seeking exist, confusion and every evil thing are there."

Broken, strife-torn homes, in which parents are in bitter conflict with each other and/or have little time for their children, provide an atmosphere that invites the presence and activity of demons. Most young children lack the necessary emotional and spiritual defenses to withstand such demonic pressure. My personal observation (as I have said) is that most demonic problems begin in childhood.

In families in which the father has been an alcoholic, or cruel and dominating, or violent and abusive, girls often develop an intense hatred of men, which opens the door for the demon of hate. This is particularly true if the father has abused his daughters sexually. I have often speculated that this was the root cause of Esther's problems (described in chapter 6). It would account for the powerful hold that the demon of hate had over her.

Other demons that commonly exploit such children are rejection, anger, fear, rebellion, misery, loneliness, depression, and sometimes suicide. In the West there has been an alarming increase in the number of teenage suicides. In the U.S., from 1952 to 1992, the incidence of suicide among adolescents and young adults nearly tripled. In 1992 more teenagers and young adults died from suicide than from cancer, heart disease, AIDS, birth defects, strokes, pneumonia, influenza and chronic lung disease combined. In almost all these cases, according to my diagnosis, the demon of rejection opened the way for the demon of suicide.

4. Emotional Shock or Sustained Emotional Pressure

In 1 Peter 3:6 the apostle explains that Christian women may qualify as daughters of Sarah "if you do good and are not afraid with any terror." The Greek word translated "terror" has a wide range of meanings. One lexicon describes it as "any vehement emotion; passionate excitement." Another renders it either actively as "intimidation" or passively as "terror."

Women often, but not always, have weaker emotional defenses than men. They are especially subject to fear. One woman I prayed for told me that the spirit of fear had entered her when a frightening automobile accident took place right in front of her.

Today the vast coverage of the media means that millions around the world are exposed to sudden, shocking incidents. A brutal murder or a bus blown up or a building exploding may leave an indelible impression not only on the victims who survive, but on all the men, women and children who view the horror again and again on television.

Men as well as women are subject to many other forms of emotional pressure. Both men and women are subject, for example, to the passionate excitement of sexual desire. Sudden, unpremeditated yielding to such desire can often open the door to a spirit of lust. Indulging in sexual fantasies or watching pornography can have the same effect.

It sometimes happens, too, that a child or young person subjected to sexual assault may in that way unwittingly open up to a demon of lust. The demon has no respect for "innocence," but simply uses this moment of weakness to force its way in. From that moment on, the child or young person is subjected to pressures of lust that are not the expression of anything in his or her character.

But it is not always a sudden surge of emotion that opens the way to a demon. It may be some persistent, unrelenting pressure. A man who through no fault of his own has to spend many weary months without employment may begin to brood over his inability to provide for his family. Discouragement may affect him in various ways. Some tactless remark by his wife or trivial disobedience by his children may provoke a sudden outburst and open the way for a demon of anger to slip in. Or the continuing pressure of enforced inactivity may open him up almost imperceptibly to a dark spirit of depression or hopelessness.

Similarly, a woman whose husband continually belittles and criticizes her may finally yield to a spirit of hopelessness. Or a mother seeking to protect her child from dangers that are often more imaginary than real may project a spirit of anxiety on the youngster, until the spirit forces its way in and takes up residence in the child.

Obviously, there are many kinds of emotional shock or pressure to which people may be subjected. But these few examples may alert you to this form of demonic attack and help you build up your defenses against it.

5. Sinful Acts or Habits

Sometimes a single decisive act may open the way to a demon. The decision of Judas Iscariot to betray Jesus was such an act. When he went out from the Last Supper with this intention, Luke records, "then Satan entered Judas" (Luke 22:3). Judas himself opened the door that he could not afterward close.

Actions much less heinous than that of Judas may open the way for a demon. My late friend Don Basham was once praying for a woman who needed deliverance from a spirit of lust. When Don commanded the demon to come out of her, it answered, "She invited me in!"

"When did she do that?" Don asked.

"When she went to that dirty sex movie," the demon replied.

The woman had to repent and ask forgiveness for her sin before the demon could be compelled to leave her.

We need to remember that Satan is a legal expert. When some sinful act has opened the way for a demon, it will not leave until the sinful act has been confessed and canceled by God's forgiveness.

Any act of deliberate wrongdoing may open the way for a demon. Many such acts are possible – telling a premeditated lie, for instance, or shoplifting, or cheating on exams.

Again, it may not be a single act that opens the door. It may well be the deliberate, persistent practice of a sinful act that eventually becomes a habit. Secret sins like repeated masturbation or fornication or pornography almost inevitably open the way for demons. But other, more "respectable" habits can have a similar effect. Frequent overeating opens the way for a demon of gluttony. Persistent daydreaming opens the door to a spirit of fantasy. Habitual exaggeration in conversation opens the way for a lying spirit.

6. Laying On of Hands

Laying hands on a person in prayer is not just a picturesque religious ritual. It can be a powerful spiritual experience, a temporary interaction between two spirits through which supernatural power is released. Normally the power flows from the one laying on hands to the one on whom hands are laid, but at times it can flow the other way.

The power may do either good or evil. It may emanate from the Holy Spirit or from a demon, depending on the one from whom it flows. For this reason, Paul established certain safeguards. "Do not lay hands on anyone hastily," he wrote, "nor share in other people's sins; keep yourself pure" (1 Timothy 5:22). In other words, be careful with whom you allow your spirit to interact!

The laying on of hands should be done reverently and prayerfully. Any person participating should make sure he or she is not thereby, in Paul's words, sharing in another person's sins.

It is a mistake to turn a group of people loose and encourage them to lay hands indiscriminately on one another. The following brief testimony from Ruth illustrates the danger:

> In 1971 I was attending a charismatic meeting, and the speaker asked people to stand if they wanted prayer for healing. I had a bad cold, so I stood. He then instructed people seated nearby to lay their hands on us and pray for our healing. Four or five prayed for me.
>
> When I awoke the next morning, my cold was

better – but my fingers were all curled up and stiff and hurting. Immediately I thought, *Someone with arthritis laid hands on me last night!* I renounced the spirit of arthritis, and within five minutes all the symptoms were gone.

I was a very young believer, less than one year old, and I have been so grateful to God for teaching me then to be careful who lays hands on me.

7. Idle Words

This is an area in which many of us are caught off guard, yet one about which Jesus gave us some of His most solemn warnings.

> *"But I say to you that for every idle word men may speak, they will give account of it in the day of judgment. For by your words you will be justified, and by your words you will be condemned."* Matthew 12:36–37

What are "idle words"? They are words we utter thoughtlessly, words that do not express our real thoughts or intentions. When we are called in question concerning such words, we often excuse ourselves by saying, "I didn't really mean it," or, "I was only joking," as though this releases us from responsibility. Yet it is precisely these idle words that Jesus warns us against.

The fact that many Christians are habitually guilty of speaking idle words does not make it less serious. In fact, anyone who considers this warning of Jesus to be unimportant needs to repent.

Idle words can open the door to demons. In a fit of exasperation a person may say, "I'm sick and tired" of whatever it may be. He does not mean it literally, but he may be opening the door to a demon of sickness or tiredness. Words concerning death are particularly dangerous. Many times people say, "I nearly died laughing," or, "You'll die when you hear this one!" Death is a dark, evil power, and we are foolish to treat it lightly.

In a temporary fit of grief or discouragement, a person will often say, "I wish I were dead," or, "I'd be better off dead." Words like that are a direct invitation to the spirit of death. I have ministered to hundreds of people who opened themselves up to the spirit of death by such words carelessly spoken. (I will say more about the spirit of death in chapter 20.)

Making Jesus Lord

These seven examples illustrate some of the ways we and our children may be exposed to demonic influence. We need to remember, too, that demons are extremely persistent. A demon may be driven out but still seek to force its way in again. Jesus warned of this:

> *"When an unclean spirit goes out of a man, he goes*
> *through dry places, seeking rest, and finds none.*
> *Then he says, 'I will return to my house from which I*

came.' And when he comes, he finds it empty, swept,
and put in order. Then he goes and takes with him
seven other spirits more wicked than himself, and
they enter and dwell there; and the last state of that
*man is worse than the first.... "*Matthew 12:43–45

The unclean spirit returns to "his house" – that is, the person it formerly occupied – and it finds it "empty, swept, and put in order." Then it takes "seven other spirits more wicked than himself," reenters the house with them and occupies it once again.

What was there about "the house" that opened the way for the demon to reenter? The house was "swept" – that was no problem. It was "put in order" – that was no problem, either. But it was "empty" – that was the problem! The man had left his house vacant. He had never taken Jesus in to be his Lord.

When a person commits himself to Jesus as his Lord, he can look to Jesus for supernatural power to keep demons out. But without Jesus as Lord, he does not have the strength to protect his "house." When the demon assaults him, it may quickly break down his ineffective resistance. Then, when the demon reenters, it brings with it seven other demons, each more wicked than itself, and the person is worse off than he was before.

Let me illustrate with an example that became vivid to me. In the 1960s I generally traveled by car with Lydia to my preaching assignments in the U.S. Sometimes this meant a journey of two or three days. At evening, as we drove into a city, we would look for a neon sign with one word: *Vacancy*. When we saw that sign, we knew there was a motel open to receive us.

In the spiritual realm, Satan's demons roam around looking for the same sign: *Vacancy*. When they see it, they say to themselves, *Ah! Here's a person who hasn't made Jesus Lord of his life. Perhaps we'll be able to force our way in.* There is only one safeguard: making sure Jesus truly is Lord of every area of your life.

At the beginning of this chapter, I explained how a family background in the occult can open the way for demons. In the next chapter I will deal more fully with the whole area of the occult, emphasizing the even greater danger of any form of direct, personal involvement.

Questions for This Study

1. List the seven avenues by which a demon may enter a person.
2. Give an example of each one of these avenues.
3. When people open themselves up to a demon by committing a sinful act, what must take place for the demon to leave?
4. According to Derek, what transpires during the laying on of hands?
5. There is only one way to keep spirits from returning to "house" that they have been expelled from. What is that way?

Life Application

As you consider the seven avenues through which demons may gain access, please write down situations you have experienced that may have opened your life to their entry.

Memory Verse

For he who sows to his flesh will of the flesh reap corruption, but he who sows to the Spirit will of the Spirit reap everlasting life.   Galatians 6:8

Faith Response

Father, because of Your love for me, I place my faith in You to bring me fully into Your Kingdom through Your Son, Jesus and the work He did on the cross.

Answers are on page 412

FOURTEEN
What Is the Occult?

ONE MAIN CHANNEL THROUGH WHICH DEMONS gain access to humanity is the *occult*. If we do not understand the almost universal influence of the occult on the human race, we will not be able to deal effectively with demons.

Somewhere in every one of us is a deep longing to make contact with the unknown, with some "higher power" – something greater or wiser or more powerful than ourselves. This is true at all levels, from the teenage girl reading her horoscope, to the witch doctor in some remote tribe who has never seen a white man, to the scientist probing outer space and seeking to discover the secrets of the universe.

It was God who placed this longing within us, but His archenemy, Satan, has devised a way to divert seekers into deceptive, evil systems that bring them into bondage to himself. These deceptive systems can take countless different forms, but the generic name for them all is *the occult*. This raises the fourth question commonly asked concerning the realm of the demonic: What is the occult?

The word *occult* is derived from a Latin word that means "concealed" or "covered over." The power operating through occult practices or systems derives from Satan and is evil. But most people caught up in them do not know this. They have been enticed by labels or claims that make them appear highly desirable.

This is vivid to me because of my own experience. I was fascinated, as I said in chapter 10, by all things connected with India, and at Cambridge I actually attempted to become a yogi. No matter how hard I tried, however, I could never attain the release or fulfillment I was searching for. This indefinable longing was finally satisfied when, by the grace of God, I had a supernatural encounter with Jesus, the Son of God.

Scripture calls turning away from the one true God to false gods "spiritual adultery." Thus the Bible's strong warnings against immorality and adultery also apply to all forms of involvement with the occult. The "strange [immoral or adulterous] woman" described in Proverbs vividly depicts the lure of the occult.

In Proverbs 5:6 we are warned against trying to study her ways, because they are "moveable" (KJV), "unstable" (NKJV), and "crooked" (NIV) – all of which apply to the occult. I have observed that as one deceptive error is refuted, two new occult practices or false religions rise up in its place. Rather than attempt to give a full list, therefore, I will point out ways by which they operate. *Truth is the best defense against error.*

The tragic end of those who permit themselves to be enticed and deceived by a "strange woman" is described in Proverbs 7:25–27:

> *Do not let your heart turn aside to her ways,*
> *Do not stray into her paths;*
> *For she has cast down many wounded,*
> *And all who were slain by her were strong men.*
> *Her house is the way to hell,*
> *Descending to the chambers of death.*

Scripture emphasizes that the victims of this "strange woman" are *strong men.* It is characteristic of these deceptive forces that they primarily target men with leadership capacity. Satan hates such men. Strong men become vulnerable when they place their confidence in their own strength and in their past successes.

The Two Main Branches of the Occult

The two main branches of the occult are identified in Scripture as *divination* and *sorcery.*

Divination

Divination provides knowledge through supernatural means about people, events and situations. Frequently it predicts future events. The contemporary terms for this are *fortunetelling, psychic predicting* and *extrasensory perception (ESP)*.

A clear example is offered by the slave girl in Acts 16:16–22, who was said to be "possessed with a spirit of divination" (NKJV) or "a spirit by which she predicted the future" (NIV). Actually, the Greek merely says "she had a python spirit." In classical Greek culture the python was often associated with the practice of divination or fortunetelling. The modern term for such a person is *psychic*.

This slave girl was the first person in Philippi to discern the identity of Paul and Silas. "These men are the servants of the Most High God," she cried, "who proclaim to us the way of salvation" (verse 17). Everything she said was true, yet her knowledge came from a demon. When the demon was expelled, she lost the ability to tell fortunes and her masters lost their source of income.

This is what makes fortunetelling so deceptive and dangerous. A person – and it is usually a woman – who has a python spirit can actually be a channel of supernatural knowledge concerning the past or future. This measure of truth is the bait on Satan's occult hook by which he seeks to capture and enslave his victims.

Fortunetelling (divination) is truly occult (hidden). It conceals the satanic source of the power. Among those who seek to know the future are highly placed political leaders – and even professing Christians. Yet that contact inevitably exposes them to demons. I will describe just a few examples from my own personal observation.

Mary had listened to one of my teachings and believed she was under demonic power. She was a member of an old-line church that adhered to the Gospel of Christ. But one day an older woman, considered the most spiritual in the church, came to Mary and said, "Let me read your palm." When Mary acquiesced, the older woman told her, "You will have a baby, but it will be born dead."

It happened just as she said. Mary's baby was born with its umbilical cord wrapped twice around its neck and did not survive. By the sin of consulting a fortuneteller, albeit a professing Christian, I believe Mary opened the way for a satanic force that took the life of her baby.

Once Mary understood how she had exposed herself to demonic power, she was able to claim the benefit of Christ's sacrifice on her behalf and be delivered. But that did not bring her baby back!

How many other churchgoing Christians have unknowingly been caught in Satan's coils through fortunetelling?

The prediction of a psychic about the course of a person's life often amounts to a declaration of Satan's destiny for that life. In chapter 11 I mentioned that one main function of the *daimons*, who operate on the higher level, is to assign people their destiny – that is, Satan's destiny for them. The *daimon* communicates this destiny through a *daimonion* operating on the earthly plane. (This is the essence of fortunetelling.)

This was brought home to me vividly while I was trying to help a woman who had come to me for deliverance. She told me she had been a spiritist but claimed she had repented. After praying for a while, I paused to seek direction from the Lord. Suddenly the woman turned to me and said, "I see you in a car and it's wrecked against a tree."

I stiffened. *That's the demon speaking!* I said to myself.

Then I said aloud, "Satan, I refuse your destiny for my life. I shall not be in any car that's wrecked against a tree."

More than thirty years have passed since then, and it has never happened. Suppose, however, that I had allowed fear to enter, thinking, *One day I'm going to be in a car that's wrecked against a tree!* I would have been accepting Satan's destiny for my life, and I believe he might have killed me. I thank God I was alert.

A young Christian woman came to me once in great distress. A year or two previously, against her own better judgment, she had visited a fortuneteller who had told her, "You're going to be a young widow." Shortly afterward her husband was killed in a freak accident.

This young woman was overcome by guilt at the thought that her visit to the fortuneteller had somehow exposed her husband to the accident that had taken his life. She pleaded desperately with me to reassure her. I felt great compassion for her and did my best to comfort her, but I could not honestly give her the assurance she asked for. I could not rule out the possibility that she had, in fact, accepted Satan's destiny for her husband and herself.

My own wife, Ruth, had an experience before she came to know Jesus as her Messiah. A friend told her about a psychic who had predicted certain things in his life, all of which had come to pass. He suggested that this woman could give help and comfort to Ruth, who was struggling as she raised three children alone. Ruth, an active member of her synagogue, had never heard anything forbidding fortunetelling.

The psychic, who had never seen Ruth before and knew nothing about her, told her three things: "You were not able to bear children; you have three adopted children; and your husband has left you." Every one of those statements was correct. But the revelation did not come from God; it came from Satan. He intended to use this measure of truth as a bait to entice Ruth further into the occult.

In His mercy Jesus intervened in Ruth's life. Later, when she realized her error, Ruth repented and canceled Satan's power over her.

My first wife, Lydia, used a simple illustration to warn people of Satan's snare. "You can give me a glass of pure water," she would say, "but if you put in just one drop of poison, the whole glass is poisoned." No inspired "revelation" from a fortuneteller is worth having your whole life poisoned.

Country fairs, and even some churches, often have fortunetelling booths as a side show, "just for fun." But there is no such thing as harmless fortunetelling. Poison is poison, even when it is not labeled.

Another form of this demonic activity can be even more deceptive. I call it "charismatic fortunetelling." There are some ministers and speakers at conventions who offer personal prophecy and encourage Christians to come expecting "a word from the Lord." Undoubtedly some words are from the Lord, but many more proceed from the soul of the person ministering or even from a demon of divination. This can have a disastrous effect on the lives of those who are ensnared by it.

Most people want to know what the future holds. Fortunetelling caters to this desire. But God requires us to "walk by faith, not by sight" (2 Corinthians 5:7), not knowing what the future holds but trusting His unfailing faithfulness. There may, however, be times when God will give us some sovereign revelation concerning the future, without our desiring or seeking it. When He takes the initiative, the result will serve His purposes.

Another snare, which poses as a game, is the Ouija

board. I recall teaching on the nature of the occult in an Episcopal church in New England and praying for many who needed deliverance from demons. At the closing meeting on Sunday morning, the rector began by saying that his wife had asked him earlier in the day what had caused the smell of burning in their home. "It was me," he went on, "burning our family Ouija board!"

The use of Ouija boards and other occult practices has now permeated many branches of our school systems. In one school a group of girls began playing with a Ouija board just as an experiment – to see what would happen. One day it spelled out this sentence: *Within a week one of you will be dead.* That week one of the girls was killed in an accident. The rest of the girls were terrified, not knowing what would happen next.

Another way many people are exposed to divination is through horoscopes. A generation or two ago, many newspapers carried a daily portion of Scripture. Today the same pages often carry a daily horoscope reading. Casually scanning "your" horoscope in the newspaper with an unguarded mind can expose you to demonic influence.

Here again, many Christians are deceived. They consider such activities harmless, not recognizing the snare. I ministered to a Christian woman once who needed deliverance from a spirit of divination. She could not understand how such a spirit could have entered her. As I questioned her, she eventually acknowledged that she read her horoscope occasionally in the daily newspaper. She was shocked to realize that she had opened herself to a demon of divination.

Another potential door-opener for demons is involvement in the martial arts. Ruth and I ministered to a man who had excelled in karate. After a deliverance session, he discovered to his surprise that he could no longer do the karate kick. He had not realized that his ability came from a demon. We need to bear in mind that all the martial arts originated in cultures permeated with idolatry and demonic activity.

Sorcery

The other channel through which the occult operates is sorcery. Sorcery can be considered the twin sister of divination, but it has its own special sphere of activity. It uses various means to make an impact on the physical senses. Some of its tools are drugs, potions, charms, amulets, magic, spells, incantations and various forms of music.

In speaking of the last days, Paul warns that "evil men and impostors will grow worse and worse, deceiving and being deceived" (2 Timothy 3:13). The Greek word translated "impostors" means, literally, "enchanters," but because enchanting (incantation) is used in various occult rituals, it came to mean "wizards" or "sorcerers." Some contemporary forms of music, such as acid rock, fall into the same category and are used as channels of supernatural satanic power. This agrees with Paul's prediction that, as the age draws to its close, there will be a great upsurge of these occult forces.

The book of Revelation describes two end-time judgments of God by which some sections of humanity will be killed. Then it closes by saying that "the rest of mankind...did not repent of their murders or their sorceries or their sexual immorality or their thefts" (Revelation 9:20–21). The Greek word translated "sorceries" means literally "drugs." The NIV renders it "magic arts." The evil actions here associated with sorcery are murders, sexual immorality and theft. Often addiction to drugs opens the door to these other evils.

In Deuteronomy 18:10–12 the Lord declares His attitude towards various forms of occult involvement:

> *Let no one be found among you who sacrifices his son or daughter in the fire, who practices divination or sorcery, interprets omens, engages in witchcraft, or casts spells, or who is a medium or spiritist or who consults the dead. Anyone who does these things is detestable to the Lord....* (NIV)

The other main category mentioned here, in addition to divination and sorcery, is witchcraft, which also includes spells. I will deal more fully with witchcraft in the next chapter.

"Interpreting omens" is a form of divination. The last three categories – "a medium or a spiritist or [one] who consults the dead" – are all classed together today as spiritism. Their usual form of activity is called a séance.

All such people are said to be detestable to the Lord. The word translated "detestable" is the strongest word in the Hebrew language for what the Lord hates and rejects. Note, too, that God places such people in the same category as those who sacrifice their children to a pagan deity. It is hard for our contemporary culture to realize how intensely God hates all these occult practices. No one can be involved in them without being exposed to demons.

False Religion

Closely related to the occult is false religion. Often the two are inseparably intertwined. Both promise what appeals to us all – peace, power, knowledge, access to God. They claim to direct us to the light, but they actually entice us into darkness.

How, then, can we protect ourselves? In John 10:9 Jesus said, "I am the door. If anyone enters by Me, he will be saved. . . . " Again He said, "I am the way, the truth, and the life. No one comes to the Father except through Me" (John 14:6). Many different doors lead into the realm of the supernatural. But there is only one door that leads to the supernatural realm of God. That door is Jesus. Those who go through any other door can enter a supernatural realm – but it is the realm of Satan, not of the one true God.

Satan will do all the damage he can to humanity through ideologies such as atheism or humanism, but false religion is an infinitely more powerful tool in his hands. To this very hour, the great majority of the human race is enslaved by false religion.

As with other forms of the occult, it is impossible to list all the forms of false religion currently being practiced. But here are some of the main features that characterize religions as false:

1. Acknowledging a plurality of gods
2. Practicing idol worship in any form
3. Teaching that human beings can ultimately become gods
4. Teaching that people can achieve righteousness by their own efforts
5. Offering some form of esoteric knowledge available only to a privileged few

1. Religions That Acknowledge a Plurality of Gods

The early Church was surrounded by a polytheistic culture, but in 1 Corinthians 8:5–6 Paul defined the Christian position:

> *For even if there are so-called gods, whether in heaven or on earth (as there are many gods and many lords), yet for us there is only one God, the Father, of whom are all things, and we for Him; and*

*one Lord Jesus Christ, through whom are all things,
and through whom we live.*

2. Religions That Practice Idol Worship in Any Form

Idolatry is the first specific sin forbidden in the Ten Commandments and the one that carries the heaviest penalties (see Exodus 20:3–5).

3. Religions Teaching That Human Beings Ultimately Can Become Gods

This was the original temptation offered humanity by Satan in the Garden of Eden: "You will be like God [or like gods]" (Genesis 3:5).

This promise contains an inherent self-contradiction. God, who has created all things, including the human race, is Himself uncreated. It is logically impossible for man, the created, to become like God, the uncreated. The created can never become uncreated. Nevertheless, this promise of becoming like God has appealed to the self-exalting pride of humanity in every generation.

4. Religions Teaching That People Can Achieve Righteousness by Their Own Efforts

Again, the appeal is to human pride. Proud people are drawn to religious systems that demand hard, unreasonable forms of work and even self-inflicted suffering. The more rigorous the demands of a religion, the greater the degree of pride a person feels in fulfilling them.

5. Religions That Offer Some Form of Esoteric Knowledge Available Only to a Privileged Few

Access to this knowledge usually requires some special rite of initiation. Already in the first century, the apostles were warning their followers about this form of deception, called by its Greek name *gnosis* (knowledge). It was against this error that Paul warned Timothy:

> *O Timothy! Guard what was committed to your trust, avoiding the profane and vain babblings and contradictions of what is falsely called knowledge [gnosis] – by professing it, some have strayed concerning the faith.*   1 Timothy 6:20–21

There are two outstanding contemporary examples of religions whose secrets are revealed only to those who have passed through a stringent process of initiation. They are Mormonism and Freemasonry. The latter includes Eastern Star (the women's affiliate of Freemasonry), the Shriners, Rainbow Girls and Demolay.

In Mormonism the temple rituals are available only to a select few. No outsider may enter the temples while services are in progress. Freemasonry is even more secretive. Except for a few "official" public appearances, it is completely closed to the uninitiated and its secrets are guarded by blood-curdling oaths.[1]

---

1. For more information see *Masonry – Beyond the Light* by William Schnoebelen (Chick Publications, 1991).

Biblical Christianity, on the other hand, is open. It has no special process of initiation and no secret rites. The basis of its faith, the Bible, is an open book. All are encouraged to study it.

All forms of false religion appeal in one way or another to human pride. The Gospel, on the other hand, emphasizes that we are saved by the grace of God, which cannot be earned, but is received only by faith, which God Himself supplies. This leaves no room for pride.

> *For by grace you have been saved through faith, and that not of yourselves; it is the gift of God, not of works, lest anyone should boast.*
>
> Ephesians 2:8–9

There is a great gulf that cannot be bridged between the worship of the true God and every form of the occult or false religion. Paul emphasizes that every form of false religion is permeated by demonic power and that Christians must not, therefore, be involved in any way:

> *… The things which the Gentiles sacrifice they sacrifice to demons and not to God, and I do not want you to have fellowship with demons. You cannot drink the cup of the Lord and the cup of demons; you cannot partake of the Lord's table and of the table of demons.*   1 Corinthians 10:20–21

Anyone who has been involved in the occult or false religion needs to repent of it, confess it as sin, and seek Christ for forgiveness, cleansing and release. In addition, any books or other objects connected with the occult or false religion should be destroyed.

Clean and Free

This brief overview of the whole area of the occult and false religions reveals just how complex and confusing it is. There is no simple way to define or describe it. You might compare it to an octopus with many tentacles, which it fastens onto its victim. Just as the victim is guarding himself against one tentacle, another seeks to fasten onto him from his blind side.

This is well illustrated by the following testimony of a young man from a Christian family who was taken captive by the occult. Eventually he gained understanding of the demonic realm, received deliverance, and became a successful pastor.

> My parents are godly, born-again Christians. Like little Samuel of old, I was dedicated to serve the Lord from my conception. My parents taught me in the ways of truth from my youth. At the age of four, I would stand and preach to my folks or anyone else who would listen. In my early years my heart was tender toward the things of God, and I was always quick to pray and repent when I wronged God or

man. My precious parents taught me the best they could to walk in God's ways, but they erred greatly because their tradition did not teach them that occult involvement was much worse than their traditional "thou-shalt-nots."

To read the funny papers on Sunday, to go to a movie at any time or to condone drinking or smoking was unthinkable. But they never dreamed that allowing me to listen to ghost stories from my grandmother would start me on a path of heartache that would last over twenty years.

I first came into contact with my grandmother's stories at the age of seven. From that point on I could find joy in little else but the study of the occult. Radio programs of the '40s and '50s such as Inner Sanctum, The Shadow and The Whistler held my undivided attention. When TV came in, Night Gallery, Alfred Hitchcock and The Twilight Zone, plus any other kind of horror show, were my delight. By the time I was in the sixth grade, Edgar Allen Poe was my favorite author. A Baptist Training Union leader had introduced me to Poe's writing after a church Halloween party.

At age eleven, I told God in one of my frequent rages to get out of my life and leave me alone. I would buy small animals on a weekly, sometimes daily, basis and torture them to death. (I did this out of sheer compulsion. Years later I found out it was an integral part of witchcraft.) As strange as it may seem, I loved animals and wanted to be a doctor of veterinary medicine.

I would walk up to Christian workers and tell them I hated them. No form of discipline, word or rod, could constrain me. Rebellion and utter hatred of God, church, Christians, school, all forms of authority, and especially my mother and father, ruled part of my being. The other part of me longed to be kind and loving.

I finally came to a saving knowledge of Jesus at the age of 25. Even though God intervened and I was born again, my relationship with my parents was very bad. I loved them because of Jesus, but I could not be civil toward them for more than an hour. After a short period of close fellowship, anger and hate would surface and my misery would spread to all those around me. I tried to suppress my inward pressures, but they showed themselves by my craving for alcohol and food. I was 5' 7½" and weighed 217 pounds.

Was I really saved? Yes! Yes! Yes! I would spend hours weeping over lost souls, memorizing Scripture, witnessing and teaching the Word. What was so tragic was that still no one had ever told me that ESP, Ouija boards and books on psychic phenomena were forbidden to me as a believer. Therefore, I taught these to my First Baptist Church Training

Union class, thus stirring up in them the same idolatry and witchcraft my grandmother had stirred up in me years before.

Praise the Lord, one day as I told a fellow believer about my ESP, he told me to leave it alone, as Scripture warned against it. Oh, how I thank God for that man! His simple warning helped me begin on the path to deliverance.

Wanting to obey the Lord, I stopped all contact with the satanic realm. This was a good beginning, but what I really needed was complete renunciation of Satan and deliverance from the demons that had entered because of my interest in the occult.

How do I know I had demons? The day I stopped flirting with Satan and started obeying the Word, my internal problems and fears intensified. The anger and hate got worse. I began to have hallucinations night and day that presented the Jesus I loved in a most defiling way. Though I was happily married, my problem with masturbation was uncontrollable. My greatest plague was that I was a latent homosexual. I never gave in to it, though I had to fight it constantly. I would have horrible thoughts of being with men, and desires to dress like a woman. When I was alone, this evil spirit would manifest and I would take on effeminate mannerisms.

I hated and loathed these things with all my might. I prayed, repented and tried to crucify the flesh, not realizing that my problems had gone past the earthly, past the soulish, into the demonic (James 3:15). I had two fountains within me: One loved souls, blessed God and yearned to serve Him. The other defiled me with unclean thoughts and desires, blasphemed Jesus and cursed the saints. I would have willingly admitted all this to anyone who could have helped me. No one I knew had the power to deal with my problems, even to the point of listening to them. So I had to keep it all in as best I could.

In December 1969 my wife and I were introduced to the deliverance ministry. When it was mentioned that Christians could have demons, I gave no argument. My spirit leaped for joy, as I knew I had found the answer to my problems. A brother in Christ ministered deliverance to me, commanding the spirits to leave. I literally felt them move up from my stomach through my mouth, coming out in sighs and yawns.

From that day to this, I have never been plagued with masturbation. Plus, my anger and hate were gone. Now I can spend hours with my mother with no schisms. I can actually hug her with love and compassion.

For several months I was on cloud nine. Then suddenly the latent homosexuality and hallucinations started again. To be exact, it was about two o'clock one morning when I was awakened by demonic harassment from within and without. By this time I knew how to cast out demons and resist Satan, but my relief was only temporary.

Just when I was about to lose hope, I heard a Derek Prince tape saying occult sins had to be confessed and renounced by name. This was something I had not done. I immediately did so, realizing where most of my problems had come from. Shortly after this I went through my greatest deliverance service.

One day I was driving from Columbus, Georgia, to Montgomery, Alabama (a little over one hundred miles). During a time of horrible harassment by demons, I called on Jesus with all my might. He took me back in mental visions to instances that began at age four when demons first entered me. As He showed me each instance, I would renounce the sins involved and command the demon to come out. For more than an hour, demons came out of my mouth, the top of my head and shoulders. By the time I got to Montgomery, I felt wrung out, but I was free – free for the first time in years.

Since that time my spiritual growth has progressed rapidly. My time and energy can be directed toward fruitful ministry rather than wrestling continually to suppress desires and thoughts that used to threaten my very existence. Also, the Lord has taken me from 217 pounds to 155 happy pounds.

Praise the Lord! Because of Jesus, I am clean and free.

Questions for This Study

1. What is the deep longing God has placed within all of us?
2. What counterfeit does Satan use to take advantage of this longing in people and bring them into his bondage?
3. What is the meaning of the word "occult"?
4. The two main branches of the occult are

   _____ and _____.
5. True or false? The information that comes from divination is always incorrect and misleading.
6. The prediction of a psychic about the course of a person's life often amounts to what?
7. False religions may contain any one or all of what five characteristics?

Life Application

1. Was there any time in your life when you were involved in an occult practice, even if it was "just for fun" or "you didn't really believe in it"? List anything that comes to mind, renounce it and ask the Lord to cleanse you through the blood of Jesus.
2. To the best of your knowledge, have any of your ancestors ever participated in occult activities? This would include involvement in Masonic practice and false religions. List any you know of. Repent of these

on behalf of your ancestors, and in the name of Jesus declare yourself free from their influence.

Memory Verse

Now thanks be to God who always leads us in triumph in Christ, and through us diffuses the fragrance of His knowledge in every place. 2 Corinthians 2:14

Faith Response

I will take a stand and will refuse to receive any supernatural knowledge or strength from any source other than the Scriptures and the Holy Spirit.

Answers are on page 413

FIFTEEN

Is Witchcraft Still at Work Today?

AS WE TRACE THE TORTUOUS, DECEPTIVE PATHS of demonic activity and the occult, we discover that they all proceed from one primal source: *witchcraft*.

Witchcraft is the universal, primeval religion of fallen humanity. When the human race turned from God in rebellion, the power that moved in was witchcraft. As the Bible says, "Rebellion is as the sin of witchcraft" (1 Samuel 15:23). Each people group practices its own distinctive form of witchcraft, but certain elements are common to almost all of them.

In many parts of the world, the open practice of witchcraft has continued unchanged for centuries. In nations with a Christian history, primarily in the West, witchcraft has adapted itself to the culture and takes certain special forms. Previously confined to a small minority, in these last decades it has become continually more blatant and aggressive.

The supernatural element in witchcraft fascinates many people in our contemporary, materialistic Western culture. Where people are familiar only with a form of religion (whether church or synagogue) that operates solely on a material and intellectual plane, they are prone to look for an alternative that offers the supernatural, particularly if it offers *power*. This is why multitudes of such people are now turning to some form of witchcraft.

One purpose common to all forms of witchcraft is control. Whenever any religious activity seeks to control other people, the influence of witchcraft is probably at work. Some reading this chapter know exactly what I am talking about because they have escaped from Satan's clutches. Others will grasp at this opportunity to find their way out. Still others will utilize this information to help set people free.

The primitive practice of witchcraft normally contains the following elements: a priesthood (witch doctor, medicine man, shaman); a ritual or liturgy (which may take various forms); a sacrifice (animal or human); some characteristic form of music (often incantation or drumbeats); and some form of covenant binding the participants to one another and to whatever satanic being is the focus of their activity. The word *coven* (a gathering of witches) is probably derived from the same root as *covenant*.

These are the four main aims of witchcraft:

1. To propitiate a higher spiritual being, often regarded as capricious or malevolent
2. To control the forces of nature, such as rain or good weather for harvest
3. To ward off sickness and infertility, as in Africa, where almost every barren woman will go to the witch doctor for a potion or charm
4. To control other human beings – to terrify enemies in battle or to produce sexual desire in one person toward another

Four Levels of Modern Witchcraft

The Westernized, "modern" practice of witchcraft contains the same elements. It operates on at least four levels:

1. Open, public, "respectable"
2. "Underground" – covens
3. Fifth column, disguised within society and the Church
4. A work of the flesh

1. Open, Public, "Respectable"

Operating in its real nature, witchcraft teaches and practices the worship of Satan. The Church of Satan has its own web site on the Internet, which presents it as a "respectable" church. But those who have come out of its clutches will tell you that the central satanic ceremony is a "black mass" – a blasphemous parody of a Christian Communion service. The dominant motivation is a deliberate, conscious hatred and rejection of Jesus Christ. The main enemy is the Christian Church.

2. "Underground" – Covens

Witchcraft covens usually meet at night to offer sacrifices and to initiate new members. One central element in the practice of witchcraft (as we saw in the testimony at the end of the last chapter) is sacrifice. Usually the sacrifices are animal – a dog, cat, rat or some other small animal. According to my understanding, however, the sacrifice is, whenever possible, human, usually a baby. There are also reported incidents of young people being required to kill and even behead victims as part of their initiation into witchcraft.

The "god" of witchcraft is Satan. Its adherents are bound to him and to one another by a covenant committing them to absolute secrecy concerning their activities.

What attracts people to Satanism? I believe it is the offer of supernatural power. Once convinced of the power they have acquired, Satanists are often bold and aggressive.

A Christian friend of mine was sitting on an airplane next to a woman who refused all the food that was served. The woman told my friend she was fasting and praying.

"I'm a Christian, too," my friend said, "and sometimes I fast and pray."

"Oh, no!" the woman replied. "I'm not a Christian, I'm a Satanist." She went on to explain that she had two main objectives in her prayer: the breakup of Christian marriages and the downfall of leading Christian ministers.

Statistics released in recent decades must surely have encouraged her to believe that her prayers were very effective.

I once received a pathetic letter from a woman in Texas who listened regularly to my radio broadcast. She was a witch, she said, and had been assigned to a certain church to plant doubt and unbelief in the hearts and minds of new or weak Christians. She had succeeded in drawing away three such people. Then she wrote, "Do you believe I can be forgiven and receive salvation from Jesus?" I replied that God is infinitely merciful, even though it might be a struggle for her to be totally free, and I directed her to a local pastor.

3. Fifth Column, Disguised

I will not attempt to present all the forms taken by witchcraft to entice innocent people into the worship of Satan. I will merely offer some examples.

Rock Music

Rock music is one of the main channels, and its potential for harm is fearsome. Here is a letter I received recently from a 33-year-old man. (A member of my staff responded and sought to help him.) I obtained permission to quote it:

> Dear Mr. Prince,
>
> I am writing to you today to tell you of my struggles with demonization. I know what I write probably won't be new for you, but to friends, family and church leaders, I must look like a psychopath.
>
> It all started when I was sixteen and started listening to one of my brother's rock albums. This was not just any rock album, but a very demonic album. The album was by Black Sabbath, and the cover had 666 on the top with a demonic-looking creature peering at you. On the inside of the album was a picture of a man in bed with several demons (at least six or seven) around him as if to pounce on him. The look on the man's face was pure agony. I only listened to it once or twice, but that was too many.
>
> One day I heard a very peculiar noise coming from the stereo cabinet. When I bent over to reach for the doors, a force went in me or through me and pushed me back. This was a very distinct force, and I am sure that demons were involved. I had a thought

that I should hide the album so no one could throw it away – surely this was from the demons. To this day I can't remember where I hid it, even though I pray for remembrance.

Well, ever since then my life has been a living hell. These demons hold me down and paralyze me when I start to fall asleep. I can't move, speak or open my eyes. All I can do is cry out mentally for Jesus to help me. These demons are vicious; they rape me in every way imaginable. (I could get graphic and give a more detailed account, but I don't think that would be appropriate at this time.) This was an every-night ordeal for me from the time I was sixteen until I was 31. The sexual abuse started to subside when I started attending Bible study and church regularly.

Now, I know what you're probably thinking: "Are you saved, and is Jesus Lord of your life?" I said the Lord's Prayer when I was twelve with my mother at my side and have said it hundreds of times since then. This is due mainly to the fact that Christian friends, and everyone in any of the churches and Bible studies I've been to, tell me this can't happen to a Christian. So, you see, I'm waiting for signs of my salvation by the evidence of my life getting back to normal. It is hard to believe or have faith when you are bombarded with so many conflicting reports. I can't even think straight anymore, or hold down a job for more than six to twelve months. I'm not stupid; I earned an engineering degree. I'm just confused.

I come from a so-called Christian family; both my parents are born again, along with one of my two sisters. My only brother is not. My parents are supporters of your ministry but I don't think they believe in demonization of people. I think this is because every time I bring it up, my father will weakly and timidly tell me to rebuke it in the name of Jesus and turn and walk away. My mother, on the other hand, refuses to acknowledge it and has even told my sister to stop discussing it with me. My mother's side of the family has a potential demonic nature; her father (dead) was a Freemason and her mother (also dead) and two surviving sisters (living) out of three are involved with Eastern Star.

I know this letter sounds really crazy, but I hope it makes a little sense to you, and I wish I could tell you more, but that would mean writing a book.

Isn't this tragic? A professing Christian is tormented by demons but receives no understanding, much less help, from fellow Christians. (I mentioned the danger of Freemasonry and its women's affiliate, Eastern Star, in chapter 12.)

Obviously, the young man was foolish to expose

himself to forces so obviously satanic. But others are exposed to similar satanic forces in less obvious forms. The combined elements at a rock concert or disco-theque, for example, also open the way for demons: deafening music with an insistent, repetitive beat; lyrics that range from mindless to blasphemous; strobe lights constantly fluctuating in color and intensity. The impact can break down a person's ability to reason or exercise moral judgment, and thus open the way for demons, especially if alcohol or drugs are involved.

New Age Cults, Religions and Practices

The fifth column operation of witchcraft is continually expanding. One major "front" is the strange assortment of cults, religions and philosophies grouped loosely under the banner of the New Age. Unfortunately, many who sincerely think of themselves as Christians are being drawn in by its seductive promises and deceptive terminology. Some who desire to stay healthy and fit, for example, do not realize that many health food stores are permeated with New Age products and teaching materials.

Likewise, many people are drawn into the occult and opened up to demonic forces through hypnosis. Some people are intrigued by hypnosis as "innocent" entertainment, perhaps on TV. Others come under Satan's power through a medical practitioner, for treatment of psychiatric problems or as a form of "anesthesia" for surgical procedures.[1]

Another occult practice that opens the door to demons is acupuncture. Some physicians and other medical personnel today justify its use on the ground that "it works!" But an analysis of its occult background reveals that acupuncture will never ultimately promote the well-being of those who submit to it.

The following warning comes from a Chinese doctor in Malaysia:

> About eight years ago, at a retreat in Singapore, God spoke to me about the dangers of acupuncture and its link to the occult, especially its inseparable origin with traditional Chinese religion. I immediately renounced my practice of acupuncture – a skill I learned in Hong Kong and practiced successfully for five years.
>
> As soon as I came back home, I announced to my startled staff of doctors, nurses and patients that

---

1. In late 1997 more than 700 people, mostly schoolchildren, were taken to the hospital with convulsions triggered by watching an animated cartoon on television. According to Reuters, "The blame was put on a scene depicting an explosion followed by five seconds of flashing red lights from the eyes of 'Pikachu,' a rat-like creature.... Children went into a trance-like state, similar to hypnosis, complaining of shortness of breath, nausea, and bad vision when the rat-like creature's eyes flashed."

acupuncture is dangerous and that I had renounced it and would not practice it anymore. I gathered all my machines, needles, books, diploma and charts and made a great bonfire of them publicly. The total cost of the items was about $15,000 – but the blessings after that were priceless because:

1. My wife, who had suffered from chronic migraine and had acupuncture, done by me many times before, was immediately healed without medicine or prayer.
2. My unexplained fear of darkness immediately vanished.
3. My medical practice, instead of suffering a loss, received a doublefold increase in blessings.

About three years ago we saw a very unusual case during a healing rally in Kuching, East Malaysia. A Christian lady came forward for prayer regarding her rheumatism. As soon as we started, the Lord gave a word of knowledge that she had submitted herself to acupuncture treatment in the past. She confirmed it, but each time she tried to renounce it, she was thrown onto the floor screaming in severe pain.

We realized that she was being tormented by demons that had gained entry to her body through acupuncture. After we took authority over the demons and cast them out in the name of the Lord

Jesus Christ, she was delivered and totally healed. She then told us that each time she had tried to renounce acupuncture, invisible needles began to pierce her over the parts of her body where she had previously submitted herself to treatment.

Let me end by relating a tragic case. The Christian brother who taught me acupuncture suffered from severe depression and committed suicide under mysterious circumstances. The world does not know the whole truth, because he had everything in life, but I think I know: He came under a curse and paid for it with his life.

4. A Work of the Flesh ("Sinful Nature," NIV)

Now that we have examined three main forms of witchcraft as a supernatural force (the open, public form; the underground form; and the fifth column), we must expose the root. It is the least recognized operation, but it permeates society and the Church.

In Galatians 5:19–21 Paul lists the works of the "flesh" ("sinful nature," NIV). In the middle he mentions "idolatry, sorcery" (NKJV) or "idolatry and witchcraft" (NIV). As I said at the beginning of this chapter, the root of witchcraft lies in our flesh – our fallen, rebellious, sinful nature.

This nature often manifests itself, even in infancy, in efforts to control other people. We feel secure if we can control others. Then they do not threaten us; they do what we want. God, on the other hand, never seeks to control us. He respects the free will He has given each of us, although He does hold us responsible for how we use that freedom.

There are three ways the desire to control others expresses itself: *manipulation, intimidation* and *domination*. The goal is domination. People who recognize that they are weaker than those they seek to control tend to manipulate; those who feel stronger tend to intimidate. But the end purpose is the same: to dominate – that is, to control others and get them to do what we want.

Many family relationships portray this. Husbands intimidate their wives by fits of rage or actual violence. Wives manipulate their husbands by tears and hurt feelings, and often by making them feel guilty for their shortcomings. Parents frequently intimidate or manipulate their children. But, alternatively, children can become extremely adept at manipulating their parents.

One main tool of manipulation is *guilt*. A mother may say to her son, "Honey, if you love Mother, you'll run to the store and get me a pack of cigarettes." How does that affect the child? He is made to feel guilty if he does not do what Mother asks. It will be taken as a sign that he does not love her. That is not a fair way to treat a child.

Alternatively, however, a child may manipulate his mother. When she is entertaining guests, he comes and asks to watch a forbidden TV program. He knows Mother is very careful to protect him from harmful influences, but he calculates that she will not risk his tantrum by refusing him in front of her guests.

Once we learn to recognize the desire to control others as an evil, manipulative force, we will see it at work in many different areas.

In religion it may be in the way a preacher appeals for an offering: "God has shown me that there are ten people here tonight who will each give a thousand dollars." Or he shows tear-jerking pictures of starving children in a distant land, and anyone who does not respond is made to feel guilty: *Perhaps I am one of those ten people* or *If I don't give something for those children, I must be a heartless person.*

In politics it may be in the way a candidate subtly appeals to racial prejudice in order to win votes. In business it is often expressed in advertising that entices people to want what they do not need and to buy what they cannot afford. In every case it is evil.

Once we recognize these devices as disguises of witchcraft, we realize that in our contemporary culture we are being exposed continually to its pressure. This gives new meaning to Paul's statement in 2 Corinthians 4:4 that "the god of this age has blinded the minds of unbelievers" (NIV).

Repeated yielding to any fleshly lust can open the way for a corresponding demon to enter. This applies to all the works of the flesh listed in Galatians 5:19–21. A person who yields regularly to fornication or jealousy or envy (to name but three) will probably be taken over by the corresponding demon.

This applies no less to witchcraft. People who habitually use manipulation or intimidation to control others will be taken over by a demon of witchcraft. After that they will be unable to relate to anyone apart from these tactics. Now it will be no longer just the flesh at work, but a new, supernatural power that can bring the person(s) they control into a condition of spiritual slavery.

I have seen this demonic power at work between mother and daughter. A mother may decide that her daughter should marry a man from a certain racial background or social level. Then, if the man the daughter chooses does not meet the mother's criteria, the spirit of witchcraft in the mother will cause her to react in such a way that she actually puts a curse on her daughter and prospective son-in-law. The curse may take a verbal form: "If you marry that man, you'll never have enough. He'll never provide for you." As a result, the couple will find themselves struggling continually against pressures and frustrations for which they can find no obvious cause.

The demon of witchcraft can also work in many other kinds of relationships. Sometimes a pastor seeks to control the members of his staff or even his whole congregation. Or a business executive may intimidate his subordinates. Or a political leader diverts the attention of his people from their own desperate need by stirring up hatred against some "enemy" nation.

Whenever this kind of controlling relationship exists between two people, the person being controlled almost invariably needs deliverance from witchcraft. Likewise, the person exercising control needs deliverance. But each person must meet the conditions for being delivered. On one side, the person exercising control must repent and renounce his or her desire to control. On the other side, the person being controlled must repent of submitting to such control and must sever the binding relationship.

The Way Out

In chapter 21 I will give thorough teaching on how to be set free, but let me say at this point that people who have participated in satanic worship and have exercised the power Satan gave them must be very determined (as I told the woman from Texas) if they are to be set free. The spiritual struggle will probably be intense.

Lydia and I were once part of a small group ministering to a young woman who told us she had been a priestess of Satan but had repented and longed to be free. At one point she showed us her ring symbolizing her marriage to Satan. At our urging she finally removed it – but then the demon compelled her to swallow it! One of our workers, a young man, received a supernatural anointing of faith and commanded the woman to regurgitate the ring, which she promptly did. The young man then picked up the ring and threw it into a nearby lake.

The young woman's deliverance was consummated when she made a public confession to a group of Christians and burned every garment she had ever worn while worshiping Satan. This was in line with the biblical exhortation to "[hate] even the garment defiled by the flesh" (Jude 23).

The actual experience of deliverance, however, is not the end of the conflict. A person who has made a conscious, unreserved commitment to Satan is still regarded by him as his property, held by him in eternal bondage. He will seek continually to reestablish his control, using every kind of demon under his command.

So, Satan's former victim will need the help of a committed company of believers to stand with him. He needs to learn to resist every pressure, continually affirming and reaffirming the Scriptures that guarantee deliverance and victory. In this Jesus Himself is our example. Each time He was approached by Satan with a temptation, He countered with one, all-sufficient response: "It is written ... " (Matthew 4:1–11). Satan has no answer to the written Word of God.

In the wisdom of God, this process of continually resisting every demonic pressure serves a positive purpose. When a person has been enslaved by Satan, the inner walls of his or her personality have been broken down. After deliverance, in order to retain freedom, the protecting walls must be rebuilt. The continuously repeated assertion of appropriate Scriptures gradually rebuilds the walls. Once they are firmly in place, the satanic pressures will gradually diminish and eventually cease. Satan is too clever to send his troops into a battle he knows he can no longer win.

How can people protect themselves from deception? There is only one door (as I explained in the previous chapter) that leads into the Kingdom of God: Jesus, who is "the way, the truth, and the life" (John 14:6). Those who enter the realm of the supernatural through any other door find themselves in the kingdom of darkness, not of light.

We must be on our guard, as I will explain in chapter 16, that we are not deceived into following "another Jesus" – one who does not correspond with the Jesus portrayed in the Bible and who will not lead us into the truth.

There is also only one absolute standard of truth. In John 17:17 Jesus says to the Father, "Your word is truth." Anything that does not harmonize with the Bible is error. For this reason, it is important that we study the basic truths and principles of the Bible, so that we are always ready to apply this test to anything that claims our credence. But again, we must be on our guard. Not everyone who glibly quotes the Scripture practices obedience to it. (See my book *Protection from Deception*.)

Questions for This Study

1. The one, primal, universal religion of fallen man to which all demonic activity and the occult can be traced is called what?

2. All forms of witchcraft have one common purpose. What is that purpose?

3. What is the main enemy of witchcraft?

4. Give a reason why people are attracted to Satanism.

5. List some of the forms witchcraft takes to draw people in.

6. The three means that fleshly witchcraft uses to control people are: _____ , _____ , and _____ .

7. What is the main tool of manipulation?

Life Application

1. Think back through your life and determine whether you ever felt controlled through manipulation, intimidation or domination. List those experiences and how they affected your behavior.

2. Is there any current relationship in which you feel controlled? If so, ask the Lord what steps you should take to be set free.

Memory Verse

For if by the one man's offence death reigned through the one, much more those who receive abundance of grace and of the gift of righteousness will reign in life through the One, Jesus Christ. Romans 5:17

Faith Response

Lord, please show me any way in which I may be trying to control others through manipulation, intimidation or control. Show me as well any situations where I have yielded to the illegitimate control of others.

Answers are on page 414

SIXTEEN

Do Christians Ever Need Deliverance from Demons?

THIS SIXTH QUESTION IS THE ONE I HAVE BEEN asked more than any other. Often it is asked in an incredulous tone of voice, implying that the answer expected is *No!*

At one time an official publication of a major denomination classified Don Basham and me as heretics because we were casting demons out of Christians. "What are we supposed to do?" I asked Don. "Leave the demons in them?" The charge against us was based, of course, on the assumption that Christians could never have demons that would need to be cast out. (Later this charge was apparently forgotten, because churches belonging to that denomination have since invited me to minister deliverance.)

In more than thirty years, I have never heard or read a reasoned, scriptural presentation of the doctrinal position that Christians can never need deliverance from demons. Those who believe this, as I said in chapter 5, seem to consider it so obvious that it needs no support from Scripture. But the implications of such a position can be, to say the least, surprising.

A Christian young man told me that Brother Jones, a well-known evangelist, had prayed for him and that he had been delivered from a demon of nicotine.

"I thought Brother Jones doesn't believe a Christian can have a demon," I replied.

"You're right," the young man answered. "But when Brother Jones prayed for me, he didn't know I was already a Christian."

That left me pondering.

In that case, I said to myself, *it would seem that unbelievers have an "unfair" advantage over Christians, because they can receive prayer for deliverance from a demon. But once they become Christians, they are no longer eligible!*

The term *Christian* means different things to different people. So, before I proceed, I need to clarify my use of the word. I will base my definition on John 1:11–13:

> [Jesus] *came to His own, and His own did not receive Him. But as many as received Him, to them He gave the right* [literally, authority] *to become children of God, even to those who believe in His name: who were born, not of blood, nor of the will of the flesh, nor of the will of man, but of God.*

By *Christian* I mean someone who has repented of his or her sins and, through personal faith, received Jesus as Savior and Lord. As a result, this person has been born of God – that is, "born again" (see John 3:5–8).

Another way to describe a Christian is someone who has fulfilled the condition for salvation stated by Jesus in Mark 16:15–16:

> *And He said to them, "Go into all the world and preach the gospel to every creature. He who believes and is baptized will be saved; but he who does not believe will be condemned."*

Such a person has heard and believed the Gospel, been baptized and is therefore saved. Can a person like this subsequently need deliverance from demons?

This depends partly on how the person was brought to salvation or the new birth. In the ministry of Philip in Samaria, the people received manifest deliverance from demons and later believed and were baptized in water (see Acts 8:5–13). It would be reasonable to assume that most of them needed no further deliverance.

Yet even here there is one noteworthy exception. Simon the sorcerer was among those who believed and were baptized. Later, however, when he offered Peter money for the power to impart the Holy Spirit to people, Peter said to him, "Your money perish with you.... You have neither part nor portion in this matter, for your heart is not right in the sight of God" (Acts 8:20–21). It would be rash to assume that Simon no longer needed deliverance from demons, even after he believed and was baptized.

Suppose, however, that Philip had followed a different pattern of evangelism – one that is common in our day. Suppose he had preached the Gospel to the people of Samaria and then, without dealing with demons, had invited the people to come forward, say a prayer, sign a decision card or receive instruction from a counselor. What would have been the result? They would have been saved or born again, but they might still have needed deliverance from the demons that were in them before they became Christians.

I want to emphasize that I am not criticizing this kind of evangelism. I have practiced it myself. I am merely pointing out that it does not necessarily produce the results that followed the ministry of Philip in Samaria. It leaves open the possibility that the people who respond may still have demons that need to be dealt with. This does not mean they are not Christians. It means that some of them may still need deliverance.

What Happens with the New Birth?

We need to analyze more precisely, therefore, what happens when a person is born again. What is the minimum that happens? And what is the maximum? When people receive "the right [or more literally, as we saw above, authority] to become children of God," that authority is effective only in the proportion that it is used. A teacher may have authority, but if he does not use it, his pupils will be unruly and disorderly. If a police force does not use its authority, crime will continue unchecked.

So it is with the new birth. Its potential, I believe, is unlimited, but its development depends on the use each believer makes of his or her God-given authority. One person may choose the minimum and simply become a respectable church member. Another may reach for the maximum and become an active, dedicated winner of souls – even a preacher who reaches multitudes or an intercessor who brings many to birth in prayer. The difference lies in the degree to which each uses his or her God-given authority.

One specific form of authority that goes with the new birth is the authority to drive out demons, either from ourselves or from others. When the disciples told Jesus, "Even the demons are subject to us in Your name," He replied, "Behold, I give you the authority ... over all the power of the enemy" (Luke 10:17–19). This authority is effective, however, only insofar as we use it. Sometimes demons go out automatically, but usually they have to be driven out.

There are two different sets of circumstances that may confront a Christian with the need to deal with demons:

1. Demons were already in him before he became a Christian.
2. Demons entered him after he became a Christian.

When Demons Are Already in the Person

Let us consider first the case of a person who already has demons when he or she seeks salvation. I have not been able to find any passage of Scripture suggesting that demons will automatically leave at that time. In fact, the ministry of Philip in Samaria suggests the opposite. If the demons left automatically when the people believed and were baptized, why would Philip have spent time and energy driving them out? He could simply have baptized the new believers, which would have eliminated the demons.

Logically, then, if an evangelist does not follow Philip's pattern of both preaching the Gospel and casting out demons, many will believe and be baptized without being delivered from demons. This could apply to many contemporary Christians.

So, without specific reference to demons, let us consider more generally what happens when a person is born again. The Scripture does not suggest that new Christians are automatically exempt from all the consequences of what happened to them before they became believers. Consider a woman who suffers from chronic sinusitis caused by bacteria. She becomes a Christian but the sinusitis continues. The natural explanation would be that the sinusitis is still caused by the same bacteria. No one would dispute that conclusion on doctrinal grounds.

Now let us consider a man who has severe emotional problems caused by demons. The man becomes a Christian but the problems continue. Is there any scriptural reason to question that his emotional problems are still caused by demons? The child of alcoholic parents, for instance, may have been exposed to demons of anger and fear. If he later becomes a believer but continues to be subject to uncontrollable fits of anger or fear, the obvious explanation is that the demons of anger and fear still need to be driven out.

The same applies to those who have exposed themselves to demons through involvement with drugs, alcohol, sexual immorality or the occult. If, when they become Christians, they are still held in bondage by some of the evil forces to which they exposed themselves previously, the explanation is simple: They need to be delivered from the demons that cause the bondages.

But God be thanked! As Christians we have available the authority of Jesus Himself, and we can deal with all the forms of demonic pressure to which we may have opened ourselves. That authority is not effective, however, until it is exercised in active faith.

The doctrine that Christians are no longer subject to demonic activity can lead to one or the other of two unfortunate results. Either a believer may yield to demonic pressures with some comment like "I can't help myself; that's just the way I am." Or he or she may seek to suppress the pressures within, and in so doing expend much spiritual energy that could have been used for more positive purposes. In either case the practical and scriptural remedy is for such a person to treat demons as demons and to use his or her God-given authority to drive them out.

Having said all that, we must always leave room for God's sovereignty. My own experience of salvation is a case in point. As I said earlier, I came to the Lord out of a background of Greek philosophy, and had been involved in yoga. During the night that I had a sovereign encounter with Jesus Christ, I was on my back on the floor of my barrack room for more than an hour. First, I sobbed convulsively; then a well of joy sprang up within me and began to flow out in waves of laughter.

Before this experience I could acknowledge Jesus as a great teacher and wonderful example, but not the Son of God. The next morning, however, I knew, without any process of reasoning, that Jesus *is* the Son of God. Years later, after I had begun to minister deliverance to others, I realized that I had been delivered that night from a demon of yoga, which had kept me from being able to believe in Jesus as the Son of God.

Others have received deliverance from a demon of nicotine or alcohol by praying a simple prayer, without even knowing that demons exist. Again, a child of God-fearing Christian parents may receive salvation at a very young age without ever being exposed to demons.

We have no scriptural basis, however, for assuming that this freedom comes about automatically. Wherever we encounter demons, the scriptural response is to expel them, exercising the authority Christ has given us.

When Demons Enter the Person Later

Now we come to the second question: Can demons enter a person after he or she has become a Christian?

It would be naïve to assume that being born again means we shall never again be subjected to demonic pressure. On the contrary, Satan is more likely to increase his pressures against us when we become Christians, especially if we become a serious threat to his kingdom. This is doubly true of those whose previous way of life kept them in strong bondage to him.

As we consider relevant passages from the New Testament, we need to remind ourselves that all the epistles were addressed specifically to Christians, not to unbelievers. The promises and warnings alike apply to Christians. It would be illogical to claim the promises for ourselves but apply the warnings to unbelievers. Furthermore, we must remind ourselves that we have no right to claim any promise unless we have fulfilled the specific condition attached to it.

There are many warnings to Christians to be on their guard against the attacks of Satan. Peter, speaking specifically to Christians, says:

> *Be sober, be vigilant; because your adversary the devil walks about like a roaring lion, seeking whom he may devour. Resist him, steadfast in the faith, knowing that the same sufferings are experienced by your brotherhood in the world.*   1 Peter 5:8–9

There are two parts to Peter's admonition. First, we are to be self-controlled and vigilant. Otherwise, we will not detect the presence or activities of demons. Second, we are to resist demonic pressures, taking an active stand against them. If we obey these instructions, we shall be victorious. But if we are not self-controlled and vigilant, we will fail to recognize and resist our enemies. Then they will invade us and seek to destroy us. The most serious mistake we can make is to act as if there is no danger.

Certain passages in the New Testament warn us explicitly against exposing ourselves to demons. One tool Satan uses regularly for this purpose is deception. In 1 Timothy 4:1 Paul's warning is urgent: "Now the Spirit expressly says that in latter times some will depart from the faith, giving heed to deceiving spirits and doctrines of demons."

Paul speaks here about people who, through yielding to the influence of demons "depart from the faith." Obviously, they could not depart from the faith unless they had been *in* the faith. As Christians they had apparently opened themselves up to deceiving demons and consequently turned away from their faith in Christ. Our only safeguard is to be vigilant at all times and to resolutely reject all demonic pressures and deceptions that come against us.

Paul gives a similar urgent warning to the Christians at Corinth – even though some today teach that Christians should be delivered from all fear of deception. Obviously, Paul had not received that teaching! Speaking to Christians who were the fruit of his own ministry, he writes, "*I fear, lest somehow, as the serpent deceived Eve…so your minds may be corrupted from the simplicity that is in Christ*" (2 Corinthians 11:3, emphasis added).

In the next verse Paul warns against any false teacher who may come along: "For if he who comes preaches another Jesus whom we have not preached, or if you receive a different spirit which you have not received, or a different gospel which you have not accepted, you may well put up with it!" (verse 4).

There are three parts to Paul's warning. First, the deceiver preaches "another Jesus." Second, those who accept this deceitful message "receive a different spirit" than the one they received previously. And third, they embrace "a different gospel" from the original.

Through Paul's ministry these Christians had received the Holy Spirit. Therefore, when he spoke of a "different spirit" that they had not received, he was referring to a spirit that was unholy – that is, a deceiving demon.

Here is a clear example of how Christians, who have been born again and received the Holy Spirit, can be tempted into receiving a false spirit – a demon. What would open the door to the demon? Clearly, accepting a message that presents "another Jesus." This is the root of the problem. Once Christians put their faith in "another Jesus," they receive a "different spirit" – that is, a demon – and begin to believe a "different gospel."

It is logical, therefore, to ask whether there are teachers in the Church today who are preaching "another Jesus." The answer is an emphatic *Yes!*

There is a "Jesus," for instance, popular in some South American countries. He is pictured as a Marxist revolutionary, championing the cause of the poor and prepared to organize an armed revolution against the capitalists.

Another "Jesus" is popular in New Age circles. He is an Eastern guru who blends the Gospel message with the esoteric teachings of Hinduism or Buddhism. But the biblical Jesus, who is both the Creator of all things and the Judge of all men, is never presented.

Then there is a "Jesus" who appeals to those with humanistic leanings. He speaks continually about love and forgiveness but makes no mention of either hell or repentance. He represents Jesus only as Savior and never as Judge, and has no place for the parable about the nobleman closing with the words "But bring here those enemies of mine, who did not want me to reign over them, and slay them before me" (Luke 19:27).

There is also the "Father Christmas" version of Jesus telling people that all they have to do is believe and they will receive everything they ask for, from the best-paying job to an expensive automobile and a house with a swimming pool. But he, too, like the humanistic "Jesus," never mentions hell and never calls for repentance or holiness.

Tragically, many contemporary Christians are being lured into accepting a false, unbiblical "Jesus" in one or another of these forms. Through accepting "another Jesus," they are receiving a "different spirit" – that is, a demon. This is not a theoretical, doctrinal issue for abstract discussion. It is a matter of eternal life or death concerning which the true ministers of Christ are obligated to warn God's people.

Christians are vulnerable to this kind of deception, in part because of a wrong doctrinal emphasis in much contemporary preaching. This places disproportionate stress on certain single, one-time experiences, but never teaches people about the changes they must make in their lifestyles, which alone can validate those experiences.

THEY SHALL EXPEL DEMONS

The Need for Ongoing Obedience

The new birth is a marvelous experience – perhaps the most important that can ever happen in a person's life. But it is only a birth. Its value lies in the new life to which it is the gateway. Christians who go no further in their experience are like children whose parents continually celebrate their birthdays but do not provide them with the nurture and training they need to become responsible adults.

Other Christians place great emphasis on the baptism in the Holy Spirit but make no room for the ongoing work of the Spirit in their lives. Jesus said that receiving the Spirit would cause "rivers of living water" to flow out of a believer's life (John 7:38–39). Yet some Christians never get more than a "puddle," or at best a "pond." There is no continuing flow of the Spirit in their daily lives.

Again, some Christians place little emphasis on the need for a life of continuing obedience and holiness. Yet Jesus challenged the people of His day with this question: "Why do you call Me 'Lord, Lord,' and do not do the things which I say?" (Luke 6:46). To call Jesus "Lord" without obeying Him is hypocrisy and provides no protection from the attacks of Satan.

Some Christians claim they are automatically protected from demonic attack by the blood of Jesus. God does indeed offer us total protection through the blood.

But here again, this provision depends on our meeting His conditions.

The apostle Peter tells us we are "elect according to the foreknowledge of God the Father...for obedience and sprinkling of the blood of Jesus Christ" (1 Peter 1:2). An obedient lifestyle is the condition for being protected by the blood of Jesus. His blood is not sprinkled on those who persist in disobedience. This is exemplified by the record of the first Passover in Egypt, when Moses told the Israelites:

> "And you shall take a bunch of hyssop, dip it in the blood that is in the basin, and strike the lintel and the two doorposts with the blood that is in the basin. And none of you shall go out of the door of his house until morning." Exodus 12:22

The Israelites were protected not because they were Israelites, but because they obeyed God's instructions concerning the blood, and stayed inside their houses. They were on the right side of the blood. If the firstborn had gone out of their houses, they would have suffered the same fate as the Egyptians.

The same applies to us as Christians. Our protection from Satan does not depend solely on our being Christians, but on our obeying God's directions. The blood, as I said, does not protect those who continue in disobedience.

The apostle John wonderfully affirms the power of the blood of Jesus to deal with sin in our lives: "But if we walk in the light as He is in the light, we have fellowship with one another, and the blood of Jesus Christ His Son cleanses us from all sin" (1 John 1:7).

There are some important points to notice here. First, the opening word *if* indicates that there is a condition to be fulfilled. If the condition is not fulfilled, the promised results no longer apply. The condition is *if we walk in the light*. The two results are *we have fellowship with one another* and *the blood of Jesus Christ…cleanses us from all sin*.

Second, all the verbs are in the continuing present tense: "If we continually walk…we continually have fellowship…the blood continually cleanses us.…" John is not speaking about a once-for-all experience that never needs to be repeated. The fact that we fulfilled the conditions yesterday is no guarantee that we are fulfilling them today. Just as with the pattern of the Passover, God requires moment-by-moment obedience if we are to claim the protection of the blood.

We need to notice, too, that the first result of walking in the light is that we have fellowship with our fellow believers. If we neglect this, we are no longer walking in the light. And if we are out of the light, then the blood of Jesus is no longer cleansing us. The blood does not cleanse us while we walk in the dark.

Strange as it may seem, the demonic pressures Satan

directs against us may actually work for our good. They can serve as reminders of our need to walk before God in moment-by-moment obedience. Perhaps this is one reason God permits them.

A Man Who Loved Jesus

God's mercy in providing the ministry of deliverance is wonderfully illustrated in the following testimony from a worker in a psychiatric hospital in the U.S.:

One of the most controversial questions within the charismatic move today appears to be whether a Christian can be possessed of a demon. I had only recently received teaching concerning demons and deliverance when I began working in a large state psychiatric hospital. One of my first patients was an intelligent, thirty-year-old man who had spent over ten years of his life in some of the best treatment facilities in the country.

The outward manifestation of his illness was the uncontrollable behavior of dashing his head against walls and sharp objects, often seriously hurting himself. This behavior occurred irrespective of treatment or of the man's frame of mind. The problem became so serious that the patient was fitted with a football helmet, strapped to a bed, and the bed bolted to the floor in the center of his room.

This young man was a handsome, well-liked

person, well-known to the entire hospital staff. The tragedy of his case and what disconcerted me was his love for Jesus Christ. He was a Christian, openly professed Christ, and would weep for joy when we spent time singing, praying and sharing in the Word together. However, for several weeks I was unaware that after I departed from our fellowship, he would go into a rage, calling me profane names and trying desperately to harm himself.

After these reports I feared for his safety and discontinued the visits, relying on God to answer my prayer for his recovery. Yet the fellow became so despondent without my visits that I felt compelled to return. As I opened my Bible to share with him, the Spirit suddenly moved on me to command the demon to leave. Though the words I spoke were almost inaudible, the reaction was immediate.

Never had I witnessed such a gnashing of teeth, screams of profanity against Christ, and evil facial expressions. Not only that, but in spite of being strapped securely to the bed, his body became rigid and rose more than a foot above the bed, suspended in mid-air. The change in the patient was so sudden and violent that I became afraid. I left the room quickly, hoping this would ease his violent reaction.

Several moments passed before I realized the connection between the words I had spoken commanding the demon to leave and the violent display.

The Holy Spirit quickened me to return. This time the demonic manifestation did not dismay me. I commanded the demon to leave in the name of Jesus, reminding it of Mark 16:17. Though it continued to manifest, I returned to my office with Christ's assurance.

From that day forward, this man was completely free of that demon and its violent manifestation. Not only that, but he took his Bible and went throughout the hospital to staff and patients, praising God for his "deliverance from the demon." Subsequent hospital investigations attested to the miraculous deliverance.

Indeed, it was not my prayers, our fellowship or my sharing the Word that brought restoration in the Christian man's life, but the casting out of a demon according to Mark 16:17.

Questions for This Study

1. How does Derek define a "Christian"?
2. What was Philip's pattern when dealing with demons?
3. List a Scripture that indicates a Christian *cannot* have a demon.
4. True or false? When someone becomes a Christian, demonic pressures will lessen.
5. List some examples of "another Jesus" who is being preached today.
6. What may happen if we embrace "another Jesus"?

Life Application

1. List some teachings or preaching that might fit the definition of preaching about "another Jesus."
2. How are you using the authority given you to grow and mature as a child of God?

Memory Verse

Be sober, be vigilant; because your adversary the devil walks about like a roaring lion, seeking whom he may devour. Resist him, steadfast in the faith, knowing that the same sufferings are experienced by your brotherhood in the world.

1 Peter 5:8–9

Faith Response

Lord, I set my face to know Jesus fully as He is revealed in the New Testament, and to walk in obedience and fidelity to Him.

Answers are on page 414

SEVENTEEN

Will the Holy Spirit Indwell an Unclean Vessel?

THE CHRISTIANS WHO ASK THIS QUESTION, LIKE those who ask whether believers can ever need deliverance from demons, usually imply by their tone that the answer obviously must be *No!*

Contrary to many people's thinking, however, the answer to this seventh and final question is *Yes!* The Holy Spirit will dwell in a vessel that is not totally clean, provided that He has been given access to the central, controlling area of human personality: *the heart.*

One unchallengeable example of this is provided by King David. According to the record of 2 Samuel 11, David was guilty of the sins of adultery and murder. First, he committed adultery with Bathsheba; then he procured the murder of Bathsheba's husband, Uriah. Undoubtedly David was grossly defiled by these two sins. Yet when Nathan the prophet came to confront him with his sins, he repented. Later, in bitter anguish, he prayed to the Lord, "Do not take Your Holy Spirit from me. Restore to me the joy of Your salvation" (Psalm 51:11–12).

The wording of David's prayer is significant. He asked God to *restore* to him the joy of his salvation, but not to restore the Holy Spirit to him. Rather, he asked God *not to take away His Holy Spirit*. David had lost the joy of salvation and prayed for it to be restored, but he had never lost the presence of the Holy Spirit. Amazing as it seems, even through the sins he had committed, the Holy Spirit had remained with him.

Because God had not withdrawn His Holy Spirit, David was still able to repent. Without the Holy Spirit's urging, he could not have repented. On the other hand, if David had rejected the Holy Spirit's prompting, then God would almost certainly have taken the Spirit from him.

This is clear, scriptural evidence that in certain cases, the Holy Spirit will indwell an unclean vessel.

Every born-again, Spirit-filled Christian needs to thank God for this demonstration of His mercy and grace. Without it few of us would have any hope that the Holy Spirit would remain with us. Adultery or murder are not the only sins that can defile us, as Jesus made clear in Mark 7:21–23:

> *"For from within, out of the heart of men, proceed evil thoughts, adulteries, fornications, murders,*

*thefts, covetousness, wickedness, deceit, licentious-
ness, an evil eye, blasphemy, pride, foolishness. All
these evil things come from within and defile a man."*

Let us focus for a moment on five of the sins in
Jesus' list: evil thoughts, covetousness, deceit, pride,
foolishness. I have been associated with Christians for
more than fifty years and I cannot think of one to whom
I could point and say with confidence, "This person has
never been guilty of any of these defiling sins." Certainly,
I would not claim that for myself.

Yet God in His mercy does not take His Holy Spirit
from us. He continues to indwell us, defiled though we
are, but at the same time He pleads with us constantly to
repent. I am grateful that the New Testament does not
paint an idealistic, unrealistic picture of Christians!

The Continuous Struggle against Sin

Paul challenged Christians to a life of separation and
holiness:

> *Therefore*
>   *"Come out from among them* [unbelieving
> Gentiles]
>   *And be separate, says the Lord.*
>   *Do not touch what is unclean,*
>   *And I will receive you.*
>   *I will be a Father to you,*

And you shall be My sons and daughters,
Says the LORD Almighty."

2 Corinthians 6:17–18

But immediately afterward Paul continued: "Therefore, having these promises, beloved, let us cleanse ourselves from all filthiness of the flesh and spirit, perfecting holiness in the fear of God" (2 Corinthians 7:1).

Paul said, "Let us cleanse *ourselves.*" God will not do the cleansing for us. We are responsible to do it for ourselves. We must use the means of grace He has provided: We must confess our sins, repent and meet God's conditions for forgiveness and cleansing.

Note, too, Paul's words "Let *us* cleanse ourselves." Great apostle though he was, he included himself among those who needed cleansing. Nevertheless, the Holy Spirit continued to indwell Paul and the Christians to whom he was writing, even though they were not yet fully cleansed.

Paul was uncompromising about God's standard of holiness, but equally clear that he had not yet attained it. In Philippians 3:12–15 he described his personal pursuit of holiness:

Not that I have already attained, or am already
perfected; but I press on, that I may lay hold of
that for which Christ Jesus has also laid hold of
me. Brethren, I do not count myself to have appre-
hended; but one thing I do, forgetting those things

which are behind and reaching forward to those things which are ahead, I press toward the goal for the prize of the upward call of God in Christ Jesus. Therefore let us, as many as are mature, have this mind; and if in anything you think otherwise, God will reveal even this to you.

Each of us can do no better than follow Paul's example: acknowledge our need of cleansing, reach out to God for it and then press on to attain the standard God has set before us.

I must emphasize that I have no intention of trying to lower God's standards of holiness. They are forever fixed and unchangeable. But we need to be honest and realistic about the degree to which most of us have succeeded in attaining to those standards.

The teaching that every area of a person's life must be totally clean before the Holy Spirit will indwell him may produce one of two undesirable consequences. It may deter some sincere believers from seeking the infilling of the Holy Spirit, since they say to themselves, *I'll never be able to reach that standard.* Or this kind of teaching may pressure others who have received the baptism of the Holy Spirit into a form of self-righteous hypocrisy. Their reasoning goes something like this: *I must have been perfect to have received the Holy Spirit, so now I've got to go on being perfect all the time.*

The result is a make-believe Christian lifestyle. Such

people still lose their tempers but now they call it righteous indignation. They still criticize their minister or their fellow Christians but they call it discernment. They still overindulge their physical appetites but they justify it by saying, "All things are lawful."

We need to remember that the Holy Spirit is also the Spirit of truth. He is pleased when we are honest about ourselves, even though it hurts our pride. Conversely, He is grieved when we hide behind a religious front.

You may ask, "Are you implying that God has no requirements for those who receive the Holy Spirit?" Certainly not! But we need to be clear as to just what they are.

The Divine Requirement

In the book of Acts we see a divine precedent: the experience of the Gentiles in the house of Cornelius who received the Holy Spirit when Peter visited them (see Acts 10:24–48). These were not Jews seeking to follow the Law of Moses. They were Gentiles, and this was probably the first time any of them had heard the Gospel. Yet the Holy Spirit fell on them and they began to speak with tongues. It would be unrealistic to think that every area of their lives had been brought into line with God's standards by this one experience, or that they were totally free from the defilement of their Gentile background. Yet Peter commanded them to be baptized, thereby acknowledging their right to become members of Christ's Church. Speaking of this experience later, Peter said, "[God] made no distinction between us [Jews] and them [Gentiles], purifying their hearts by faith" (Acts 15:9).

Here, then, is the essential requirement for receiving the Holy Spirit: *a heart purified by faith.*

Solomon counsels us, "Above all else, guard your heart, for it is the wellspring of life" (Proverbs 4:23, NIV). All that we do and the way that we live spring from one source: the heart. It is characteristic of God's practical nature that His redemptive purposes begin with the heart. Once He has purified the heart, He works outward from there with His sanctifying grace, until He has brought the whole personality under the control of His Spirit.

Does this happen immediately? Listen to Hebrews 10:14: "For by one offering [sacrifice] He [Jesus] has perfected forever those who are being sanctified." To describe the sacrifice of Jesus, the writer uses the perfect tense: He *has perfected.* It is finally and forever complete. Nothing needs to be added to it and nothing can ever be taken away from it.

In describing the work of sanctification, on the other hand, the writer uses a progressive tense: They *are being sanctified.* Becoming holy is a stage-by-stage appropriation of what has already been made available to us by the sacrifice of Jesus. In this process the Holy Spirit (as His title indicates) is our Helper.

The Holy Spirit is realistic about our failings. He gently points out our mistakes and sins, and helps us to change. At times He may powerfully convict us, but He never condemns us.

This realism about the continual struggle of Christians against sin is presented forcefully in the New Testament. In Hebrews 3:13 the writer says: "Exhort one another daily...lest any of you be hardened through the deceitfulness of sin." Again, in Hebrews 12:1 the writer speaks about "the sin which so easily ensnares us." And in verse 4 he says, "You have not yet resisted to bloodshed, striving against sin."

Dealing with sin is a life-and-death struggle. It is not shameful to acknowledge that sin is still at work in our lives. On the contrary, our great danger lies in refusing to acknowledge it, which leaves us unprepared to resist temptations when they do come.

If the Holy Spirit were to wait until we are perfect to take up His dwelling within us, it would be like a professor saying to his students, "I'll start teaching you when you have passed your exams." His students would respond, "But professor, that's not what we need! We need you to start teaching us now, so we'll learn what we need to pass our exams."

It is *now* that we need the Holy Spirit, so that we may have His help available to us continually to overcome the power of evil and to attain to God's standard of holiness. One particular area of conflict in which we need the Holy Spirit's help is in dealing with demons. The Holy Spirit does not withhold His help if He discerns that there are demons within us. On the contrary, He sees our need more clearly than we do ourselves, and He empowers us to expel them. Because He has compassion on us, He is willing to take up His dwelling within us, and to work with us to establish Christ's victory over all the power of the enemy. Our progress depends on the degree to which we cooperate with the Holy Spirit within us.

Let me emphasize once again: The Holy Spirit does not come to indwell us because we are already perfect. He comes to help us so that we may become perfect.

Certainly, the Holy Spirit will not help us in our struggle with demons if we intend to continue living in sin. But if we recognize our sins and sincerely repent, He will fight with us against the demons that enslave us. With His help we will be able to expel them and be set free.

Cleansing the Vessel

In the testimony that follows, a congressional aide in Washington, D.C., speaks frankly of her personal struggles:

> I was baptized in the Spirit about seven years ago. In late June of last year, in a church in Washington, D.C., I received an instant healing of nerve deafness.

Then in August my doctor confirmed that I was healed of cysts and tumors in the breasts.

I was top staff member for a Congressman and, while he personally was thrilled with my experience of healing, my testimony was not well received in the political circles in which I moved. In September I resigned from my job and spent the next few months resting and taking time with the Lord.

Then in mid-December I became depressed and despondent. The first week of January was horrible! One day I lost my temper. I was here all alone, and it related to a most trivial matter. I realized instantly the sin I had committed – anger. And as I tried to pray for forgiveness in English, I felt choked... not from emotions, but a distinct pressure on my throat – a very real physical force.

A friend suggested that I might need deliverance. So, I bought your tapes dealing with deliverance and demonology.

I have always shied away from anything concerning spirits, demons, ghosts and what-have-you, believing that if I left them alone, they would surely leave me alone. I just did not want any truck with spirits and demons! Still, I listened to your tapes on deliverance. I had my Bible on the table and kept pace as you followed through the Scriptures. At the end of the tape, when you gave the instructions to your class, I decided to follow also. Then you started the prayer for deliverance, but the tape ended abruptly – and almost the last thing you said on the tape is, "Remember, Jesus is your Deliverer."

I did not know what to expect or what to do. So, my prayer to the Lord was that I didn't know what to do, but that since He was my Deliverer, I was committing myself completely to Him. I named those things not of the Lord that I felt were evil and sinful and which I did not want to be part of me – resentment, unforgiveness, doubts, anxieties, fears, etc.

As I have said, I didn't know what to expect. Within a very few minutes, not more than two or three, I began to heave and gag in the most desperate kind of way. After about ten minutes or so, I felt that my abdominal region would never be the same! But I did not feel or believe that I was completely released. Then I asked the demons or spirits to name themselves and I commanded them to come out. This did not happen. Why, I don't know.

Then I asked the Lord to tell me if there were more, and what the names were, so I could ask deliverance from them. The first one was suicide, and the force was something terrific. I felt it all the way to the top of my head. I felt some release, but not completely. I asked the Lord to tell me if there were more – and I was told it was the deaf spirit. The deliverance of that was fantastic! It lasted longer than anything else, and the force actually pulled my abdomen to my back, and I physically felt the violent uprooting of my stomach, and in this also I felt the pressure in my head.

I am completely released, and ever since have known such a marvelous peace.

Questions for This Study

1. To what area of our life must the Holy Spirit have access in order to indwell us?

2. Name two men mentioned in the Bible who had the indwelling of the Holy Spirit, yet they struggled with the presence of sin in their lives.

3. We must rely on the Holy Spirit for the _____ and _____ to repent of our sins.

4. What is an essential requirement for receiving the Holy Spirit?

5. List the three steps needed to cleanse ourselves from defiling sin.

6. If you refuse to acknowledge and repent of sin in your life, it can open you up to what condition?

Life Application

1. Ask the Holy Spirit to reveal any sins which are hindering your growth in Christ; then, without feeling condemned, apply 1 John 1:9 to whatever He shows you.

2. Thank Him for the grace to overcome, and submit yourself to His power and leading.

Memory Verse

Therefore, having these promises, beloved, let us cleanse ourselves from all filthiness of the flesh and spirit, perfecting holiness in the fear of God.   2 Corinthians 7:1

Faith Response

I will give thanks to the Holy Spirit for dwelling in me and faithfully leading me into greater sanctification.

Answers are on page 415

PART FOUR
How to Recognize and Expel Demons

THE PURPOSE OF THIS SECTION IS TO OFFER PRAC-
tical directions for recognizing and dealing with demons.
It is not intended to be a complete "how-to" guide, nor
is it a set of rules to follow. I do not believe it is possible
to devise a guide or set of rules that will meet all the
needs. (At least I know I could not do it!)

Rather, in dealing with demons, we need to follow
the pattern of Jesus, who said that He "cast out demons
by the Spirit of God" (Matthew 12:28). Jesus depended
on the Holy Spirit for discernment, direction and power.
We can be effective only when we are equally dependent
on the same Holy Spirit.

After more than thirty years in this ministry, I still
find myself confronted from time to time by situations

for which I can find no precedent in my previous experience. My only security lies in consciously and continually acknowledging my dependence on the Holy Spirit. But thank God, He is always dependable!

The material in this section is drawn from two main sources: first, my study of the patterns and examples provided by Scripture; and second, my personal experience in dealing with many demonized people.

In the first two chapters I analyze the main ways demons can affect us and exercise their influence on us. At the end of chapters 18, 19 and 20, you will find personal testimonies of Christians who became involved in dealing with demons. If you follow on through the subsequent chapters, you should arrive at a point at which you can identify demonic activity in your own life or in the lives of others for whom you are concerned. Having identified it, you will be prepared and equipped to take appropriate action.

Finally, a word of caution. Nothing I say in this section should be interpreted as implying that there is no place in our lives for the help we can receive from the medical profession. For my part, I am deeply grateful for the skill and dedication with which doctors and nurses and others have cared for me. Without their help I probably would not be alive today to write this book!

EIGHTEEN

Characteristic Activities of Demons

EVIL SPIRITS OR DEMONS ARE, ACCORDING TO MY understanding, the lower echelon of the "spiritual hosts of wickedness" (Ephesians 6:12) that Satan directs against humanity. (See chapter 11.) They have three main purposes assigned to them by Satan: first, to torment and afflict us; second, to keep us from knowing Christ as Savior; and failing that, third, to keep us from serving Christ effectively.

In accomplishing these purposes, demons are normally invisible. They cannot be perceived by human eyes. We can, however, recognize their presence and activity in the same way that we recognize the presence of the wind. Actually, this is an appropriate comparison because in both Hebrew and Greek, the word for *spirit* is also the word for *wind*. We never actually see the wind, but we see the effects the wind produces: dust rising in the streets, clouds sailing across the sky, trees all bending in one direction, rain being driven across our field of vision. All these "signposts" reveal the presence and activity of the wind.

So it is with demons. We do not normally see them, but we recognize their presence by certain characteristic actions. Listed below are some of the most typical of their activities:

1. Demons entice.
2. Demons harass.
3. Demons torture.
4. Demons compel.
5. Demons enslave.
6. Demons cause addictions.
7. Demons defile.
8. Demons deceive.
9. Demons attack the physical body.

Let us look at each of these.

1. Demons Entice

Demons persuade people to do evil. Every one of us has experienced this at some time. Enticement often comes verbally. You pick up a wallet dropped on the street and you see cash inside. Then something whispers to you, *Take it! Nobody will ever know. Other people would do the same. If it were your money, they'd take it.*

Anything that has a voice is a person, and that voice

belongs to a demon that is enticing you. If you yield, Satan will have begun to break down your defenses. You will no longer have a clear conscience. You will know you are guilty. That prepares the way for Satan's next assault.

2. Demons Harass

Demons study you, follow your movements, observe your weak moments, detect your weak places. Then they engineer situations that will open the way for them to slip in.

Take, for example, a businessman who has had a terrible day at the office. Everything has gone wrong. He tripped on the staircase, his secretary spilled coffee on him, the air conditioning failed, an irate customer came in threatening to sue. Then, on the way home, he spent an hour sitting in his car in a traffic jam. When he finally reaches home, supper is not ready and the children are running around screaming. This is when he loses control and starts to shout at his whole family.

He is a kind, gentle man, and his wife and children are shocked. They forgive him quickly when he apologizes. His outburst could simply have been a loss of self-control. But the demon of anger was watching, and now it waits for a similar opportunity. When the man loses control again, the demon seizes that unguarded moment and slips in.

Soon his wife notices a change in him. His love for

his family has not changed, but there are times when something else takes over. His eyes reveal a strange glint. When the demon of anger gains control, he abuses his family, actually hurting those he loves the most. Afterward he is ashamed and remorseful. He says, "I don't know what made me do it."

This is just one of many examples of how demons will harass a person until they can find a place or moment of weakness through which they can gain entrance.

3. Demons Torture

Jesus related the parable of a servant whose master forgave him a debt of several million dollars, but who then refused to forgive a fellow servant a debt of just a few dollars. The parable concludes with a judgment on that unforgiving servant: "And his master was angry, and delivered him to the torturers until he should pay all that was due to him" (Matthew 18:34). In the next verse Jesus applied this parable to all Christians: "So My heavenly Father also will do to you if each of you, from his heart, does not forgive his brother his trespasses."

The torturers, I believe, are demons. I have encountered hundreds of Christians who are in the hands of the torturers for one simple reason: unforgiveness. They have claimed forgiveness from God for the incalculable debt of all their sins, yet they refuse to forgive another person for some offense, real or imagined.

After Jesus taught His followers the model prayer we have come to call the Lord's Prayer, He added only one comment:

> *"For if you forgive men their trespasses, your heavenly Father will also forgive you. But if you do not forgive men their trespasses, neither will your Father forgive your trespasses."*   Matthew 6:14–15

There are various forms of torture to which we may be subjected. There is, for instance, physical torture. One example is arthritis: twisting, torturing, crippling, binding. I am not suggesting that all arthritis has a demonic cause. Yet it is remarkable how often arthritis is actually associated with an inner attitude of resentment, unforgiveness, bitterness. (In chapter 20 I will give a remarkable example of deliverance from arthritis.)

Then there is mental torment. One common form is the fear of going insane. I have been surprised by how many Christians are tortured by this fear. Frequently they are ashamed to confess it to anyone.

Like the enticement to do evil, this demonic attack may also take a verbal form: *Your Aunt Lois just entered a mental institution, and your neighbor had a nervous breakdown. And you'll be next!* Usually this fear is the work of accusing demons that continually bombard the person's mind.

Another form of spiritual torture is an inner accusation that says, *You've committed the unforgivable sin.*

When a person tells me he is being assailed by this thought, I always answer, "That's nothing but an accusation of a lying spirit. If you really had committed the unforgivable sin, you would be so hardened that you wouldn't care. The fact that you are concerned about it proves that you have not committed it."

4. Demons Compel

No word is more characteristic of demon activity than the word *compulsive*. Behind most compulsions is a demon – for example, compulsive smoking and compulsive consumption of alcohol or drugs. It is well established that these activities produce a chemical reaction in the brain. This opens up a place of weakness in a very sensitive area through which demons can easily enter.

Compulsive eating can also be demonic. But gluttony is "respectable." You may not find many alcoholics in the contemporary Church, but you will find many gluttons! Compulsive eating usually starts with the loss of self-control. Then one day gluttony slips in. Christians are often unwilling to acknowledge that they are compulsive eaters. But acknowledging the sin is the essential first step to deliverance.

Once, at the end of a deliverance service, a woman came to me and confessed that she had a demon of gluttony. When she was delivered, she vomited onto the carpet. She was embarrassed, of course, and everyone was concerned about the carpet. Later I asked myself, *Which is more important? To have a clean carpet and a dirty woman? Or a dirty carpet and a clean woman?*

There are many other forms of compulsion. One is garrulousness – compulsive talking. There are many warnings against this in Scripture. For instance: "In the multitude of words sin is not lacking. But he who restrains his lips is wise" (Proverbs 10:19). Excessive talking will always end in some form of sin. Again, the apostle James said that if anyone "does not bridle his tongue ... this one's religion is useless" (James 1:26). If you have not kept your tongue under control, you may have opened the way for a demon. Two demons that might seize such an opportunity are gossip and criticism. Both are at home in religious circles!

We all need to stop and check on ourselves: *Are there things I do simply out of compulsion?* We may have become so accustomed to our habits that we are hardly aware of them – yet they may be demonic. After one deliverance service, I received a letter from a woman who said, "For the first time in 25 years, I've been a week without biting my nails!"

5. Demons Enslave

Let us take an example from an area that few in church talk about: sex. Suppose you have committed sexual sin. You repent and meet God's conditions for forgiveness. You know you are not only forgiven but justified – "just-as-if" you had never sinned (see Romans 8:30). But you still have an intense desire to commit the same sin, even though you hate it. You are sure you have been forgiven, but you are not free. You are enslaved.

One very common example is masturbation. Some psychologists say masturbation is normal and healthy. It is not worthwhile to argue about that. I simply know there are thousands of people, both men and women, who masturbate and then hate themselves for doing it. Each time they say, "Never again!" But it happens again. They are enslaved.

In chapter 5 I spoke of Roger, whom Lydia and I failed to help. Years later, while conducting deliverance services in various parts of the world, I often heard people – men and women alike – saying the same kind of things he said: "I can feel it in my fingers. They're tingling. They're getting stiff!"

How grateful I am to the Lord that I have learned the answer! Now I tell people in my teaching, "You can be set free from masturbation. Just be determined. Come against it in the name of Jesus. Shake it out of your fingers until you can feel they're free."

Over the years I have seen hundreds of people delivered in this way from the tormenting demon of masturbation.

Let me add that marriage does not necessarily resolve the problem of masturbation, as we read in the testimony in chapter 14. If either partner still has a demon of masturbation, the demon will seek to obtain for itself the physical satisfaction that should be enjoyed by the other partner. This is one reason the sexual relationship in some marriages does not provide the physical satisfaction that each partner should expect.

When we combine *compel* and *enslave*, we arrive at a particular form of enslavement.

6. Demons Cause Addictions

I have discovered that an addiction is often like a branch growing out of another, larger branch. To help people, we may have to go beneath the addiction and discover the larger branch out of which it grows. Two common examples are continuing personal frustration and a deep emotional need that is not being fulfilled.

Let us take, as an example, two married women, one an Episcopalian and the other from the Church of God. Each is aware that her husband runs after other women, spends money on himself that she needs for housekeeping, and shows little interest in his family. Each is reaching out desperately for some source of comfort.

The Episcopalian walks across her living room to the cocktail cabinet and becomes an alcoholic. The woman from the Church of God, who would never go near an alcoholic beverage, goes to the refrigerator and eats everything in sight. She becomes a foodaholic – a glutton.

In either case, deliverance from the addiction,

whether alcohol or food, will probably not be complete unless the branch that supports the addiction – each woman's frustration with her husband – is dealt with. The best solution would be for the husband to repent and change. But even if he does not, the wife cannot expect to be set free unless she forgives him and lays down all her bitterness or resentment against him.

In the U.S. today more than fifty percent of all households are singles. As a result, the deep emotional need for loving companionship may be left unsatisfied. If a person feels betrayed and cut off by a parent, spouse or friend, he or she may turn instead to a dog or cat or some other pet. (Animals are often more loyal than humans – and also less demanding!) This longing for companionship may result in a strange kind of addiction.

Some years ago, Ruth knew a Christian woman in Jerusalem named Joanna who had no living relatives but kept seventeen dogs in her house. She could not see a stray dog without taking it home. Wherever Joanna went, her dogs went, too. Some of them slept in bed with her. She was, in fact, "addicted" to her dogs.

When Joanna was suddenly taken ill and hospitalized, her dogs went crazy. They rushed continually to and fro, barking loudly. Eventually an exasperated neighbor threw some poisoned food to the dogs and they all died. Soon afterward Joanna died, too. She had nothing left to live for.

In other cases we may not become addicted ourselves, but we may be the cause of addiction in another. Busy parents may discover to their dismay that a teenage child has become addicted to one of the many drugs that are so easily available. Too late they discover that their son or daughter has turned to drugs as a substitute for the love and companionship they were too busy to provide.

Almost anything that is both compulsive and enslaving is an addiction, and there is no limit to the forms that addictions may take. In 1 Corinthians 6:12 Paul said, "All things are lawful for me, but all things are not helpful. All things are lawful for me, but I will not be brought under the power of any."

This provides us with a scriptural definition of addiction: *A person is addicted when he or she has been brought under the power of anything that is not helpful.* I believe that addictions, so defined, are almost always demonic.

In attempting to solve their problems, people sometimes trade one addiction for another. It often happens, for instance, that a person gives up smoking and immediately puts on excessive weight. He or she has traded nicotine for gluttony.

Pornography is a tragic example of an addiction. The man enslaved by pornography finds himself compelled to tune in to those TV channels that satisfy the demon within. He cannot walk past a magazine or video display in a store; it draws him like a magnet. One pastor said to me, "When I travel, the demon wakes me up at two A.M. when the X-rated movies come on. I have to turn it on. I cannot control myself." His whole body convulsed when the demon came out. But some years later he told me he was completely free.

Television is a largely unrecognized addiction. Some people cannot walk into a room without switching on the TV. It is not a reasoned action. These people may have no idea what they want to watch. They reach for the television set without thinking, just as an alcoholic reaches for a drink. In the long run, the social results of television addiction may be even more disastrous than those of alcoholism.

More recently the World Wide Web is spawning addictions. People have been classified as "addicts" because of social withdrawal and loss of control. Psychologists have discovered that addicts include such varied groups as housewives, construction workers and secretaries. Side effects range from plummeting job performance to broken marriages.

Some forms of addiction have no recognized name. Lydia and I dealt with a young woman once who was a member of a Pentecostal church. She had a compulsive desire to sniff nail polish. "When I walk into the cosmetics department of a store," she told us, "I've got two options. I can either buy nail polish or I can run out of the store. But I've got to do one or the other." When she was delivered, the demon threw her down and came out screaming, just as it did from the man in Mark 1:26.

Another, more familiar addiction is sniffing airplane glue or a similar product. This is amazingly common among young people, and often not recognized by parents.

Some addictions are more powerful or dangerous than others, but none is beneficial. Two socially acceptable beverages that can become addictive are coffee and soft drinks, especially caffeinated drinks like colas. According to statistics, the average American consumes 37 quarts of soft drinks in a year. Sometimes a person who stops drinking coffee or cola goes through withdrawal symptoms similar to those of a person going off hard drugs.

A decisive factor in the marketing of a commodity is the fact that it can become addictive. Once a person has become addicted, the producer is guaranteed a customer for life. Some tobacco companies in the U.S. acknowledged recently that they deliberately altered the nicotine content of their cigarettes in order to ensure addiction.

7. Demons Defile

That demons defile is not surprising since the Bible calls them "unclean spirits." One main area that demons defile is our mental lives – our thoughts and imaginations. This can take the form of impure, lustful images or fantasies that project themselves unbidden into our minds. This may happen especially when we are trying to focus on the things of God, either in worship or in Bible reading. Any strong, lustful impulse that rises up in our minds at such moments is almost certainly demonic. Demons oppose our communion with God.

Another area of personality regularly defiled by demons is that of speech. Many men (and women, and even some children) cannot speak three sentences without using obscene or blasphemous language. For five and a half years in the British Army during World War II, I was surrounded by such men. In fact, until the Lord saved me, I was one of them.

That was another element in the powerful, supernatural deliverance I received when I was saved. One day I could not speak without blaspheming and cursing. The next day that language no longer came out of my mouth. This was not the result of an effort of my will. It was just gone! Only later did I realize that God had released me supernaturally from defiling demons. The demons of blasphemy and unclean speech had to go, in the same way that the demon of yoga had gone.

8. Demons Deceive

I believe demons are behind almost every form of spiritual deception. In 1 Timothy 4:1 Paul says, "Now the Spirit expressly says that in latter times some will depart from the faith, giving heed to deceiving spirits and doctrines of demons."

As I pointed out in chapter 16, people cannot depart from the faith who have never been in it. These are Christians who have been enticed out of sound, biblical faith into some form of doctrinal error. Spiritual deception, I believe, is the greatest single danger that threatens Christians in these latter times. And behind each form of deception is a corresponding demon. Any doctrine that detracts from the holiness of God, or that attacks the person, nature and work of Christ, or that undermines the authority of Scripture, is demonic. (We looked in chapter 16 at the deception of preaching "another Jesus.")

Already in the first century Jude found it necessary to exhort the Christians of his day "to contend earnestly for the faith which was once for all delivered to the saints" (Jude 3). The need for such earnest contention has increased exponentially since the time of Jude.

Demonic deception, however, goes beyond distortions or aberrations of the Christian faith. It includes all religions, cults or philosophies that set aside any of the great central truths of the Bible, especially anything that concerns Jesus Christ. We need to remember that demons are always trying to conceal or distort who Jesus is.

Another way demonic deception manifests itself is by causing Christians to mimic the behavior of animals. I call such demons "animal spirits."

In chapter 9 I described how various animal spirits

manifested themselves in our meetings in Zambia. Such manifestations occur in churches in more "civilized" nations, too, and are attributed to the Holy Spirit. By way of illustration, let me quote briefly from a letter I received in June 1996 from a friend who pastors a predominantly white Pentecostal church in South Africa. Describing a movement that had developed in his area, he wrote:

> Within a short space of time, a brother emerged out of this movement who, together with his church, led the whole thing into bizarre, unclean behavior.... So, it was not therefore uncommon to hear brethren bark, crawl on the floor like animals and make other related animal noises, all under the power of an uncontrollable force. These phenomena were all attributed to the work of the Holy Spirit.
>
> For instance, in one church men were crawling around on all fours on the ground (like dogs) and lifting their legs against chairs as if in a urinating position.... In our church a lady arrived one night and began to cackle like a hen at the back of the church. This went on for some time until, in a total frenzy, she jumped up and began to lift her blouse and expose herself. Needless to say, as you can imagine, I have never seen leaders scramble so fast in order to remove the lady from the church.

This account vividly illustrates the power of demonic deception. All the Christians involved in this movement came from churches claiming to believe the Bible. The tragedy is that behavior of this kind was attributed to the Holy Spirit, who is "the Spirit of holiness" (Romans 1:4). I deal with the question of a counterfeit Holy Spirit in my book *Protection from Deception*.

9. Demons Attack the Physical Body

In chapter 20 I will trace the connection between demons and physical sickness. Here I will simply mention some other ways demons may affect us physically.

There is, for instance, a demon of tiredness. Some years ago, I was involved in a lengthy deliverance session with a woman who, after a while, began to say, "I can't go on with any more of this. I'm too tired. I can't take any more!"

I began to feel sorry for her. Then I wondered if it was a demon speaking, not the woman. I challenged it and the demon replied, "That's right. She's always tired. She's tired when she gets up. She's tired when she goes to bed. She's too tired to pray, too tired to read her Bible."

It seemed that this particular demon was acting as a cover for other demons. If it could persuade me to stop, the others would not have to face the authority of the name of Jesus and be expelled. Once I discerned the ruse and drove out the demon of tiredness, then the other demons also came out, one by one.

Another physical effect that demons can produce is

unnatural sleepiness. Isaiah speaks about "the spirit of deep sleep" (Isaiah 29:10). Sometimes, when a Christian wants to pray or read his Bible at ten PM, he is fast asleep by 10:15. Yet the same person can stay up watching TV until the early hours of the morning. Many Christians have testified to being affected by a supernatural force that opposes them when they seek to read the Bible or pray.

Unnatural sleep can also be a means of escaping unpleasant life situations. I knew a woman who sometimes slept as much as sixteen hours at a stretch when she was under pressure at home. When the demon was expelled, it protested, "You can't cast me out. I'm her salvation!" There was perverted logic in the demon's words. Sleep was this woman's way of escaping life's unpleasant realities. It was a false salvation!

If we go beyond specific symptoms of demonic activity, such as those listed in this chapter, we can discern one general characteristic of most people who are demonized: restlessness. A person who can maintain an attitude of serene composure in all the troubled circumstances of life is probably demon-free. But there are not many such people!

Delivered from a Spirit of Death

The testimony that follows is from an American businessman delivered from a spirit of death:

About three years ago, unbeknownst to me, I entertained the spirit of death. It came to me in the guise of a spiritual happening – i.e., directions from God. Essentially it was impressed on me that I would die before I became sixty, or in about three years, and that I needed to get my life in shape. I had seen a vision of a body in a casket – unrecognizable at first, but gradual recognition came that it was me. The impression became clearer, and I was convinced God was showing me that I would die within three years. So, I started doing those things one needs to do to get ready, such as a two-day meeting with my eldest son to give him the "good news"; letters of preparation to others in the family; updating the will.

I commenced to "live to die," which affects every area of your life. In recent years I have become very familiar with death. Since I became a believer in 1964, I lost my grandparents (old); my wife (age 33) and a son (7) in a tornado; father (68); brother (41); nephew (41); nephew (10) in an automobile accident; six-week-old granddaughter in a premature birth, caused by an accident; and currently I have a granddaughter with cystic fibrosis. Previously my mother died at age 41. In addition, my father-in-law died, and my business partner and close friend was killed in 1988 after falling from a ladder. I became so accustomed to dealing with death and its results that I thought God had given me the gifts necessary to be a witness for Him at that critical time.

Starting in early 1987, I withdrew from involvement in much of the spiritual activity around me. I became negative about my business. My health started deteriorating. I had previously had open heart surgery in 1981 and came through with flying colors. But in 1987 the coronary vessels began to close, one after another, so that I had my first angioplasty surgery (the balloon procedure) in November 1987 – my seventh angioplasty procedure in October 1989. On October 18, 1989, I had open heart surgery for the second time. Three of the same vessels involved in the 1981 operation were replaced, along with a new vessel.

Back in the summer, we had signed up for your conference that began on November 19, 1989. Derek, as you began to speak of the spirit of death, spiritual revelation came on me like a slap across the face. As soon as you said spirit of death, I knew immediately whom I had entertained – who had deceived and was deceiving me. I got delivered with severe coughing (quite painful, I might add, due to the recent open heart surgery). I chose to live, not die. I was delivered from the spirit of death – no ifs, ands or buts, right then and there.

In addition, as you began to speak on curses, I became convinced that my familiarity with death

was no accident but due to a curse that was
handed down to my children and their chilc
met the qualifications and decided to do w
took to break the curse.

Deliverance and breaking the curse over my life
were like being resurrected. I was living to die – but
now I am living to "live, and declare the works of
the LORD" (Psalm 118:17).

Questions for This Study

1. Demons seek to break down our _____, and to entice us to do _____.
2. Why do demons harass us?
3. What types of demonic torture are discussed in this chapter?
4. What are some compulsive behaviours that may be demonic?
5. Addiction often grows out to what two larger "branches"?
6. What is one reason demons seek to defile us?
7. Derek believes the single greatest threat to Christians in latter times is _____ _____.
8. What is one general characteristic of most people who are demonized?

Life Application

1. Stop for a moment and consider: *Are there behaviors I do simply out of compulsion?* Please list them.
2. What compulsive behaviors have you observed in those around you? Describe some of these.
3. What other forms of compulsive behavior have you experienced that were not mentioned in Derek's list?

Memory Verse

All things are lawful for me, but all things are not helpful. All things are lawful for me, but I will not be brought under the power of any.   1 Corinthians 6:12

Faith Response

Lord, reveal any force in my life that has acquired illegitimate mastery over me. Release me from any such force that could disrupt my relationship with You and Your Word.

Answers are on page 415

NINETEEN

Areas of Personality Affected by Demons

WHOEVER HAS NO RULE OVER HIS OWN SPIRIT IS like a city that is broken down, without walls" (Proverbs 25:28). Solomon is comparing the human personality to a city, the walls of which have all crumbled. A person such as Solomon describes has no inner defenses.

The personality of a drug addict, for example, has been so broken down that demons of all kinds can come and go freely. There are no defenses left that can keep them out. Such a person needs more than a one-time experience of deliverance. He needs to undergo a process of rehabilitation while his spiritual walls are being rebuilt. This may take months or years.

The analogy of a city may also apply to people not enslaved by drugs. Inside every one of us is something analogous to a major city, with all its different localities and residents. I lived for a while in Chicago, for example, which has many major areas – department stores and fashionable shops; bus and train terminals; banking and commercial institutions. One street was frequented largely by prostitutes and homosexuals. There were also ethnic neighborhoods whose residents were mainly Polish, Swedish or Jewish. There were also expensive residential areas and slum areas.

Using a city as a pattern, I will briefly outline some of the main areas of human personality, indicating the kinds of demons that take up residence in each area. This, I believe, will help you in your own further study, meditation and prayer.

1. Emotions and attitudes
2. The mind
3. The tongue
4. Sex
5. Physical appetites

Then I will devote much of chapter 20 to the ways demons assault the physical body.

1. Emotions and Attitudes

This area of the human personality is assailed by numerous demons, some of which I will mention below. I have come to the conclusion that every negative emotion or attitude opens the way for the corresponding demon. A person who has an outburst of anger or sudden fright is, as I said before, not necessarily under the influence of a demon of anger or fear. But if these emotions become obsessive or habitual, then quite probably there is a demon at work.

Demons tend to operate in gangs. Typically, one particular demon is a "door-opener" – that is, it holds the door open for a succession of other demons to follow. One of the most common door-openers is rejection – a sense of being unwanted, unloved, unimportant.

Every human being is born with a deep, innate longing for love and acceptance. When this is absent, the heart suffers an inner wound. I discussed some possible causes in chapter 13. It may be that the mother did not want the baby she was carrying in her womb. Or the parents did not love their child, or perhaps they did not know how to demonstrate their love. Undemonstrated love does not meet a child's emotional need. Or the sense of rejection may be caused by the breakup of a close relationship – perhaps a divorce. Whatever the cause, a demon of rejection has gained entrance.

There are two different reactions to rejection. One is passive. A person yields to this condition and goes through life with it, but becomes more and more unhappy and withdrawn. The other reaction is aggressive. In this case a person fights back, adopting a don't-care attitude and developing a shell of outer hardness.

If a person's reaction to rejection is passive, the "gang" that presses in through this open door includes some or all of the following: self-pity, loneliness, misery, depression, despair and finally suicide. Virtually every suicide, I believe, is motivated by a demon. It is obvious that a demon of suicide does not enter because a person has already killed himself. It comes to drive a person to suicide.

This is usually also true of a demon of murder. It does not come in because a person has already committed murder. Rather, it enters to drive a person to commit murder. Remember that the Bible defines murder primarily as an inner attitude: "Whoever hates his brother is a murderer" (1 John 3:15).

A woman who has had an abortion almost certainly has a demon of murder, even if she did not realize she was taking human life. She probably cannot be set free until she confesses her sin and repents. This is often also true of those who enabled her to abort her child.

On the other hand, if a person's reaction to rejection is aggressive, it opens the door to a gang that includes anger, hatred, rebellion, witchcraft, violence and finally murder. I have already referred to 1 Samuel 15:23: "Rebellion is as the sin of witchcraft [or divination]." When people open up to rebellion, witchcraft is likely to follow. This is well illustrated by the many young Americans in the 1960s who went into rebellion and, almost without exception, ended in the occult. I thank God that I personally came to know hundreds of these who were gloriously saved and delivered.

For some time, I worked with a young man whose life vividly illustrated the result of an aggressive response to rejection. When he was about fifteen, his mother said something that gave him the impression she did not care about him. He went to his room, threw himself on his bed and sobbed convulsively for about half an hour. Then he went to his mother, looked her in the face and said, "I hate you!" After that he began to take drugs, and many demons entered him. He became a leader of a notorious gang in a major U.S. city.

Thank God, that was not the end of the story. When he encountered Jesus, he was wonderfully delivered and transformed. He became a minister and helped many others to be delivered from drugs and demons.

2. The Mind

This is probably the main battlefield of the human personality. Some of the characteristic demons are doubt, unbelief, confusion, forgetfulness, indecision, compromise, humanism and insanity. Usually, the people who rely most on their mental abilities are those most open to this kind of demonic attack.

I recall a mild, well-mannered minister of an old-line denomination who came to me for counseling. After we talked, I said, "I believe your problem is compromise." He replied, "Yes, that's always been my problem." I said, "It could be a demon." When we prayed for deliverance, the demon proved to be surprisingly powerful. It actually threw him from one side of my study to the other before it finally came out.

Then there was the Ph.D. candidate from one of the Ivy League universities who came to a conference where I was teaching. Christopher had heard something about my ministry of deliverance, but vowed before the conference that he would leave just the same as he had come. He attended my meetings and observed all that was going on. But true to his vow, he left the same as he came.

While he was in the plane returning to school, however, he experienced such intense pain in his head that he actually thought he was going to die. In his agony he began to pray, and the Lord showed him that it was a demon of doubt. Furthermore, he realized when that demon had entered him. A fellow student, taunting Christopher for being a Christian, had said to him, "Do you really believe Christ fed five thousand people with five loaves and two fishes?" Christopher had replied, "Well, whether Christ really did that or not is not important. It doesn't affect my faith in Him." That, he realized, had opened the door to the demon of doubt.

In his agony, Christopher cried out to the Lord for deliverance. Then he felt the demon go out through his left ear. Turning to the woman sitting next to him, a total stranger, he said, "I believe Jesus Christ fed five thousand people with five loaves and two fishes!"

Christopher had stumbled onto a vital spiritual principle: *If we have opened the door to a demon by saying the wrong thing, we need to cancel the wrong thing by saying the right thing.* Peter denied the Lord three times, but after the resurrection Jesus led Peter to unsay his denial by affirming to the Lord three times that he loved Him (see John 21:15–17).

3. The Tongue

A demon that operates in the area of either the mind or the tongue is a lying spirit. It may speak either to a person's mind or through a person's tongue.

As an example of the first, I recall a woman who came to me once for help, complaining, "I've been seeking salvation for six months, but I just can't get saved!" I asked her to tell me which churches she had been attending. When she cited them, I recognized that they all preached a sound, scriptural message of salvation.

Without saying anything to the woman, but under my breath, and in the name of Jesus, I bound the lying spirit that was speaking to her mind, telling her God did not love her and that she could not be saved. Then I led her in a simple prayer for salvation. She came through immediately to an assurance of salvation, which she has never, to my knowledge, lost.

The authority to "bind or loose," which I exercised in this case, is an important tool in dealing with demons. In Matthew 12:29, speaking about driving demons out of a person, Jesus said, "Or else how can one enter a strong man's house and plunder his goods, unless he first binds the strong man? And then he will plunder his house."

If there is a "gang" of demons, the "strong man" is usually the leader, who controls and dominates the rest. In the process of deliverance, it will generally be the first to manifest itself.

Further on, in Matthew 18:18, Jesus gave His disciples the authority to "bind" or to "loose" spiritual forces: "Assuredly, I say to you, whatever you bind on earth will be bound in heaven, and whatever you loose on earth will be loosed in heaven."

The authority to bind or loose can be very effective in dealing with demons, but its exercise must be safeguarded by the application of important scriptural principles. (In chapter 25 I outline these principles.)

The lying spirit in the woman I was dealing with was speaking to her mind. On the other hand, a lying spirit may also speak *through* a person's tongue. For instance, there are people who are compulsive liars. They are not aware of the lying demon within them, and often they do not even know when they are lying.

Ronald, a Christian businessman, used to visit Lydia and me in our home. As he sat in our living room, his talk would become more and more interesting and more and more improbable. After a while my head would begin to swim. *Does he believe what he is saying?* I would ask myself. *Do I believe it?* Yet he was completely sincere, not in the least conscious that he was lying.

Later I discovered how that lying spirit came in. Ronald was the adopted son of wealthy parents who had no other children. They had great expectations for him. If Ronald came home from school with poor grades, his parents displayed their disappointment. So he began to lie about his grades. Eventually he became so used to lying that he did not even know when the lying spirit came in and took over. I later lost contact with Ronald and have no assurance that he was ever delivered.

Compulsive liars are people controlled by lying demons. They deceive others and are themselves deceived. They may even pass a lie detector test.

Other demons in the area of the tongue are exaggeration, gossip, criticism and slander. Exaggeration is a demon that particularly targets evangelists – hence the phrase "evang-elastically speaking." Gossip and criticism are two demons that feel quite at home in church.

4. Sex

Some Christians view sex as inherently impure. They are ashamed even to think about it, much less talk about it frankly. Yet this is not a scriptural attitude. God created Adam and Eve sexual beings, then declared that everything He had created was very good – obviously including sex (see Genesis 1:31).

The sexual urge in human beings is so strong, however, that it is a prime target for Satan. He knows that if he can gain control in this area, he has a powerful tool to influence every other area of behavior.

I have found that virtually every form of compulsive sexual aberration is the outcome of demonic pressure. This would include masturbation, pornography, fornication, adultery, homosexuality, lesbianism, effeminacy and all sorts of perversions concerning which Paul says, "It is shameful even to speak of those things which are done...in secret" (Ephesians 5:12).

There are various ways such demons can gain entrance. I recall a married woman, a Sunday school teacher in a mainline denomination, who confessed to Lydia and me that she had twice been involved in adultery. Yet she was desperately ashamed and apparently contrite. Seeking to discover the source of her compulsion, we learned that her father had been involved in an adulterous relationship at the time she was conceived. It seemed that the demon of adultery from her father had entered her at that moment. When Lydia and I prayed for her on that basis, she received a powerful deliverance.

"Do I need to confess what I've done to my husband?" she asked, adding, "He's a Green Beret[1] and always carries a gun."

1. An elite American military commando force.

"That's a decision you must make," I replied. "We cannot make it for you. But I believe God will not fully bless your marriage unless there is complete honesty between you and your husband."

Later she did confess to him and he forgave her. As a result, she told us that their marriage relationship was better than it had ever been.

The moment of conception is a very decisive moment. (The Chinese calculate a person's age from this moment.) Children conceived outside of marriage are often born with a spirit of fornication. This pressures them, as they grow up, to commit the same sin.

5. Physical Appetites

This is another area open to demons. The two most basic are eating and drinking, which some Christians see as purely natural, with no spiritual significance. Yet the New Testament depicts these activities as important elements of our Christian lifestyle.

The new believers added to the Church following the day of Pentecost, for example, "ate their food with gladness and simplicity of heart, praising God and having favor with all the people" (Acts 2:46–47). There was something about the way these Christians ate and drank that impressed their unconverted neighbors. Would that be true of contemporary Christians?

Again in 1 Corinthians 10:31 Paul says, "Therefore, whether you eat or drink, or whatever you do, do all to the glory of God." This raises a very practical question: Is it possible to *overeat* to the glory of God?

This issue confronts Christians of the Western world in particular, where overeating has become a lifestyle. How many would even consider that they might be enslaved by a demon of gluttony? Yet surely this explains why multitudes switch from diet to diet, never achieving their goal of stable, moderate weight. They are as much in bondage to food, as I said in chapter 18, as others are to alcohol or nicotine. Furthermore, the spiritual and physical consequences of overeating may be no less harmful than those associated with nicotine or alcohol.

Solomon offers a prayer that would be suitable for Christians in bondage to such appetites:

Catch us the foxes,
The little foxes [the little demons] *that spoil the vines,*
For our vines have tender grapes.

Song of Solomon 2:15

Unimportant though they may seem, these little, foxlike demons may spoil the tender fruits of the Spirit that God looks for in our lives. One form of spiritual fruit that inevitably suffers from the little foxes is the fruit of self-control. It cannot coexist with self-indulgence. We need to remember the warning of Jesus in John 10:10:

"The thief does not come except to steal, and to kill, and to destroy." Demons may come through various appetites or lusts, including alcohol, nicotine or food. But regardless of the door through which they enter, all have the same motivation: to do all the harm they can.

Often the unrecognized barrier to receiving deliverance is *pride*. It can be difficult for churchgoing Christians to call their problem by its right name and to acknowledge that they need to be delivered from a demon. The woman whose demon of gluttony came out through vomiting was embarrassed. But surely that temporary embarrassment was a small price to pay for deliverance from such a humiliating and destructive bondage.

In addition to these lusts of the flesh, there is also "the lust of the eyes" (see 1 John 2:16). Specific demons enter through the eye gate. One demon already mentioned, which is projected regularly through the media, is pornography. This word is derived from *porne* – the Greek word for *prostitute*. Some men commit fornication through their eyes.

Jesus Himself said that this is one way a man can commit adultery: "But I say to you that whoever looks at a woman to lust for her has already committed adultery with her in his heart" (Matthew 5:28). I have been shocked to discover how powerful the influence of pornography is within the professing Church.

There are many other forms of lust, however, that

open the door to demons in both men and women. In Titus 3:3 Paul includes himself among those who at one time were "foolish, disobedient, deceived, serving [enslaved by] various lusts and pleasures...." How wonderful is the grace of God that has provided a way of deliverance from these demonic snares!

In the dramatic account that follows, a pastor in Florida describes his experience in dealing with a young homosexual:

> "Pastor," the young man in my office wept, "somebody's got to help me! I can't go on any longer." He bent forward in the large platform chair. "Two years ago, I was born again. I really love the Lord, but I still have a powerful lust for other men."
>
> We waited until he regained his composure.
>
> "Before I was saved, I was a homosexual. Since then I haven't committed that sin – but the desire is still in me, and I'm afraid I can't keep it under control much longer. I went to my pastor for deliverance, but he says it's impossible for a Christian to have a demon of homosexuality, and that I'll just have to exercise discipline."
>
> He looked at me with distress gripping his face. "But discipline isn't the answer! I know there's a perverse spirit in my body. It is there! Deliverance is the only hope I have. Can you help me?" He began weeping again.

I waited until he had regained his composure. Then I explained, "I wish it were true that Christians were immune to demonic invasion. Unfortunately, our corruptible has not yet 'put on incorruption,' and our mortal has not yet 'put on immortality,' as it says in 1 Corinthians 15:54. Until that happens, our minds and bodies will still be vulnerable to the enemy. A demon can go anywhere that sin and disease can go. If a Christian can have either of these, he's also subject to having a demon."

He listened intently.

"Receiving ministry today obligates you to a series of follow-up appointments in the future. This is not a one-time session. Jesus warned that when the unclean spirit leaves a person, it goes through dry places seeking rest and finds none. Ultimately it will return to the same person and try to gain reentry. If it succeeds, that person's final condition will be worse than before. You absolutely must guard against that happening. To prevent it, you have to maintain a life of devotion to God, fellowship with other Spirit-filled believers, and sincerely read your Bible. Doing that will strengthen your relationship with the Lord."

He agreed.

"I want you to lean back in the chair and listen carefully to what I say," I went on. "If you comply with God's terms, you will be set free. The Scripture promises that whoever calls on the name of the Lord will be delivered. That promise cannot fail. God will fulfill His covenant word to you. Just be certain you're in perfect submission to Him."

Then I led the young man in a proclamation renouncing every occult, unclean activity in which he had ever been involved. Then he verbally forgave everyone who had ever harmed him, including the men who had abused him sexually in childhood.

"Forgiving them does not mean you agree with what they did," I explained. "It simply means that through forgiveness you cut the ropes that keep you tied to the injury they brought into your life.

"It's important that you understand I will be speaking directly to the spirit," I continued, "and not to you. You must listen carefully, but stay out of the way. Don't allow the demon's threats to intimidate you, and don't protect it."

He leaned back, eyes closed, as we began.

In a quiet but authoritative voice, I started quoting Scriptures to the spirit. I chose verses reminding it of Satan's failure and Jesus' victory. For example: "Inasmuch then as the children have partaken of flesh and blood, [Jesus] Himself likewise shared in the same, that through death He might destroy him who had the power of death, that is, the devil, and release those who through fear of death were all their lifetime subject to bondage" (Hebrews 2:14–15).

I reminded the spirit that it was as powerless to hinder the success of this ministry as it had been to stop the resurrection of the Lord Jesus.

"And these signs will follow those who believe," I told the demon, quoting Mark 16:17, "for Jesus said, 'In My name they will cast out demons.'" And again, "'I give you the authority to trample on serpents and scorpions, and over all the power of the enemy, and nothing shall by any means hurt you'" (Luke 10:19).

For about twenty minutes I continued quoting Scripture.

"The weapons of our warfare are not carnal," I went on, quoting 2 Corinthians 10:4–5, "but mighty in God for pulling down strongholds, casting down arguments and every high thing that exalts itself against the knowledge of God...."

Several times the young man smiled at me with a seductive, sexy grin. Recognizing that this was merely a manifestation of the spirit, I continued. Suddenly, when I quoted Romans 16:20, "The God of peace will crush Satan under your feet shortly," something amazing happened. The young man twisted sideways in the chair, grabbed the arm with both hands and went into a violent, epileptic-like seizure. His body lurched forward in a furious, hammering fashion, vibrating sideways at the same time. I held him around the waist, giving him as much support as I could. It was ugly. Yes, demons are ugly.

The sound coming out of him was equally astonishing. A bellowing noise, like that of a wounded bull, roared from his body. The events of Philip's preaching in Samaria immediately came to mind: "Unclean spirits, crying with a loud voice, came out of many who were possessed" (Acts 8:7); and Jesus' delivering the afflicted child when "the spirit cried out, convulsed him greatly, and came out of him" (Mark 9:26).

The seizure lasted several minutes as I continued to rebuke the spirit, commanding it to be quiet and to go. Then, as suddenly as the seizure had begun, the young man collapsed back in the chair, physically and emotionally spent. The room became quiet. The spirit was gone.

Slowly, reverently, as in worship, the youth raised both arms over his head, weeping and laughing, "It's gone! It's gone! I felt it go. Praise God, I'm free! It's gone!"

A moment later he rose from the chair, spending the next half hour walking through the offices, singing, laughing, shouting. "Thank You, Jesus! It's gone! It's gone! Thank You, Jesus!"

In that brief period of time, the tormented lifestyle of homosexuality ended. Only its memory would remain.

I had particular reason to rejoice with this young man. For nearly thirty years of traditional ministry, I had been unable to help people with such crushing problems. I had stood by helplessly and watched as church members were torn apart by situations that deliverance ministry could easily have solved. Some of them even died. That failure, common to most of us pastors, radically changed when I received the baptism of the Holy Spirit and learned about deliverance ministry. Thankfully this young man did not become another of my casualties. The truth had set him free.

Questions for This Study

1. Using a city as pattern, list some of the areas of the human personality where a demon might take up residence.

2. What is a "door-opening" demon?

3. The two different responses to rejection are _____ and _____.

4. The mind is the main battlefield of the human personality. Name some of the demons that attack this area.

5. In the process of deliverance, which demon is usually the first to manifest itself?

6. The spiritual fruit of self-control cannot coexist with what?

7. One of the most common barriers to receiving deliverance is _____.

Life Application

Read Romans 1:28–32. As you consider our modern culture, list several ways in which some of the demonic influences named in this passage may be given a foothold through the popular value systems of the media and entertainment industry.

Memory Verse

Inasmuch then as the children have partaken of flesh and blood, [Jesus] Himself likewise shared in the same, that *through death He might destroy him who had the power of death, that is the devil, and release those who through fear of death were all their lifetime subject to bondage.*Hebrews 2:14–15

Faith Response

Lord, grant me discernment to be aware of and stand against the demonic influences that would seek to gain entrance through the culture that surrounds me.

Answers are on page 416

TWENTY

Demons of Sickness and Infirmity

ANOTHER AREA WE NEED TO CONSIDER IS THE body. In chapter 3 I pointed out that Jesus made no hard-and-fast distinction between healing sickness and expelling demons.

Luke describes the first occasion that Jesus ministered to the sick:

> *All those who had anyone sick with various diseases brought them to Him; and He laid His hands on every one of them and healed them. And demons also came out of many, crying out and saying, "You are the Christ, the Son of God!"* Luke 4:40–41

This account makes it clear that *many* of their sicknesses were caused by demons.

Demons can, I believe, be the cause of almost every

kind of physical pain and sickness, but it takes discernment to distinguish between sicknesses or pains that have a demonic cause and those that are purely physical. With our limited understanding, we may find it difficult to envisage how a spiritual entity such as a demon can occupy a physical space, such as an area of the human body. But whether we understand it or not, the fact is that it happens and that it is depicted frequently in Scripture.

The gospels record that Jesus healed the mute, deaf and blind by expelling demons (see Matthew 9:32–33; 12:22; Luke 11:14). In Luke 13:11–16 Jesus met a woman who had suffered from what we might call spinal curvature or scoliosis for eighteen years. Although her condition seemed to be purely physical, Jesus declared that she had been bound by a "spirit of infirmity." On that basis He set her free and she was completely healed. In Mark 9:17–29 Jesus dealt with a boy who had the symptoms of epilepsy. He confronted it, however, as "a dumb and deaf spirit" (verse 25). When the demon was expelled, the boy was healed.

Nearly two thousand years have passed, but the same principles still apply. Over more than thirty years, I have seen hundreds healed from many kinds of sickness or infirmity through deliverance from demons. I will mention just a few cases.

Epilepsy

In the early 1970s a young woman of eighteen came to Lydia and me for prayer. She had been diagnosed with epilepsy, which was controlled by medication. When she heard some of my teaching, she wondered if her epilepsy might be caused by an evil spirit.

When Lydia and I prayed for her and commanded the demon of epilepsy to leave her, it came out. But then I felt the Lord telling me, *Your job isn't finished.* So I asked the girl, "How did your seizures start? Was it through a physical injury?"

"Yes," she replied. "I was struck on the head by a baseball, and after that the seizures started."

I explained to her that the physical injury opened the "door" by which the spirit of epilepsy entered. "Now that the spirit has gone out," I said, "we need to close the door so that it can't come in again."

So, Lydia and I laid hands on her head and prayed for the healing of her brain.

We remained in contact with the young woman for about two years. During that time, she took no further medication and suffered no further seizures.

A few years ago another woman came to me with her daughter of about eighteen.

"Mr. Prince," she said, "ten years ago you prayed for me and I was delivered from the spirit of epilepsy. Here's my daughter. She has the same problem. Please pray for her."

Ruth and I prayed for the daughter, commanding the demon of epilepsy to leave, and she was healed, just as her mother had been.

A friend of mine, an evangelist, was asked to pray for someone with epilepsy. When he came against the epileptic spirit, the spirit – not the person – replied, "You fool! I've been medically certified." [1]

Demons know how to adapt to modern medical procedure and terminology!

I should add here that two members of our large combined family, not related to one another, have received healing from epilepsy through prayer without any outward manifestation – so Jesus still has different ways to deal with people today!

When people come to me for prayer for deliverance from epilepsy, I usually tell them, "You need to know that the demon may put up a fight before it leaves. Are you prepared to fight for yourself? If so, I'll fight together with you and we'll win. But if you are not prepared to fight for yourself, I'm not going to fight on my own." In every case that I can remember, the person has been willing to fight, and God has given us the victory. I have no faith, however, for people who

---

1. In fact, there is another "medically certified" demon called Tourette's syndrome, by which people mutter curses and oaths in public against their will.

simply remain passive, without taking their own stand against the enemy.

As a general rule, I do not pray for those who expect to be released only on the basis of my prayers. A person unwilling to take an active stand against the demon will probably not have the defenses to keep it from returning. Matthew 12:43–45 warns us that the evil spirit will return, bringing "seven other spirits more wicked than himself... and the last state of that man is worse than the first." The experience of Esther described in chapter 6 provides an example of demons trying to return. (In chapter 23 I will give instructions about how to stay free.)

Blindness, Deafness, Muteness and Arthritis

In Hawaii a young man brought to Ruth and me his grandmother, who was about eighty and blind. She was from French-speaking Switzerland, and her mother tongue was French. Although I was not conscious of having any great faith, Ruth and I began to pray for her. Then, speaking in English, I commanded the spirit of blindness to leave the woman. After a few moments, the woman turned to me and said in French, "*Je vous vois*" ("I can see you"). I was both amazed and delighted!

In 1985 Ruth and I led a ministry team to Pakistan. Because it had been advertised that we would pray for the sick, people came from all over Pakistan. Most of them were illiterate and quite undisciplined. One day the women, who in that culture are seated separately, were extremely noisy and disorderly. Seeking to establish some discipline, I announced, "This morning we will pray only for men."

Immediately about two hundred men rushed up to our team, all wanting prayer. Ruth and I encountered a man who touched first his lips, then his ears, indicating that he was a deaf mute. Recalling that Jesus had expelled an evil spirit from a deaf mute, I decided to do the same. I cannot say I had any special faith.

"You, deaf mute spirit," I said, "in the name of Jesus, I command you to come out of this man."

I knew the man could not hear me, nor would he understand English. But the demon understood!

When I said to the man, "Now say hallelujah," he opened his mouth and shouted, "Hallelujah!" I took him to the leader on the platform, who began to tell the people in Urdu about the miracle.

This report stirred up faith, and people began to bring other deaf mutes to us. (In a Muslim nation there is an unusually high proportion of such cases.) In the next few minutes Ruth and I cast out deaf mute spirits from at least ten more men or boys, and all were healed. One exciting case was a boy of about five whose first word was *umma* (mama).

In 1980, at a large conference in South Africa, I was asked to conduct a seminar on healing and deliverance for about a thousand people. The first day I taught on healing, then began praying individually for the sick.

The power of God was present and there were several dramatic healings.

Then a woman came forward with arthritis. I said to her, "I believe that your arthritis is a demon. Are you prepared to have it cast out?"

She nodded, so Ruth and I laid hands on her and commanded the demon of arthritis to go. Within a few minutes she said, "All my pain has gone! I'm healed."

As the people applauded and thanked Jesus, I sensed that their collective faith had risen so that it was no longer necessary to minister to each person individually. I asked all those suffering from arthritis to stand. About thirty people all over the auditorium rose to their feet. After explaining to them what I intended to do, I took authority over every demon of arthritis and commanded them to go in the name of Jesus. Then I told the people standing not to sit down until their pain had left and they knew they were healed.

As Ruth and I went on praying for people with other sicknesses, those with arthritis began to sit down one by one. After about fifteen minutes, none was left standing.

Some weeks later, traveling around South Africa, Ruth and I met several of these people individually, and they confirmed to us that they had been healed that day.

Death

In chapter 6 I recounted that both Esther and her daughter, Rose, were delivered from a spirit of death. The spirit had entered Esther when she had nearly died on the operating table – a moment of special weakness. We need to remember that Satan is a murderer (see John 8:44). He uses the spirit of death to kill a person who would not die through purely natural causes.

This was corroborated by a Christian doctor, head of a clinic, who came to me after a meeting. "What you taught us about the spirit of death," he said, "has helped me understand people who die without our finding any sufficient medical cause of death. Now I realize that they are victims of the spirit of death."

One of my grandsons, himself a minister, had an amazing experience. Here is his testimony:

Our daughter, Rebecca, was born with a hole in her heart. When she was six, in January 1993, she had open heart surgery to repair it.

We were permitted to visit the Intensive Care ward for only ten minutes every hour. Before entering the ward, it was necessary to obtain permission from the head nurse. One morning we were waiting in the hallway with twenty other anxious parents. When we were refused entry, we realized something was amiss. I picked up the house phone to inquire, and the nurse replied that they were having difficulties with one of the children and that we would have to continue to wait. I told the other parents, and every face went pale. Suddenly the double door swung open and out came the doctor and hospital chaplain. They spoke to the couple standing opposite us, and immediately the mother burst into tears. They were ushered quickly into the counseling room.

Shortly after this traumatic scene, we all were allowed to enter and visit our children. When we entered the ward, we noticed a doctor standing at the foot of the bed right next to our daughter. The twelve-year-old boy in the bed, who had undergone surgery that morning, was the son of that couple! Glancing at his heart monitor, we saw that it was a flat line.

Standing between the two beds, I grabbed my wife's hand and said in a low voice, with urgency, "I come against the spirit of death in this place in the name of Jesus." Our attention then turned toward our daughter, who was awake and in need of our care.

The next morning, as I was walking down the corridor, I saw the boy's father with a smile on his face. I stopped and asked him what had happened. The father told me in amazement, "The doctors had given my son no hope, and just like that he turned around. This morning he sat up in bed and gave me two thumbs up!"

My wife and I both know God delivered that boy from the spirit of death. Thank God we knew what to do!

Natural or Demonic? Discerning the Cause

In the previous chapters I have spoken about lying spirits that attack people's minds. In 1994 Ruth and I experienced a different kind of attack from lying spirits. After battling a series of major illnesses for several years, Ruth had received a word from the Lord: *Your time of sickness is over.* A few weeks later, on a day we had set aside for prayer and fasting, Ruth was attacked by pain in every area of her body, from her head to her feet. She said, "O Lord, please, not again!"

Through these years Ruth and I have learned not to give way to infirmity, but to stand on God's promises. So, she said to me, "I know I would feel better if I could worship the Lord, but I don't have the strength. Would you put on the Russian worship cassette from the conference we did in Moscow last year? I believe it will help me."

Ruth was on the floor of our bedroom, and as she began to relax and worship the Lord, she exclaimed, "These are lying symptoms – lying spirits – trying to steal God's promise from me!"

When we took our stand together, in the name of Jesus, against those lying spirits, Ruth was completely delivered from pain.

In God's amazing grace, He went on to grant us a special serendipity for which there is no natural explanation. In Ruth's words:

> I rose to my feet and went to the kitchen for a glass of water. Suddenly Derek called to me, "Come quickly!"

When I returned to the bedroom, I gasped! The whole room and adjoining bath were fragrant with the scent of roses – like an English garden. It was as if the Lord Himself was there. I fell on my face on the floor in adoration.

God had made Ruth and me "more than conquerors" (Romans 8:37). We came out of that trial with more than we had when we went into it.

This experience brought to my mind other Christians who had received a genuine healing from the Lord, against whom Satan had apparently directed lying spirits to undermine their faith and destroy their testimony. We need to "put on the whole armor of God, that [we] may be able to stand against the wiles of the devil" (Ephesians 6:11).

I need to emphasize, however, as I said in chapter 10, that not all sicknesses are caused by demons. Many have other, natural causes. This makes it important to identify sicknesses that are directly caused by demons.

In 1 Corinthians 12 Paul lists nine supernatural gifts of the Holy Spirit available to believers. Of these there are two that may help us to identify demons: literally, *a word of knowledge* and *discernings of spirits* (see verses 8, 10).

I have given a literal translation of these two phrases because the text indicates that each word of knowledge and each act of discerning is an individual gift. Each, too, operates on a supernatural plane, not as the product of natural reasoning or intelligence.

In Hebrews 4:12 the writer says:

For the word of God is living and powerful, and sharper than any two-edged sword, piercing even to the division of soul and spirit, and of joints and marrow, and is a discerner of the thoughts and intents of the heart.

It is this kind of insight that can come through a word of knowledge. It can penetrate the invisible areas of human personality and reveal the identity of evil forces lurking there. Often the revelation comes in the form of a single word or phrase impressed on the mind of the person ministering deliverance, or sometimes of the one receiving deliverance. A demon thus identified might be colitis, crippling, asthma, schizophrenia or cancer.

The presence of a demon, however, may not necessarily be revealed supernaturally. It may simply come about in the normal course of personal counseling, in the same way that a doctor may diagnose a disease from the symptoms a patient describes. This chapter and the preceding nine provide a fairly comprehensive survey of some of the most common symptoms of demonic activity. One thing I have found particularly helpful is to identify, if possible, the moment or place of weakness through which a demon gained entrance.

There is another way demons can be contributory causes of sickness. In chapter 19 I spoke about negative emotional spirits. While not actually causing sickness, they can produce an attitude of mind that either opens the door to sickness or else prevents sick people from receiving their healing by faith. Some examples of such negative spirits are rejection, fear, grief, unforgiveness, discouragement, disappointment and despair. In such cases, it is usually necessary to expel the negative spirit before seeking to minister physical healing.

I have related just a few of the occasions on which I have seen the authority of Christ used with great effectiveness against demons of sickness and infirmity. But I still regret the many occasions on which I did not follow the pattern of Christ's aggressive approach to such demons. I have learned that moving on this supernatural plane requires continuing, day-to-day dependence on God, trusting Him for discernment and authority. In this ministry we must affirm with Paul that "we walk by faith, not by sight" (2 Corinthians 5:7).

Deliverance from Multiple Sclerosis and Stroke

I will close this chapter with two remarkable accounts of people delivered from demons of sickness or infirmity. The first comes from a lay worker in an American church:

A young woman from our church – we will call her Jane – had developed multiple sclerosis (MS). She heard teaching on faith, claimed her healing and was greatly improved. But she continued to have symptoms and to stumble while on her feet. She testified to her healing during a church service, but added, "I still stumble some, and I know there is something more I need."

Jane and her sister came to us for prayer about 2:30 one afternoon. She said they had gone through all the prayers to obtain release. Then we started to work. Jane named at least one hundred spirits. I was too busy to count them. I have recalled a lot but not all of them. We worked from three until 6:15 P.M.

I thought there would be a spirit of MS, but instead she named spirits of all the symptoms: tiredness, weakness, stumbling, trembling, crying, weeping, mourning, blindness, deafness, choking, suffocation, coldness, paralysis, numbness, torment, fatigue, laziness, idleness, headaches, ear pain and more!

As we prayed, all the manifestations of MS grabbed her body, preventing her from standing. She also said she was numb all over. As the spirits came out, she would tell me what part of her body was getting warm and having the sense of feeling return.

She got free to her waist and to her hips, then to her knees and legs. Finally, she said, "The remaining ones are in my feet." She took off her boots; her feet felt rigid and cold. She would tell us as the demons were leaving her feet. Finally, she said, "There are just two more in my toe." I do not remember the first one, but the second one was "complaining." When it left, she jumped up and danced around the room. Jane was totally freed from MS.

The other remarkable account of deliverance from a demon of sickness comes from a New Zealand evangelist with an international ministry:

On June 10, 1992, while I was conducting a meeting in Katikati, New Zealand, the Lord drew my attention to a woman with crutches, whom I called up to the stage. She climbed the stairs with difficulty.

She was in terrible pain, she said. She had bad osteoarthritis, circulation trouble in her heart, and had suffered from diabetes for 41 years. She had also had a stroke after losing her husband two years earlier. The left side of her body had been affected. She limped, was unable to write properly, and was hardly able to converse. She loved singing, but her throat was contracted. In her youth, she added, she had had trouble with her periods, and had her first D&C – dilation and curettage – at age fourteen. Later she had had miscarriages.

I commanded every spirit affecting her to flee, particularly the spirit of stroke. Following my prayer she almost ran down the stairs from the platform.

Her hands were in the air and she was clearly full of the Holy Spirit.

Three years later, on June 14, 1995, she came to another meeting in a nearby town and testified.

As she had gone back to her seat in Katikati, she told us, she had felt God's healing. For the next week she had experienced jolts in her body as though something was moving in and out. Now she was able to run up and down the stairs. She was able to write, and the left side of her body was totally healed from the effects of the stroke, including her eye. And after three years the doctors still could find no trace of the diabetes she had had for 41 years.

Unquestionably she had received a miracle as the demonic power was cast out.

Questions for This Study

1. True or false? All illnesses are caused by demons.

2. A _____ spirit will try to convince someone that he or she has _____ a healing.

3. Once a person has been delivered from a demon, what is the next step he or she must be willing to take?

4. What is required to determine if a particular illness is caused by a demon?

5. Derek found it was helpful to identify the _____ or _____ of weakness through which a demon gained entrance.

6. List what you must do to be able to move effectively in the supernatural realm.

Life Application

Consider any physical problems from which you may be suffering. Begin to consider how you will be able to discern which ones, if any, may have a demonic cause. Write them down. This may be an ongoing journey of discovery.

Memory Verse

It is because of him that you are in Christ Jesus, who has become for us wisdom from God – that is, our righteousness, holiness and redemption. Therefore, as it is written: "Let him who boasts boast in the Lord."

1 Corinthians 1:30–31 NIV

Faith Response

Lord, I commit myself to live in day-to-day dependence on You, trusting in You for the discernment and authority to move in the supernatural.

Answers are on page 416

TWENTY-ONE
Preparing for Deliverance

PERHAPS, AS YOU HAVE BEEN READING, YOU HAVE recognized that there are demons at work within you. You did not previously understand the pressures you were enduring, but now you have been able to identify them. Thank God! You no longer need to endure those pressures passively.

In this chapter I will show you the way that leads to deliverance and to victory. The wonderful secret is this: You do not have to win the victory for yourself. You can enter into the victory that Jesus, by His death and resurrection, has already won for you.

On the cross Jesus paid the full and final penalty for all the sins of all people of every age and of every race. He was the Lamb of God who carried away the sin of the world (see John 1:29). By raising Him from the dead, God demonstrated to the universe that His justice was fully and finally satisfied by the propitiation Jesus had made for our sins.

The sacrifice of Jesus on your behalf is the one all-sufficient basis on which you can claim a full release from every demonic force Satan has directed against you. Once you realize this and act in faith on it, you will be able to say with Paul, "But thanks be to God, who gives us the victory through our Lord Jesus Christ" (1 Corinthians 15:57).

If you decide to claim the deliverance God has provided for you, you have two options: to seek ministry from your pastor or fellow Christians, or to turn directly to the Lord for the help you need.

If you have access to a church or other ministry willing to help you, then by all means seek their help. It is important to make sure, however, that they are sincere, Bible-believing Christians and that they understand what is involved in dealing with demons. If you, as a Christian, approach them and discover that they do not believe a Christian can have a demon, then obviously they will not be able to help you.

In our U.S. office we receive letters regularly from people who have come to realize they need deliverance from demons and are asking us to recommend some church or ministry in their area that will help them. Regrettably, more often than not, we do not know anyone to whom we can conscientiously direct them. It reminds me of a scene in the ministry of Jesus:

But when He saw the multitudes, He was moved with compassion for them, because they were weary and scattered, like sheep having no shepherd. Then He said to His disciples, "The harvest truly is plentiful, but the laborers are few. Therefore pray the Lord of the harvest to send out laborers into His harvest."   Matthew 9:36–37

The ministry of deliverance is a harvest field in which many properly equipped workers are needed. I realize, therefore, that many who read this book may not have any human source of help to whom they can turn. But thanks be to God, the way is always open to the One who is *the* Deliverer – Jesus! If you decide to take this route, I have outlined for you a series of nine steps that can lead you through to the deliverance and victory you need:

Step No. 1: Personally affirm your faith in Christ.

Step No. 2: Humble yourself.

Step No. 3: Confess any known sin.

Step No. 4: Repent of all sins.

Step No. 5: Forgive all other people.

Step No. 6: Break with the occult and all false religion.

Step No. 7: Prepare to be released from every curse over your life.

Step No. 8:   Take your stand with God.

Step No. 9:   Expel!

First, however, it is important to make sure of your personal relationship with God. If you do not already know you are a born-again child of God, with all your sins forgiven through Jesus' sacrifice, then you can, by the very act of following these steps, enter into a direct, personal relationship with God as your Father. If, on the other hand, you already have a personal relationship with God, going through these steps will strengthen your faith and give you a solid, scriptural basis on which to seek the help that you need from Him.

Read carefully through the nine steps in this chapter, step by step, until you are sure you fully understand each of them. Then, in chapter 22, I will provide you with a form of prayer by which you can claim your deliverance from every demonic oppression. You are protected by the blood of Jesus, as I said in chapter 16, only when you are rightly related to Him and walking in obedience. Be sure, therefore, that you have prayed the prayer in faith before you take your stand against the demons.

Step No. 1: Personally Affirm Your Faith in Christ

Jesus is the "High Priest of our confession" (Hebrews 3:1). The Greek word translated *confession* means "saying the same as...." Therefore, we say the same about what

Jesus has done for us as the Bible has already said. We make the words of our mouths agree with the Word of God. We proclaim the victory of Jesus in a bold and personal way on our own behalf. When we do so, we invoke His ministry as our High Priest to bring our need before God the Father, thus releasing the whole authority of heaven on our behalf.

If we fail to confess our faith in this way, we give Jesus no basis on which to intervene for us.

Step No. 2: Humble Yourself

"God resists the proud,
but gives grace to the humble."

Therefore humble yourselves under the mighty hand of God....

1 Peter 5:5–6, emphasis added

If we approach God with an attitude of pride, He resists us and we have no access to Him. So our first step toward God must be to humble ourselves, to say to God, "I need you!"

God never offers to make us humble. Throughout the Bible He places the responsibility on us. God can humiliate us, and sometimes He may have to; but only we can make ourselves humble. If we are willing, however, God will supply all the grace we need.

When we seek deliverance from demons, there may come a point when we have to choose between dignity and deliverance. If dignity becomes more important than deliverance, we have not really repented of our pride.

I was approached once by a doctor's wife in the Deep South of the U.S. – an old-style, genteel lady who said, "Mr. Prince, if I understand you rightly, when I seek deliverance the way you describe it, I may end up screaming."

"It could happen," I replied.

"But I was brought up that a lady doesn't scream in public."

"Well," I said, "suppose you were in a river drowning, about to go down for the third time, and you thought there might be somebody on the bank who could rescue you. Would you be too ladylike to scream?"

I needed to say no more.

If you are not prepared to humble yourself, you will not be willing to take the steps that follow.

Step No. 3: Confess Any Known Sin

Nowhere in the Bible does God commit Himself to forgive sins that have not been confessed. But for those who confess, His promise is clear: "If we confess our sins, He is faithful and just to forgive us our sins and to cleanse us from all unrighteousness" (1 John 1:9). God is faithful because He has promised. He is just because Jesus has already paid the penalty for our sins.

If you are troubled about some specific sin, be honest about it. Do not call it by some fancy psychiatric name. Most of the names for our basic sins are not pretty. And God forgives them only when we acknowledge them as *sins*. He never promises to forgive "problems." If you have a "problem" with overeating, call it by its name: the sin of gluttony. If it is lust, call it lust. If it is hatred, call it hatred. If it is gossip, call it gossip.

Remember, too, that once you have told God the worst about yourself, you have not shocked Him. He knew it all before you told Him. Furthermore, He still loves you!

I referred in chapter 13 to God's warning that He visits the sins of the fathers on their children to the third and fourth generations (see Exodus 20:3–5). This may apply in your case. The sins of your ancestors do not make you guilty, but they can be causing you to suffer from their consequences. It may be advisable for you to confess and disassociate yourself from any sins that your ancestors committed. This applies particularly to the occult or a false religion.

It is not wise, however, to indulge in self-analysis. Simply relax and let the Holy Spirit bring to your mind any specific sins you need to confess. Remember, He is your Helper.

Step No. 4: Repent of All Sins

It is necessary to confess your sins, but that by itself is not enough. You must also repent for your sins. "He who covers his sins will not prosper, but whoever confesses and forsakes them will have mercy" (Proverbs 28:13). You must first confess, then forsake your sins. To forsake your sins means to turn away from them completely.

A young man said to me once, "I think I have a spirit of lust, but I rather enjoy it. Do you think God will deliver me from it?"

"Definitely not!" I replied. "God delivers us from our enemies, not from our friends. But if you will make your friend your enemy, then you can ask God to deliver you. You need to ask Him to help you hate that sin as He hates it."

Repentance involves two things. First you must accept personal responsibility for what you have done. You cannot hide behind some other person – a parent, spouse or minister, perhaps – and hold him or her responsible for the wrong things you yourself have done. Nor can you blame demons for your sin. Your attitude must be: I am guilty, and I acknowledge it.

Second, you must take the same stand against your sin that God Himself takes. Do not try in any way to minimize or excuse it. Hate it as God hates it! Then sin will have no more power over you.

Step No. 5: Forgive All Other People

In Mark 11:25–26 Jesus established an unvarying spiritual law:

"And whenever you stand praying, if you have anything against anyone, forgive him, that your Father in heaven may also forgive you your trespasses. But if you do not forgive, neither will your Father in heaven forgive your trespasses."

If we desire forgiveness from God for our sins, we must unconditionally forgive all those who have sinned against us.

In chapter 18 I mentioned the parable Jesus told about a servant whose master forgave him a debt equivalent to several million dollars, yet he himself refused to forgive his fellow servant a debt of just a few dollars (see Matthew 18:23–35). When we consider the incalculable debt each of us owes God for the sins we have committed against Him, the most that any fellow human being owes us is, by comparison, just a few dollars.

The judgment on the unforgiving servant was to be delivered "to the torturers" (verse 34). In chapter 18 I compared the activity of demons to that of the torturers. If you want to be delivered from the torturers, you must freely forgive all those who have offended or harmed you in any way.

Remember that forgiving another person is not primarily an emotion. It is a *decision* of the will. First you must make a firm decision. Then you must verbalize it: "I forgive So-and-so of all the wrong he [or she] did to me. I lay down all bitterness, all resentment, all hatred."

Deciding in your heart, then speaking it out with your mouth, makes your act of forgiving effective.

Step No. 6: Break with the Occult and All False Religion

I explained in chapter 14 how intensely God hates any doctrine or practice that puts some other person or thing in the place of undivided loyalty and whole-hearted worship that belongs solely to God. Somewhere in the background of all these other systems lurks the one who is the archenemy of God and man. If you want to draw near to God, you must sever all contact with Satan.

This includes removing from your possession, and from where you live, anything that in any way links you to the occult or to the satanic. This includes books, souvenirs, charms and objects of art. Remember Moses' warning to Israel: "Nor shall you bring an abomination into your house, lest you be doomed to destruction like it..." (Deuteronomy 7:26).

The best way to dispose of such things is, if possible, to burn them. Remember, this is how the Christians in Ephesus responded when they realized their occult scrolls linked them to the power of demons. Follow their example!

If your circumstances prevent you from doing this immediately, make a commitment to God to do it just as soon as you have the opportunity.

Step No. 7: Prepare to Be Released from Every Curse over Your Life

The Bible has much to say about the power of blessings and curses. Altogether it mentions them about six hundred times. Contemporary Western Christendom has tended to focus on the blessings and to regard the curses as a superstitious carryover from the Middle Ages. But this is unscriptural and unrealistic.

I have compared a curse to a dark shadow over our lives that shuts out part (at least) of God's blessings. Two of the blessings that may be excluded by a curse are physical healing and deliverance from evil spirits.

Over the years I have compiled a list of some problems that commonly indicate that a curse is at work:

1. Mental or emotional breakdown
2. Repeated or chronic sicknesses (especially if hereditary)
3. Barrenness, a tendency to miscarry or related female problems
4. Breakdown of marriage and family alienation
5. Continuing financial insufficiency
6. Being "accident-prone"
7. A family history of suicides or unnatural or untimely deaths

There is, as I have said, one all-sufficient scriptural basis for release from a curse: the sacrifice of Jesus on the cross by which He took on Himself every curse due to us, that in return we might inherit the blessings of Abraham, who was blessed by God in all things (see Genesis 24:1; Galatians 3:13–14). (For further instruction, refer to my book *Blessing or Curse: You Can Choose!*)

If you sense there is some curse over your life, seek release from it on the basis of what Jesus did for you on the cross when He was made a curse. (I will give you the words to pray in the next chapter.)

Step No. 8: Take Your Stand with God

Make a firm decision and speak it out: "I submit my will, my purpose, my future, my whole life to God. I take my stand with God against all sin, all evil and every kind of demon."

As soon as you take your stand with God, He also takes His stand with you. You can enjoy the confidence expressed in Romans 8:31: "If God is for us, who can be against us?"

One way God may come to your help is by revealing the identity of any demons you need to expel.

I commented in chapter 8 that dealing with a demon can be like dealing with a fierce dog. When you call the dog by its name, you have more authority over it. You may already be aware of the names of a specific demon or demons from which you need to be delivered. Or it may happen that as you enter the process of deliverance a name of a demon will come to your mind. These are two of the ways the Holy Spirit may come to your help.

At the end of one deliverance service, a young man asked me, "Is there such a thing as a spirit of tooth decay?"

"I've never heard of such a spirit," I replied, "but if the Holy Spirit says there is one, then there is."

"Well, that's what I've just been delivered from," the young man told me.

Many years later the same man, no longer young, told me the result of that deliverance.

"I would go to the dentist and have a tooth filled," he said, "but after a year or two, the tooth would decay beneath the filling and I would need a new filling. But since I was delivered from the spirit of tooth decay, I've never had that problem again."

If the Holy Spirit does give you the name of a specific demon, your next step must be to take a deliberate stand with God against the demon, and to verbalize it. Speak it out: "You spirit of lust [or rejection or confusion or whatever], I take my stand against you in the name of Jesus. I no longer submit to you. You have no more place in me. I command you to go!"

You cannot afford to be passive. Remember James 4:7: "Submit to God. Resist the devil and he will flee from you."

Step No. 9: Expel!

This is so simple and practical that it does not seem spiritual. But it works! You should not attempt to do it, however, until you have prayed the prayer in the next chapter.

I explained in chapter 11 that the word for *spirit* in both Hebrew and Greek is the word for *wind* – and also the word for *breath*. So how do you get rid of breath? You expel it, usually through your mouth.

There are, however, eight other orifices in the human body. At times a demon may come out through any one of them, or in other ways. In chapter 19 I related the story of the student Christopher and how a demon of doubt came out through his left ear. I have also mentioned that a demon of masturbation frequently comes out through the fingers. A spirit of crippling is often expelled with convulsive movements of the body.

If it happens that a demon does not come out through your mouth, but through some other orifice or area of your body, you will become aware of it. Cooperate with the Holy Spirit and He will show you what to do. But most frequently you may expect to expel a demon through your mouth.

A mother came to me once with her little boy of about four and asked me to pray for him.

"What's his problem?" I asked.

"Allergies."

"What kind of allergies?"

"Food allergies."

"What kinds of food is he allergic to?"

"Tell me what he *isn't* allergic to!"

Then I told the mother, "I'm going to deal with this as an evil spirit. Is that all right?"

She gave her consent.

Then I turned to the little boy and explained, "There's a bad spirit in you, like a breath, and it keeps you from eating the things you like. I'm going to command it to come out of you, and when I say, 'In the name of Jesus,' I want you to blow it out. O.K.?"

The boy nodded, and behaved like a well-trained little soldier. I commanded the evil spirit to leave him, and when I said, "In the name of Jesus!" the boy blew out four times. Nothing further happened. No emotion, no excitement. I wondered whether the boy had really been delivered, but I had to leave it with the Lord.

Three days later the mother came back and asked for prayer for herself.

"What's your problem?" I asked.

"Allergies," she replied.

"Tell me first what happened to your son," I said.

"He came home with me," she said, "marched straight up to the refrigerator and sampled everything in it – and nothing did him any harm!"

I remembered what Jesus said about the need to become like little children.

After you have said your prayer for deliverance and

concluded with "Amen!" *begin to expel.* That is a decision of your will, followed by an action of your muscles.

At the same time, make way for the demon or demons to come out. Keep the exit clear! Do not go on praying or start to speak in tongues. I have discovered that movement of the lips and tongue in speech acts as a barrier to keep the demon in. Think of an ambulance coming down the road, lights flashing and siren blaring. All other traffic moves off to the side of the road. Do the same in your throat. Clear the way for the demon to come out.

As you begin to expel, what comes out first may be just natural human breath. But after a short while, something other than human breath will start coming out. That is your enemy! Keep the pressure on!

There may be different manifestations as a demon emerges. It may be scarcely perceptible, just a little sigh or yawn. Or it may come with sobbing, groaning, coughing, screaming or roaring. Remember, in the ministry of Philip, the demons came out with loud cries. One woman delivered from a demon of nicotine yawned so widely that she thought she was going to dislocate her jaw! But when she closed her mouth, she was free from nicotine.

Set no predetermined limit as to how long you will go on expelling. Keep on as long as there are any demons to come out.

When a demon is coming out, some people – usually women – may go on screaming without receiving any release. This indicates that the demon has stopped in the narrow section of the throat and is holding on there to avoid being expelled. In such cases, a deliberate, forceful cough will usually dislodge the demon and force it out. In a deliverance service, sometimes a demon's screaming will distract others seeking deliverance, hindering them and even making them afraid. This is when workers need to act quickly and help the person screaming to get released.

Many different things may happen when a demon comes out. But remember, when you speak in the name of Jesus, you have authority over the demons. Do not yield to a spirit of fear. Remember, too, that the Holy Spirit is there with you to help you. Yield fully to Him and let Him guide you through to full victory!

Questions for This Study

1. What is the one, all-sufficient basis on which you can claim your release from Satan's demonic influences?

2. If we fail to confess Jesus as our _____ _____ , we give Him no basis on which to _____ for us.

3. According to Exodus 20:3–5, God warns that the sins of the father may extend to how many generations?

4. What are the two steps involved in repentance?

5. Forgiving another person is not primarily an _____ ; it is a _____ of the will.

6. What are the two blessings that may be excluded by a curse?

7. List some of the hindrances to receiving deliverance cited in this chapter.

Life Application

Write out the first eight steps Derek cites as preparation for deliverance. As you do, take enough time on each step to allow the Holy Spirit to show you how to complete that action fully.

Memory Verse

But thanks be to God, who gives us the victory through our Lord Jesus Christ. 1 Corinthians 15:57

Faith Response

Father, Jesus Christ, Holy Spirit, I believe according to Your Word that You are for me and not against me, and that You lead me to total freedom!

Answers are on page 416

TWENTY-TWO
A Prayer for Deliverance

YOU HAVE NOW REACHED THE POINT AT WHICH
you can claim your deliverance in prayer. People sometimes say to me, "I want to pray, but I don't know what
to say." So, I have prepared a pattern prayer for you to
follow.

Before you pray, however, read carefully through the
nine steps outlined in the previous chapter. Make sure
you understand them and that you are ready to meet
all the conditions.

You will find a few blank places in the pattern prayer
where you need to fill in details that apply to your individual situation – specific sins, specific contacts with the
occult or false religion, the names of people you need
to forgive. Be sure to make this latter list as complete
as possible.

I have seen hundreds, even thousands, of people
receive deliverance through this pattern of prayer. You

may wish to enlist the support of a fellow Christian. But be sure the person you choose is in agreement with your decision and will be praying out of faith, not unbelief. If there are two of you, you can also claim the promise of Jesus in Matthew 18:19: "If two of you agree on earth concerning anything that they ask, it will be done for them by My Father in heaven."

Finally, do not feel bound to stick rigidly to this pattern prayer. If the Holy Spirit prompts you to add words from your heart, do not hesitate to do so. And do not be in a hurry. Go through the whole prayer slowly and deliberately.

1. *Personally affirm your faith in Christ:*
   "Lord Jesus Christ, I believe You are the Son of God and the only way to God – that You died on the cross for my sins and rose again so that I might be forgiven and receive eternal life."

2. *Humble yourself:*
   "I renounce all pride and religious self-righteousness and any dignity that does not come from You. I have no claim on Your mercy except that You died in my place."

3. *Confess any known sin:*
   "I confess all my sins before You and hold nothing back. Especially I confess...."

4. *Repent of all sins:*
   "I repent of all my sins. I turn away from them and I turn to You, Lord, for mercy and forgiveness."

5. *Forgive all other people:*

"By a decision of my will, I freely forgive all who have ever harmed or wronged me. I lay down all bitterness, all resentment and all hatred. Specifically, I forgive...."

6. *Break with the occult and all false religion:*

"I sever all contact I have ever had with the occult or with all false religion – particularly.... I commit myself to get rid of all objects associated with the occult or false religion."

7. *Prepare to be released from every curse over your life:*

"Lord Jesus, I thank You that on the cross You were made a curse, that I might be redeemed from every curse and inherit God's blessing. On that basis I ask You to release me and set me free to receive the deliverance I need."

8. *Take your stand with God:*

"I take my stand with You, Lord, against all Satan's demons. I submit to You, Lord, and I resist the devil. Amen!"

9. *Expel:*

"Now I speak to any demons that have control over me. [Speak directly to them.] I command you to go from me now. In the name of Jesus, I expel you!"

Each time you experience a release, praise and thank God for it. Giving thanks and praise is the simplest and purest expression of faith. It also creates an atmosphere that demons find intolerable.

When you feel your deliverance is complete, or that you have come as far as you can at this time, be sure to kneel down and *make Jesus Lord of every area of your life*. Remember the warning of Jesus that if a demon comes back and finds the house empty, he will return and bring others with him. On your own you do not have the strength to keep the demons out. But if the Lord Jesus has taken up residence within you, you have His help to keep them out. This reminds me of a woman who was consistently victorious in her Christian life. When asked her secret, she said, "Whenever the devil knocks at the door, I just let Jesus answer!" Do not try to fight the demons by yourself.

If you feel your deliverance is not yet complete, wait until your strength returns or you feel prompted by the Holy Spirit. Then continue with the process of getting the demons out.

Sometimes at the end of a deliverance service, a person comes up to me and asks, "How do I know if I'm completely free?"

Usually I reply, "It's not my job to give you a certificate. If I did, it wouldn't be worth the paper it's written on! The thing that's really important is that you've discovered the reality of demons and how to deal with them. Now you are responsible to deal with them in the same way wherever and whenever you encounter them."

Finally, here is a reminder that applies to every Christian: *You never need to be ashamed of having been delivered from demons.* In the gospel record there was one person to whom God granted a unique and glorious honor: to be the first human witness of the resurrection of Jesus. The incident is recorded in Mark 16:9:

> *Now when He rose early on the first day of the week, He appeared first to Mary Magdalene, out of whom He had cast seven demons.*

Think of it! Jesus appeared to Mary Magdalene, who was identified as the one "out of whom He had cast seven demons." If Mary never needed to be ashamed, no more do you if you, too, have been delivered from demons.

There is, however, one thing of which you might need to be ashamed: if you discovered you needed deliverance from demons, but pride kept you from acknowledging your need and being set free.

Questions for This Study

1. What two responses should come after every release from demonic torment?
2. When your deliverance is complete, what specific step should you take?
3. Should there be any sense of shame about needing to be delivered from demons?

Life Application

Journal about your experience while praying the prayer of deliverance.

- Areas in which you felt release and freedom
- Areas in which you felt special resistance or conflict
- Areas where you do not yet feel entirely free and which will need further attention at some other time
- Any impressions from the Holy Spirit that you feel you need to remember for follow-up and encouragement

Memory Verse

If the Son makes you free, you shall be free indeed.

John 8:36

Faith Response

Thank You, Jesus, for being my Deliverer!

Answers are on page 417

TWENTY-THREE

How to Keep Your Deliverance

THANK GOD YOU HAVE RECEIVED DELIVERANCE! Continue to thank God! Even if you are not sure yet of all that has happened, you can express your faith by thanking Him. This is the first step to help you keep your deliverance.

You can be sure, however, that Satan will not give up on you. He will do everything in his power to reassert his control over you. You must be prepared for his counterattack. I have referred several times to the warning of Jesus that a demon that has gone out of a man will seek to return. You must make completely sure, therefore, that Jesus is dwelling in you and that He is absolute Lord of your life.

We have seen that human personality is like a city, and that demonic invasion can have the effect of breaking down the walls inside us that should protect us.

Once our enemy has been driven out, we must begin immediately to rebuild our protective walls. Here are the basic principles to help you rebuild:

1. Live by God's Word.
2. Put on the garment of praise.
3. Come under discipline.
4. Cultivate right fellowship.
5. Be filled with the Holy Spirit.
6. Make sure you have passed through the water of baptism.
7. Put on the whole armor of God.

1. Live by God's Word

In Matthew 4:4 Jesus said that mankind shall live "by every word that proceeds from the mouth of God." The word *live* is all-inclusive, covering everything we think, say or do. All must proceed from the same source: the Word of God. We must give it unchallenged preeminence in every area of our lives.

Many other influences will compete for control over us: our own feelings, the opinions of others, accepted traditions, the culture that surrounds us. But God guarantees us victory in every area – and specifically, victory over the devil – only insofar as our lives are directed and controlled by His Word.

Take to heart the directions the Lord gave to Joshua as he was about to enter the Promised Land:

*"This Book of the Law shall not depart from your
mouth, but you shall meditate in it day and night,
that you may observe to do according to all that
is written in it. For then you will make your way
prosperous, and then you will have good success."*

Joshua 1:8

These directions may be summed up in three
phrases: think the Word of God; speak the Word of
God; act the Word of God. Then God guarantees you
success.

2. Put On the Garment of Praise

In Isaiah 61:3 God offers us "the garment of praise" in
place of "the spirit of heaviness." In chapter 4 I related
how I was delivered from depression when it was identified as a spirit of heaviness. After that I gradually
learned that when I was praising the Lord, the spirit of
heaviness would not come near me. I saw that I needed
to cultivate a lifestyle in which praise would cover me
as completely as the clothes I wore.

Once when Lydia and I were having an informal
prayer meeting in our home in London, a woman from
our congregation came to our door, leading a man by
the hand.

"This is my husband," she said. "He's just out of
prison and needs to be delivered from a demon."

At that time, I had no experience in ministering

deliverance to others and no idea how to do it. So, I simply invited him to join our prayer meeting. Some of our members were offering loud, uninhibited praise to the Lord.

After a while the man sidled up to me and said, "There's too much noise. I'm going!"

"It's the devil that doesn't like the noise," I replied, "because we're praising Jesus. You've got two options. If you go now, the demon will go with you. If you stay, it will go without you."

"I'll stay," he mumbled.

A little later he approached me again and said, "It's just gone! I felt it leave my throat."

You, having received deliverance, are also "just out of prison." Enjoy your liberty! Do as the Word of God says: Put on the garment of praise. When you are praising the Lord, you trouble the devil more than he can trouble you.

3. Come under Discipline

Jesus' last order to His apostles was to "go ... and make disciples ... " (Matthew 28:19). A disciple, as the word indicates, is one who is under discipline. Jesus never instructed anyone to make "church members."

Because "rebellion is as the sin of witchcraft" (1 Samuel 15:23), and because rebellion against God has exposed our whole race to the deceptive and destructive power of Satan, we can come under God's protection only as we place ourselves under His discipline. An undisciplined life is vulnerable to demonic attack.

In 2 Timothy 1:7 Paul says God has given us "a spirit of power, of love and of self-discipline" (NIV). This is the primary form of discipline in any life – self-discipline. Unless we learn to discipline ourselves, no other form of discipline will be effective.

The first area in which this applies is our personal communion with God in His Word and in prayer. Living by God's Word demands that we give Him regular "prime time" each day. Then, with the help of the Holy Spirit, we must bring our emotions, desires and appetites under control. A man not in control in these areas is not in control of his life.

There is one decisive area we must bring under control: the tongue. In chapter 13 I pointed out that idle words open the way for demons. The control of the tongue is the mark of spiritual maturity: "If anyone does not stumble in word, he is a perfect man, able also to bridle the whole body" (James 3:2).

Obviously, you will not achieve this level of self-discipline in a few simple steps. From time to time, you will stumble. Just pick yourself up, dust yourself off and continue to move forward and upward. As long as you are moving in the right direction, Satan may harass you but he cannot defeat you.

There are various other areas in which we may need to come under discipline, relating to the family, school, church and various forms of secular government. God requires us to cultivate submissiveness in any of these areas that apply in our lives: "Submit yourselves for the Lord's sake to every authority instituted among men ... " (1 Peter 2:13, NIV).

It is true that deliverance brings us freedom, but many Christians misunderstand the nature of freedom. We are not free to do our own thing; we are free that we may bring every area of our lives under God's discipline.

4. Cultivate Right Fellowship

I pointed out in chapters 15 and 19 that a person whose walls have been broken down by demons needs the help of other Christians to stand with him as he builds up those walls.

We need to recognize that one of the most powerful influences in our lives is the people with whom we associate. This means we have to choose the kind of people we spend time with. We may live among unbelievers, but we cannot make ourselves one with them. There must always be a difference between our lifestyle and theirs.

If we are walking in the light, we will have fellowship with our fellow believers (see 1 John 1:7). There is no place for self-centered individualism in the Christian life. As Christians we need each other. The writer of Hebrews gives us an urgent warning:

And let us consider one another in order to stir up love and good works, not forsaking the assembling of ourselves together, as is the manner of some, but exhorting one another, and so much the more as you see the Day approaching.

(Hebrews 10:24–25)

On the other hand, we are also warned, "Evil company corrupts good habits" (1 Corinthians 15:33). If you sincerely desire to keep your deliverance, you must break off relationships that have a wrong influence on you, and begin to cultivate friends who will encourage you and set you a good example. It may be painful to sever ties with friends or to dissociate yourself for a time from family members whose influence is harmful. But you can trust the Holy Spirit to help you do it with grace and wisdom and to take care of the consequences. Remember, He is your Helper!

5. Be Filled with the Holy Spirit

In Ephesians 5:18 Paul gives us two words of instruction. The first is negative: "Do not be drunk with wine." The second is positive: "Be filled with the Spirit." Most Christians would acknowledge that it is wrong to be drunk. Yet how many believe it is equally wrong *not* to be filled with the Spirit?

The infilling of the Holy Spirit is an essential part of God's provision for victorious living. Paul speaks of this infilling in the continuing present tense: "Be continuously filled." He is speaking not about a one-time experience but, in the next three verses, about a lifestyle:

- Singing praises continually to the Lord
- Being unceasingly thankful to God the Father
- Being humbly submissive to one another

As the Holy Spirit fills you continuously in this way, demons will find in you no vacant area that they can occupy!

6. Make Sure You Have Passed through the Water of Baptism

Jesus told His apostles to "preach the gospel to every creature. He who believes and is baptized [immersed] will be saved..." (Mark 16:15–16). Baptism in water is not an option – some ecclesiastical ceremony that follows salvation. On the contrary, it is an outward act of obedience expressing the inward work of faith in our hearts, and thus making salvation complete. In the book of Acts there is no record of anyone receiving salvation without afterward being baptized in water.

In the New Testament, baptism is compared to two events in Old Testament history: Noah and his family in the ark passing through the waters of the flood (see Genesis 7–8; 1 Peter 3:19–21); and Israel escaping from the dominion of Pharaoh by passing through the Red Sea (see Exodus 14:15–31; 1 Corinthians 10:1–2). In each case passing through the water was an act of separation. Noah and his family were saved from the ungodly world that perished under God's judgment, and Israel finally escaped Pharaoh's oppression, since the Egyptian army could not follow them through the water.

There were two phases in Israel's salvation. First, in Egypt they were saved from God's judgment by faith in the blood of the Passover lamb, which was a type of Christ. Second, they were delivered from Egypt by passing through the Red Sea.

This pattern applies to us as Christians. We are saved *in the world* by faith in the blood of Jesus. But we are separated *from the world* by passing through the water of baptism. It is the act of being baptized that cuts us off from the kingdom of Satan. His demons have no right to follow us through the water.

If you have never been baptized in water as a believer, this is an important step you need to take to cut off demonic activity. If you have already been baptized, on the other hand, you need to stand fast on that fact and be confident that Satan's demons have no further right of access to you. (I deal more thoroughly with this subject in my book *Foundational Truths for Christian Living* in the section "New Testament Baptisms.")

7. Put On the Whole Armor of God

Now that you are wearing your garment of praise, God offers you a complete set of armor to put on over it. In case you have not yet realized it, you are a soldier in a war. You need all the armor God has provided for you.

The items of your equipment are listed in Ephesians 6:13–18, as follows:

- The girdle [belt] of truth
- The breastplate of righteousness
- The shoes of the preparation of the gospel of peace
- The shield of faith
- The helmet of salvation
- The sword of the Spirit – the word [Greek *rhema*] of God
- All prayer

We will go through these items of armor in order.

The Girdle [Belt] of Truth

In biblical times men usually wore loose clothing that hung down below their knees. Before undertaking any strenuous activity, they would gather up their loose garment above their knees and fasten it with a belt around the waist. Hence the phrase that occurs several times in the Bible: *Gird up your loins*.

Likewise, you must gather up and fasten out of the way anything that would impede your freedom to follow Jesus. The "belt" that enables you to do this is God's Word, applied in a very plain and practical way. You must become totally sincere and open and put aside every form of dishonesty or hypocrisy. You must love the truth.

The Breastplate of Righteousness

The breastplate protects your most critical and vulnerable area: your heart. This righteousness is not mere intellectual assent to a doctrine: "With the heart" – not with the head – "one believes to righteousness" (Romans 10:10). Saving faith in the heart transforms a life of sin into a life of righteousness – not a righteousness that comes from following a set of religious rules, but from Christ dwelling in our hearts and living out His life through us.

"The righteous are bold as a lion" (Proverbs 28:1). This kind of righteousness transforms timidity into boldness, doubt into confidence.

The Shoes of the Preparation of the Gospel of Peace

Your shoes make you mobile. You must be available to God at any time or place to share the Gospel with those God puts in your way. In a world of strife and tension, you must be a vessel of God's peace.

The Shield of Faith

The shield alluded to in Ephesians 6 was big enough to give protection to a soldier's whole body, but it was effective only when he had learned how to use it.

You, too, must learn to use your faith as a shield to protect your whole person – spirit, soul and body – from Satan's fiery darts. Remember, the shield will not merely ward off the flaming darts; it will extinguish them!

The Helmet of Salvation

The helmet protects the head – that is, the mind. Satan will direct more attacks against your mind than against any other area of your personality. The helmet is also called "the hope of salvation" (1 Thessalonians 5:8) – not mere wishful thinking, but an attitude of steady, continuing optimism based firmly on the truthof God's Word.

In chapter 4 I described how God taught me to put on this helmet.

The Sword of the Spirit – the Word [Greek *rhema*] of God

Rhema means primarily a *spoken* word. The Bible on your bookshelf will not protect you. God's Word becomes a sword when you speak it through your mouth in faith. Remember how Jesus used that sword against Satan, answering every temptation by quoting Scripture: "It is written...." You must learn to do the same.

The sword is provided by the Holy Spirit, but it is your responsibility to take it. When you do, the Spirit provides supernatural power with which to wield it.

The Final Weapon: All Prayer

With the sword you are limited by the length of your arm. But "all prayer" is your intercontinental ballistic missile. By this kind of prayer, you can reach across oceans and continents and strike the forces of Satan wherever they are at work. You can even reach out against Satan's headquarters in the heavenlies. But it takes discipline and maturity to learn to use such a powerful weapon.

The Divine Paradox

Perhaps you feel a little overwhelmed as you consider what you must do to maintain your deliverance. You may feel inclined to say, "Can't you put it more simply, in just a few words?"

Yes, all that I have said above can be expressed in one simple instruction: To keep your deliverance, *all you have to do is live the Christian life as it is depicted and demonstrated in the New Testament.* That is the distillation of how to keep your deliverance – but it is *radical!*

In Matthew 16:24–25 Jesus lays down two unvarying requirements for all who would follow Him:

"If anyone desires to come after Me, let him deny himself, and take up his cross, and follow Me. For whoever desires to save his life [literally, soul] *will lose it, and whoever loses his life* [literally, soul] *for My sake will find it."*

Here is the divine paradox: to save (protect) our souls, we must lose them.[1]

Before we can follow Jesus, there are two preliminary steps. First, we must deny ourselves; we must say a resolute and final *No!* to the demanding, self-seeking ego. Second, we must each take up our own cross. We must accept the sentence of death that the cross imposes on us. Taking up the cross is a voluntary decision that each of us must make. God does not forcefully impose the cross upon us.

If we do not apply the cross personally in our own lives, we leave a door open to demonic influence. There is always the danger that the uncrucified ego will respond to the seductive flatteries of deceiving demons. Pride is the main area in our character that Satan targets, and flattery is the main lever he uses to gain entrance.

We must each apply the cross personally to ourselves. In Galatians 2:20 Paul says, "I have been crucified with Christ; it is no longer I who live...." We each need to ask: Is that true of me? Have I really been crucified with Christ? Or am I still motivated by my soulish ego?

Many Christians today would feel that this solution is too radical. They would question whether this is really the only way to be secure from deception. They tend to

---

1. The next eight paragraphs are quoted from my book *Protection from Deception* [Derek Prince, *Protection from Deception* (New Kensington, Pa.: Whitaker House, 2008). Used with permission.].

regard Paul as some kind of "super-saint" whom they could never hope to imitate.

Paul, however, did not see himself this way. His ministry as an apostle was unique, but his personal relationship with Christ was a pattern for all to follow. In 1 Timothy 1:16 he said:

However, for this reason I obtained mercy, that in me first Jesus Christ might show all longsuffering, as a pattern to those who are going to believe on Him for everlasting life.

Again in 1 Corinthians 11:1 he said, "Imitate me, just as I also imitate Christ."

The only alternative to the cross is to put self in the place of Christ. But this is idolatry and opens the way for the evil consequences that invariably follow idolatry.

The cross is the heart and center of the Christian faith. Without the cross proclaimed and applied, Christianity is left without a foundation, and its claims are no longer valid. It has become, in fact, a false religion. As such, like all false religions, it is inevitably exposed to demonic infiltration and deception.

Let me close this chapter with one final comment. I have come to see that my experiences over the years in dealing with demons have had a profound impact on my own Christian life. Time and time again I have come up against the blunt, uncompromising words of Jesus.

I have come to see that in the Christian life there

are no shortcuts and no detours. If we desire immunity from demonic oppression, it is available to us on one condition only: *obedience.*

Questions for This Study

1. What three phases sum up how to practically apply the Word of God in our lives?
2. An _____ life is vulnerable to _____ attack.
3. According to Ephesians 5:18, what three actions can help us stay filled with the Holy Spirit?
4. List the two important results of water baptism.
5. According to Ephesians 6:13–18, the Lord has provided us with armor to protect us in our spiritual battle. What are the seven items of equipment we have been given?
6. What is the only condition that gives us immunity from demonic oppression?

Life Application

List the seven ways in which we "rebuild the protective walls" around our lives. After each one, write out a practical way in which you intend to put this step into action in your own life.

Memory Verse

"If anyone desires to come after Me, let him deny himself, and take up his cross, and follow Me. For whoever desires to save his life will lose it, but whoever loses his life for My sake will find it."   Matthew 16:24–25

Faith Response

Lord, I choose to follow You by denying myself and taking up my cross. Grant me the grace to fully embrace this lifestyle on a daily basis.

Answers are on page 417

TWENTY-FOUR

Why Some Are Not Delivered

MOST OF THE PEOPLE WHO HAVE PRAYED THE prayer outlined in chapter 22 have received deliverance from demons – but not all.

Here are ten possible factors that might hinder a person from receiving deliverance:

1. Lack of repentance
2. Lack of desperation
3. Wrong motives
4. Self-centeredness – a desire for attention
5. Failure to break with the occult
6. Failure to sever binding soulish relationships
7. Lack of release from a curse
8. Failure to confess a specific sin
9. Not being "separated" by water baptism
10. It is part of a larger battle

1. Lack of Repentance

Jesus began His public ministry with the words "Repent, and believe" (Mark 1:15). He never expected anyone to believe without first repenting. Faith that does not proceed out of repentance is not valid and cannot be expected to produce the results promised to true faith.

Every sinner is, by both act and nature, in rebellion against God. We do not qualify to receive God's blessings until we have renounced our rebellion and turned totally away from it. This is the essential nature of repentance: renouncing our rebellion against God. Ask yourself, *Am I submitted without reservation to the authority of Jesus Christ in my life?* If you cannot answer yes, you are still in an attitude of rebellion. There is only one remedy: repentance.

In repentance, we submit ourselves by an act of the will to the Lordship of Christ in our lives. Our repentance is proved genuine when we go on to study and obey the teachings of Jesus.

People often seek deliverance because they want to be free from the unpleasant consequences of demonic oppression. But this is not sufficient reason. If you do not commit yourself to go on after deliverance to serve the Lord, either you will not receive deliverance at all, or if you do receive it, it will not be permanent.

2. Lack of Desperation

When we are seeking deliverance from Satan's bondage,

we need to recognize the reality of our situation. We have been taken prisoner by a cruel despot who hates us with total hatred and will do everything he can to harm us and, if possible, to destroy us. When we turn to Christ for deliverance, it must be with the recognition that He is the only One who can help us.

We need to be as desperate as Peter was when he was sinking in the waters of Galilee and cried out to Jesus, "Lord, save me!" (Matthew 14:30). He realized that in another moment the water would close over his mouth and he would no longer be able to cry for help.

Several times, when a person has approached me seeking deliverance, I have said, "Deliverance is for the desperate. I don't feel that you are desperate yet. Come back when you are." Sometimes I suggest that a person fast for 24 hours before seeking deliverance.

3. Wrong Motives

The apostle James, analyzing reasons that people sometimes pray but do not get what they pray for, wrote, "You ask and do not receive, because you ask amiss, that you may spend it on your pleasures" (James 4:3).

This often applies to people praying for deliverance from demons. They have come to recognize that demonic bondage is, in varying degrees, unpleasant and frustrating. It is a barrier to their pleasures. They think they could get more enjoyment out of life if they were set free.

But this is not sufficient reason for God to respond to their prayers. When we come to Him for deliverance, He searches our motives. He offers freedom to those who will use it to serve Christ more effectively, not those who wish to continue in a life of selfish pleasure.

4. Self-Centeredness – A Desire for Attention

Some people always feel ignored and unimportant. They want to be at center stage but life keeps them in the background. They feel nobody cares about them. One possible reason: They are oppressed and suppressed by demons.

When they seek deliverance, they suddenly find themselves the center of attention and they enjoy it. But after some measure of deliverance, they drop back into the shadows. People no longer pay as much attention to them. So, they find some new aspect of their "problem" to discuss and some new area in which they need deliverance. Deep down they really do not want to be free. What they want is attention. They are like the women described by Paul in 2 Timothy 3:7, "always learning and never able to come to the knowledge of the truth."

It is right to have compassion on such people and to present clearly the conditions for receiving deliverance. But there comes a point when we must challenge them to accept full deliverance – and the responsibility that goes with it, as outlined in chapter 21.

5. Failure to Break with the Occult

It is seldom easy to make a full and final break with the occult. Satan will use every trick in his repertoire to hold onto his victims. A person seeking to break away may be like Lot's wife escaping from Sodom. She turned around for one last, regretful look at what she was leaving behind and became forever immobilized as a pillar of salt (see Genesis 19:26). Jesus held her up as a warning to all succeeding generations: "Remember Lot's wife" (Luke 17:32).

The land of Canaan into which God brought the Israelites was corrupted by idolatry and occult involvement. For this reason, God told His people, "Do not bow down before their gods or worship them or follow their practices. You must demolish them and break their sacred stones to pieces" (Exodus 23:24, NIV). The Israelites were required to obliterate every trace of occult involvement. Nothing was to be carried over from the old order to the new. God even demanded that His people's speech indicate the total break with the old order: "Make no mention of the name of other gods, nor let it be heard from your mouth" (Exodus 23:13).

The world around us today is like the land of Canaan at that time – corrupted and defiled by every conceivable form of the occult. But many Christians, as I said earlier, are slow to recognize how intensely God hates the occult. He requires that we make the same total break with all those things that He required of Israel in the land of Canaan: We must obliterate every trace of them from our lives.

The things that link us to the occult are often subtle and hard to detect. A person seeking deliverance needs to pray, "Lord, show me if there is anything in my life that still links me to the occult, and show me how to make a complete break."

6. Failure to Sever Binding Soulish Relationships

In chapter 15 I pointed out that demonic bondage can result from being manipulated or controlled by soulish pressure exercised by some other person. Release from such bondage obviously depends on severing any such controlling relationship.

Jesus warned us that "a man's foes will be those of his own household" (Matthew 10:36). This is often true in cases of such binding personal relationships. A mother, for instance, may seek to control her child. Or a young man may continually be pressured by his brother to go back to taking drugs with him.

No matter how close the family member or friend, full freedom will not come until that control is severed. The process of adjusting such relationships may be painful, but it is essential for full deliverance. Sometimes it is necessary to break all contact with the controlling person and trust God to reestablish the relationship in His time and on His terms. When this is not possible (as in the case of a spouse or a child living at home), the person seeking to stay free must be vigilant to avoid coming back under that familiar controlling power.

7. Lack of Release from a Curse

In chapter 21 I listed seven common indicators that there may be a curse over a person's life. If you recognize that any of the forces I identified are still at work in your life, it may be that you are not yet fully released from every curse.

The basis of your release is the exchange that took place at the cross. There Jesus took on Himself every curse to which our sinfulness had exposed us, that in return we might be entitled to every blessing due to His spotless righteousness.

The ramifications of this exchange are many-sided and extend into every area of our lives. For a comprehensive treatment of this subject, I direct you to my book *Blessing or Curse: You Can Choose!*

8. Failure to Confess a Specific Sin

"If we confess our sins, [God] is faithful and just to forgive us our sins..." (1 John 1:9). God does not necessarily require that we confess individually every sin we have ever committed. But at times one specific sin must be brought out into the open. Until it is acknowledged and confessed, God withholds His forgiveness and cleansing.

After David was convicted of his sins of adultery and murder, he said, "My sin is ever before me" (Psalm 51:3). David recognized the horror of the sin that had separated him from God. His only hope for inward peace and renewed fellowship with God was to bring his sin out into the open by specific confession.

When a person is seeking deliverance from demons, there may be a specific sin that has to be confessed. It may be the sin that opened him or her up to the demon in the first place. In that case God will withhold deliverance until the particular sin has been identified and confessed.

A mother once brought her teenage daughter to Lydia and me for deliverance. We succeeded in casting out a number of demons, but there was one stuck in the girl's throat that refused to move any further.

Eventually I said to the young woman, "I believe you have committed one specific sin that God requires you to confess by name."

The girl looked at me for a few moments in acute embarrassment, then blurted out, "I had an abortion."

The mother let out a gasp. She had apparently known nothing about it.

"God requires one more thing," I told the young woman. "You have to confess that abortion as murder."

She did. And the moment she correctly named her sin as murder, she was completely delivered. She received forgiveness not only from God but from her mother. Mother and daughter fell into each other's arms and cried together.

When God requires the confession of some specific sin, we must rely on the Holy Spirit to reveal it. It is His ministry, after all, to convict of sin (see John 16:8). In addition to murder, specific sins that often need to be confessed are listed in the last four of the Ten Commandments: adultery, theft, false witness and coveting (Exodus 20:14–17).

9. Not "Separated" by Water Baptism

Being baptized in water, as I pointed out in the last chapter, is the outward act by which we "complete" the salvation we have received through our faith in Christ's atonement. A person who has believed but not been baptized is "incompletely" saved. It is only "complete" salvation that grants us the legal right to be free from demonic oppression. Unfortunately, even some churches that practice baptism by immersion do not sufficiently emphasize its importance.

I want to make clear, however, that I am not speaking of baptism as a ceremony required to join some particular congregation, but simply as an act of personal obedience to Scripture. Whenever I pray for deliverance with people who have never been baptized as believers,

I warn them, "You are free now, but if you intend to retain your freedom, you must be baptized in water."

On the other hand, you may have done this without understanding the complete deliverance from Satan's power to which you are legally entitled. If you still find yourself harassed by Satan's demons, take your stand on what your baptism really means. Pray something like this: "Lord Jesus, I thank You that I have passed through the water out of Satan's kingdom and into Your Kingdom. And now, Lord, I take authority in Your name and cut off every harassing demon that has been pursuing me."

10. Part of a Larger Battle

As Christians we are involved in a vast spiritual war that spans both earth and heaven. Paul describes this as a wrestling match against satanic forces in the heavenlies (see Ephesians 6:12). At times we may find ourselves in conflict not only with demons on the earthly plane, but also with *daimons* (see chapter 11) whose headquarters are in the heavenlies.

Sometimes a person who appears relatively unimportant on the earthly plane is a strategic element in this global conflict. Satan's *daimons* are aware of this and are determined to retain control over that life and use it to oppose God's purpose. Consequently, any attempt to minister deliverance is resisted fiercely, not only by the demons in the person but also by the satanic forces in the heavenlies operating through that person. I call such a person a "battleground."

A single individual, for instance, may be the key to the salvation of a whole family or even some larger community. Or the deliverance of just one person may open the door to bring the Gospel to a hitherto unreached people group. If this is so, Satan will marshal his forces, both on earth and in the heavenlies, to retain his control over that individual.

To minister to such people, we need insight into the heavenlies – perhaps through a vision or word of wisdom or knowledge. If we have a clear picture of the forces opposing us, we can call on committed intercessors to stand together with us to claim the victory Christ has gained for us. For through His atoning death and victorious resurrection, He has "disarmed principalities and powers" of Satan that oppose us (Colossians 2:15).

It may also be, when a person does not receive deliverance, that we need to apply the words of Jesus in Mark 9:29: "This kind can come out by nothing but prayer and fasting."

Questions for This Study

1. List some of the possible factors that might hinder a person from receiving deliverance.
2. Faith that does not proceed from _____ is not _____.
3. What may be a wrong motive for seeking deliverance?
4. How must a person under demonic influence from a controlling relationship seek freedom?
5. What is the basis for being released from a curse?
6. How will we know if the Lord is requiring us to confess a specific sin?

Life Application

Ask yourself this question: *Am I submitted without reservation to the authority of Jesus Christ in my life?* Meditate on that question and allow the Holy Spirit to direct your answer.

Memory Verse

Stand fast therefore in the liberty by which Christ has made us free, and do not be entangled again with a yoke of bondage. Galatians 5:1

Faith Response

By faith, I will stand in the freedom of Christ and resist every effort to be brought under any form of bondage.

Answers are on page 418

TWENTY-FIVE

Helping Others Be Set Free

PEOPLE WHO HAVE BEEN DELIVERED FROM DEMONS
often begin to see clearly the need for others to receive
similar deliverance. Also, they can empathize with them
because they remember the pressures to which they
were subjected and the struggles involved in the process
of being delivered. As a result, many find themselves
spontaneously reaching out to others who also need
deliverance.

In Mark 16:17 Jesus opened up this ministry to
all believers: "And these signs will follow those who
believe: In My name they will cast out demons...."

As a general principle, however, deliverance should
be practiced primarily by people with apostolic, pastoral
or evangelistic ministries, or their co-workers. But any
Christian confronted by a demonized person may in
certain circumstances be called on to cast out demons.
I have seen in experience, however, that people who
engage in a regular ministry of deliverance without

observing certain scriptural conditions for exercising authority usually end up in trouble.

Here are some general principles that can safeguard the practice of deliverance:

1. Be under authority.
2. Two are better than one.
3. Do not minister alone to a member of the opposite sex.
4. Use the cross and the sword of the Spirit.

1. Be under Authority

At one point in His ministry, Jesus sent out seventy disciples to prepare the way before Him. They returned with great excitement, reporting that "even the demons are subject to us in Your name" (Luke 10:17). Jesus responded, "Behold, I give you the authority... over all the power of the enemy" (verse 19). The decisive factor in dealing with demons is the exercise of scriptural authority.

A Roman centurion who came to Jesus on behalf of his sick servant recognized that Jesus' spiritual authority was comparable to his own military authority. He summed up in one sentence the essential condition for exercising authority in any sphere: "Say the word, and my servant will be healed. For I also am a man placed under authority..." (Luke 7:7–8). To exercise authority, a person must first be *under authority*.

There are certain scriptural principles that govern the exercise of authority.

First, the supreme source of all authority is God Himself. After the resurrection, however, Jesus declared to His disciples, "All authority has been given to Me in heaven and on earth" (Matthew 28:18). This means that all authority descends from God the Father through Jesus the Son. To be under scriptural authority, therefore, every Christian needs to find his or her place in a chain of authority that stretches upward through Christ to God.

In 1 Corinthians 11:2–7 Paul uses covering the head as a symbol of authority. To be under authority is to be "covered" – that is, protected. Not to be under authority is to be "uncovered" – that is, unprotected. For every Christian, therefore, to be under an appropriate form of authority is to be spiritually protected. A Christian not under authority is spiritually unprotected and is in great danger.

God has made Christ "head over all things to the church, which is His body" (Ephesians 1:22–23). It is natural, therefore, for Him to exercise His authority in any area through the leadership of a local church. This means that a Christian who desires to be protected spiritually should take his or her place in the structure of a local church.

Ruth and I attach great importance to this issue of authority. Wherever we reside, we make ourselves part of a local congregation and come under its leadership. When we go out on ministry trips, we are sent out from our local church. In addition, our worldwide ministry is directed by an International Council in which we share leadership with a group of our co-workers who represent the various countries in which they minister. For my part, I always make it plain that I have no desire to be independent. On the contrary, I gladly recognize that I am dependent – first and foremost on God, then on the people of God.

One other main area in which God delegates His authority is the family. In 1 Corinthians 11:3 Paul depicts a chain of authority descending from God, through Christ, into every family on earth: "But I want you to know that the head of every man is Christ, the head of woman is man, and the head of Christ is God."

A married woman is normally under the authority of her husband and should not be engaged in ministering without her husband's full knowledge and approval. Peter warns us, however, that if there is not harmony between husband and wife, the husband's prayers will be hindered (see 1 Peter 3:7). An unmarried woman, if still at home, needs her father's authorization. Single women living on their own should have the authorization and oversight of mature spiritual leaders.

Men who practice deliverance, whether single or married, should be part of a fellowship or church with an effective structure of authority. This whole area of dealing with demons is a dangerous place for "lone rangers," whether male or female.

There is one key word in the question of being under

authority: *accountable*. Each Christian needs to ask, *To whom am I accountable?* A person not accountable to anyone is not under authority.

In two places Jesus speaks about authority to bind and to loose. In each case it is in relationship to the Church. In Matthew 16:18–19 Jesus says to Peter, "...On this rock I will build My church...and whatever you [singular] bind on earth will be bound in heaven, and whatever you loose on earth will be loosed in heaven."

Again, in Matthew 18:17–18 Jesus is speaking about bringing an offending brother before the Church, and He concludes, "Whatever you [plural] bind on earth will be bound in heaven, and whatever you loose on earth will be loosed in heaven." In this case binding and loosing is a collective action of the Church as a whole.

The key to the scriptural exercise of all authority is *right relationships*. This applies specifically to binding and loosing demonic forces. A person who is not in a right relationship to the Body of Christ may attempt to bind or loose demons, but the authority to make it effective will be lacking.

2. Two Are Better than One

There is no record in the gospels that Jesus ever sent anyone out to minister by himself. He always sent out His disciples in pairs. Normally only an experienced minister with authority should undertake the ministry of deliverance on his own. (Bear in mind, there is always the possibility that a person receiving deliverance may become violent.)

This principle is emphasized by Solomon in Ecclesiastes 4:9–10:

> *Two are better than one,*
> *Because they have a good reward for their labor.*
> *For if they fall, one will lift up his companion.*
> *But woe to him who is alone when he falls,*
> *For he has no one to help him up.*

3. Do Not Minister Alone to a Member of the Opposite Sex

It is unwise for a woman to attempt to minister to a man on her own, or for a man to minister to a woman on his own. Generally, the best team for this ministry is a married couple working in harmony.

In each of my two marriages God has blessed me with a wife with whom I have lived in harmony and who worked at my side every time I ministered deliverance. I owe much to the special contributions of Ruth, and Lydia before her – a word of knowledge, a gift of healing or discerning of spirits. During the period of three years between my first and second marriages, while I was a widower, I never counseled a woman alone. I was always careful to have the support and help of a mature and competent brother or sister in the Lord.

4. Use the Cross and the Sword of the Spirit

There is one – and only one – all-sufficient basis on which anyone can claim deliverance from demons: the substitutionary sacrifice of Jesus on the cross. By this, He made atonement for the sins of the whole human race and stripped Satan of his primary weapon against us: *guilt.* By faith in this sacrifice, each one of us is justified, acquitted, "just-as-if-I'd never sinned."

Lay hold of this truth and make it central in all your instruction to those you are helping.

Likewise, there is only one weapon that is invariably effective in dealing with demons. It is the sword of the Spirit – the words of Scripture spoken boldly and in faith. Demons are not frightened by denominational labels, ecclesiastical titles or theological arguments. But against the sharp sword thrust of God's Word, spoken in faith, demons have no defense.

Final Practical Points

If you are preparing to minister to someone who needs deliverance, here are twelve practical points to help make your ministry more effective. For the sake of brevity, I will refer to the person receiving deliverance as "the counselee," and I will use masculine pronouns that may apply to either sex.

1. Reread chapter 21 of this book and, insofar as possible, take the counselee through the nine preliminary steps.

2. Let the sacrifice of Jesus on the cross be the basis of all you do. Likewise, encourage the counselee to look away from himself and focus on the cross.

3. Check for the following three critical issues:

   a. *Repentance*: Has the counselee gone through a genuine experience of repentance, as defined earlier?

   b. *Forgiveness*: Is there anyone whom the counselee has not truly forgiven? Is he still holding resentment against anyone?

   c. *Renunciation*: Has the counselee totally renounced every contact with the occult and/or every binding personal relationship?

4. If the counselee is struggling, do not simply take over and do it all for him. Suggest appropriate Scriptures for him to quote on his own behalf. Encourage him to exercise and develop his own faith. This will help him face any further conflicts with Satan.

5. Sometimes the process of deliverance may encounter a kind of spiritual "logjam" in which the counselee appears to be struggling against something in himself that he does not fully understand. If this happens, ask the Lord for a word of knowledge that will identify the nature of the problem. This word of knowledge may come either to the counselee or to the one ministering. It may concern a sin that must be confessed or a binding power that must be broken (for example, a false religion). To proceed

further, the counselee must repent of the sin or break the binding power. Alternatively, the Holy Spirit may reveal the name of a certain demon resisting the deliverance. If so, instruct the counselee to take his stand in the name of Jesus and renounce that particular demon by name.

6. Demons often come out through the mouth with sobbing, crying, screaming, roaring, spitting, or even vomiting. Have a supply of tissues or paper towels or other similar materials ready that the counselee can use.

7. A woman sometimes expels demons with loud screaming. If she continues to scream without receiving any further deliverance, remember that a demon may have lodged itself in the narrow part of her throat and be holding on there. Explain this to the woman and instruct her to expel the demon from her throat with a deliberate, forceful cough (see chapter 21).

8. Do not shout at demons. They are not deaf. Even a spirit of deafness is not deaf. Shouting at them does not give you more authority; it only uses strength that could be better spent in other ways.

9. Do not waste time on attention-getters – people who go through some of the actions of a person receiving deliverance but are interested only in attracting attention to themselves (see chapter 24).

10. As you minister, Satan may attack you with a spirit

of fear. If so, affirm that "God has not given [me] a spirit of fear, but of power and of love and of a sound mind" (2 Timothy 1:7). Remember, too, the promise Jesus gave His disciples when they had to deal with demons: "Nothing shall by any means hurt you" (Luke 10:19).

11. Continually emphasize the promise of Joel 2:32: "Whoever calls on the name of the LORD shall be saved [delivered]."

12. Remember the power in the name of Jesus and the blood of Jesus. Here is a proclamation I have used many times (taken from my book *Prayers and Proclamations*) to enable Christians to apprehend and possess the victory Jesus won for us on the cross:

We overcome Satan when we testify personally
 to what the Word of God says
 the blood of Jesus does for us:[1]
Through the blood of Jesus
 I am redeemed out of the hand of the devil.[2]
Through the blood of Jesus
 all my sins are forgiven.[3]
Through the blood of Jesus
 I am continually being cleansed from all sin.[4]

1. Revelation 12:11
2. Ephesians 1:7
3. 1 John 1:9
4. 1 John 1:7

Through the blood of Jesus
  I am justified, made righteous, just-as-if-I'd never
sinned.[5]
Through the blood of Jesus
  I am sanctified, made holy, set apart to God.[6]
Through the blood of Jesus
  I have boldness to enter the presence of God.[7]
  The blood of Jesus cries out continually
  to God in heaven on my behalf.[8]

Each person ministering deliverance will discover other practical points. But theory can take us only so far. In the end we all have to learn by doing. I hope this book will help you avoid some of the mistakes I have made!

One final word of great importance. It was love that motivated God to provide deliverance for us through the sacrificial death of Jesus. Our motivation should be the same. Ask God, therefore, to make you an instrument of His love: "Let all that you do be done with love" (1 Corinthians 16:14).

5. Romans 5:9
6. Hebrews 13:12
7. Hebrews 10:19
8. Hebrews 12:24

Questions for This Study

1. List some of the general principles that help to safeguard the practice of deliverance.

2. What is the main reason for being under scriptural authority?

3. In Derek's opinion, what is the best team for ministering deliverance?

4. Demons have no defense against the sharp sword-thrust of the _____ of God spoken _____ and in _____.

5. What are the three most critical issues to emphasize when ministering deliverance?

6. True or false? Shouting at demons convinces them of your authority.

Life Application

Answer this question: *To whom am I accountable for my life and ministry?* What practical steps are you taking to draw upon the wisdom and advice of that person?

Memory Verse

Nevertheless do not rejoice in this, that the spirits are subject to you, but rather rejoice because your names are written in heaven.   Luke 10:20

Faith Response

Lord, I will look for Your scriptural, delegated authority for my life and remain accountable to that authority.

Answers are on page 418

TWENTY-SIX
After Deliverance . . . ?

THE EXPERIENCE OF DELIVERANCE IN AN INDIVID-
ual's life is a wonderful demonstration of the grace and
power of God. Sometimes I compare it to the liberation
of the people of Israel from their slavery in Egypt.

But the deliverance of Israel from Pharaoh was only
the first step in a divine process. God brought Israel *out*
of Egypt that He might bring them *into* their promised
inheritance. So it is with deliverance. It is the first, vital
step, but certainly not the ultimate purpose.

There are two important steps that must follow. The
process is described briefly in Obadiah 17:

> *"But on Mount Zion there shall be deliverance,*
> *And there shall be holiness;*
> *The house of Jacob shall possess their possessions."*

Here is God's ultimate purpose: His people "shall
possess their possessions" – that is, their God-given

inheritance. He has stated two conditions. The first is negative: *deliverance.* The second is positive: *holiness.* Any process that bypasses either of these conditions will not bring God's people into their inheritance.

There is a logical and practical reason why deliverance from demons must precede holiness. Demons display many different characteristics, but they have one thing in common: All, without exception, are the enemies of true holiness. Until demons have been driven out, neither the Church nor Israel can attain to scriptural standards of holiness.

Let me say clearly that Obadiah 17 applies first and foremost to the nation of Israel. The Church has never replaced Israel. All God's promises to Israel as a nation will be fulfilled precisely as they were given. (For more on this, see my book *The Destiny of Israel and the Church.*)

There are various places in the New Testament, however, in which the historical experiences of Israel are interpreted as types that also apply to the Church. In 1 Corinthians 10:1–11, for instance, Paul lists a series of experiences through which the people of Israel passed during and after their deliverance from Egypt, and he concludes: "Now all these things happened to them as examples, and they were written for our admonition, on whom the ends of the ages have come." The experiences of Israel during and after the Exodus, in other words, contain important practical lessons that apply to Christians in the present age.

I believe the same applies to the contemporary restoration of the people of Israel to their scriptural inheritance in the land God gave them. It contains important practical lessons for the Church.

Anyone familiar with history and biblical prophecy can see that the people of Israel were out of their God-given geographical inheritance for nearly two thousand years. But the same applies to the Church. For much of that time we, too, have been out of our spiritual inheritance. If the apostles of the New Testament were to return to earth today, they would have to search a long way to find any church that compares with the one they left behind!

Nevertheless, Scripture encourages us to look forward to "the times of restoration of all things" (Acts 3:21). For both Israel and the Church, the first step to restoration is deliverance. The step that must follow is holiness.

Holiness is the unique mark of the God of the Bible. It should also be the unique mark of His people – both Israel and the Church. In both Old and New Testaments, God says to His people, "Be holy; for I am holy" (Leviticus 11:44; see 1 Peter 1:16).

According to my personal observation – and I have ministered in many different kinds of congregations in more than forty nations over many years – churches today give scarcely any consideration to God's requirement of holiness. Not only do Christians not achieve holiness; they do not even aim at it!

I compare this to people traveling on tours to many parts of the world. Such tours include visits to a series of different cities or countries. Sometimes the organizers include an "add-on" to the tour package. For an extra payment, the tour can be extended to sites or places not normally visited. I see the contemporary Church treating holiness in the same way. It is an "add-on" for which there is an extra charge. But most people who take the tour are not interested in the add-on.

Yet holiness is not an add-on. It is an essential part of the package of salvation. The writer of Hebrews tells us, "Pursue... holiness, without which no one will see the Lord" (Hebrews 12:14). How much salvation do we have if it does not bring us into the presence of the Lord?

If God wills and I live, it is in my heart to write a book to follow this one, the title of which will be *Set Apart – The Beautiful Secret of Holiness*. Holiness is an integral and essential element of the purpose of God for His people. If God continues to spare my life, I will go on to write a third book, *Possessing Our Possessions*.

Whether I succeed in writing these two books will depend on the grace and mercy of God. But whether I write them or not, the principle is clearly unfolded in Scripture: Deliverance is only the first step in a process leading to the recovery of holiness and the restoration of the Church to her original simplicity and purity.

Questions for this Study

1. What is God's ultimate purpose for us?
2. What are two requirements for His purpose to be fulfilled?

Life Application

1. Think back over this study and all you have learned and experienced. How are you different now from when you began?
2. What will you take away from this study that you believe will have the most lasting impact on your life?

Memory Verse

But on Mount Zion, there shall be deliverance, and there shall be holiness; the house of Jacob shall possess their possessions. Obadiah 17

Faith Response

Thank you, Lord, for the price You paid that I might inherit the Kingdom of God!

Answers are on page 418

Answers to Study Questions

Chapter 1: How did Jesus do it?

1. He commissioned His followers and transmitted his authority to them.
2. Fear and ignorance.
3. It reveals the existence of two spiritual kingdoms: God's and Satan's. Also, it demonstrates the victory of God's kingdom over Satan's.
4. No. It is not scriptural to evangelize or pray for the sick without being prepared to deal with demons.
5. People oppressed by demons, and those who need to be equipped to minister deliverance to others.
6. The Scriptures, as well as Derek's personal observations and experiences in ministry.

Chapter 2: Terminology

1. Demons; unclean spirit; evil spirit.
2. Devil. "Devil" is a King James mistranslation of the Greek word for "demon."

3. Slanderer. Satan slanders God and all who represent God.
4. No. To "be demonized" does not imply ownership or possession.
5. "Subjected to demon influence" is the best way to describe someone who is demonized.
6. Areas that are not under the control of the Holy Spirit can become subject to demonic influence.

Chapter 3: The Pattern and Mission of Jesus

1. Healing the sick and expelling demons.
2. False. Most of the people out of whom Jesus expelled demons were law-keeping, religious Jews.
3. Jesus dealt with the demon, not the man.
4. To heal the sick and cast out demons.
5. The demon overpowered them, and they fled naked and wounded.
6. Casting out demons is a central part of the Christian message.

Chapter 4: My Struggle with Depression

1. Frustration, depression, and a sense that he would never succeed.
2. Scripture study, prayer, fasting, and reckoning himself dead to sin. No, they did not eliminate the problem.
3. Spirit of heaviness.
4. To keep Derek from serving Christ effectively.

5. Pessimism.
6. Using the helmet of hope and the promises of God's Word.
7. Three important lessons:
    a. The reality of demonic activity as described in the New Testament.
    b. The supernatural provision God has made for deliverance.
    c. To maintain deliverance by application of Scripture.

Chapter 5: People I Failed to Help

1. Two main reasons:
    a. Pride (he was concerned about how his congregation would react).
    b. Pentecostal doctrine, which holds that a Spirit-filled believer cannot have a demon.
2. Heretic.
3. A demonic source of "infection" is like having a shrapnel wound.
4. It had to be removed to prevent further infection.
5. The "probe" of discernment; the "forceps" of deliverance.

Chapter 6: Confrontation with Demons

1. False. Esther was a normal-looking woman.
2. Hate, fear, pride, jealousy, self-pity, infidelity and death.

3. By quoting Scripture and declaring authority in the name of Jesus.
4. "This is my house"; "If I come out, I will come back"; "My brothers will kill her"; "I've still got her daughter."
5. When she had almost died on the operating table – over three years earlier.

Chapter 7: Challenged in My Own Pulpit

1. Derek used the Scriptures to verify information and procedures.
2. He tore up a letter addressed to her brother-in-law that she had in her purse.
3. A church where people with real problems could come to receive help.
4. Instruction; deliverance.
5. Experience.

Chapter 8: Beneath the Surface

1. Humanistic; anti-supernatural.
2. Operate undetected.
3. By assigning psychological or psychiatric terminology to this activity.
4. To obtain the name of the demon you are dealing with or to deal with their responses.
5. Do not seek special revelation from a demon.
6. To seek revelation from a satanic source dishonors

the Holy Spirit. This type of interaction can expose you to deception.

Chapter 9: Lessons from an Expanding Ministry

1. Bondage; free.
2. Repentance of all sin; dependence only upon Jesus; reliance solely on what Jesus did on the cross; forgiveness for every person who has hurt or wronged them.
3. Guilt; primary weapon.
4. Unforgiveness; failure to repent.
   a. The Holy Spirit (We should flow with Him);
   b. Evil spirits (We should expel them);
   c. Human flesh (We should bring it under control.).
5. From the shed blood of Christ, His death on the cross and His resurrection.

Chapter 10: Ongoing Personal Conflicts

1. Personal experience has shown them the power in the name of Jesus; they can also empathize with other people's struggles.
2. Simple faith in Him and His Word.
3. Childhood.
4. By exposing the root and dealing with it according to the Word of God.
5. Failure; fruitful.
6. Feeding on solid food, the full revelation of God

through Scripture; practice in recognizing spiritual issues and problems in those around us.

Chapter 11: What are Demons?

1. Disembodied beings that have an intense craving to occupy physical bodies.
2. Will, emotion, intellect, self-awareness, ability to speak.
3. They are fallen angels, or disembodied spirits from a pre-Adamic race.
4. Because according to Ephesians 6:12, fallen angels still maintain their dwelling place somewhere in the heavenlies.
5. Earthbound. Descending; ascending.
6. They confronted the demons and then expelled them.

Chapter 12: Flesh or Demons?

1. Sin and demons.
2. Our old man; the flesh.
3. Lack of spiritual health; emotional weakness.
4. You cannot cast out the flesh; it must be "crucified" (put to death). You cannot "crucify" a demon; it must be cast out or expelled.
5. A healthy spiritual life, or "immune system."

Chapter 13: How do Demons come in?

1. A family background in the occult. Negative parental influences. Pressures in early childhood. Emotional

412

shock or sustained emotional pressure. Sinful acts or habits. Laying on of hands. Negative speech or pronouncements.

2. (This is a partial list.) Occult exploration (Ouija boards, horoscopes, false religions). Negative parental influences (rejection by mother or father; cruelty or abuse from a mother or father). Emotional shock or sustained emotional pressure (exposure to sudden or shocking incidents). Sinful acts or habits (lying or stealing). Laying on of hands (hands laid on to either minister or receive ministry). Negative speech or pronouncements (statements concerning one's own death or illness).

3. The act must be confessed and then canceled by God's forgiveness.

4. It is a temporary interaction between two spirits through which a supernatural power is released.

5. Make Jesus Lord over your life, and walk in obedience to Him.

Chapter 14: What is the Occult?

1. To make contact with something greater, wiser or more powerful than ourselves.

2. The occult.

3. Occult means "concealed" or "covered over."

4. Divination (sorcery); witchcraft.

5. False. This information usually contains a measure of truth.

6. Satan's plan for that person's life.

7. Acknowledging a plurality of Gods; practicing idol worship in some form; teaching that human beings can ultimately become gods; teaching people they can achieve righteousness by their own efforts; offering esoteric knowledge that is available only to a privileged few.

Chapter 15: Is Witchcraft Still at Work Today?

1. Witchcraft is the universal religion.

2. To control other people.

3. The Christian Church.

4. They desire supernatural power.

5. Rock music; New Age cults, religions and philosophies; hypnosis; acupuncture.

6. Manipulation; intimidation; domination.

7. Guilt.

Chapter 16: Do Christians Ever Need Deliverance from Demons?

1. Someone who has repented of his or her sins and, through personal faith, has received Jesus as Savior and Lord.

2. He would cast out the demons and then baptize the people once they believed.

3. There are no such Scriptures.

4. False. Demonic pressure may actually increase.

5. Jesus the revolutionary; the New Age Jesus; the humanistic Jesus; or the "Father Christmas" Jesus.

6. We may receive another spirit other than the Holy Spirit.

Chapter 17: Will the Holy Spirit Indwell an Unclean Vessel?

1. Our hearts.
2. David (Psalm 51:11–12) and Paul (2 Corinthians 8:1);
3. Conviction; grace.
4. A heart purified by faith.
5. Acknowledge your need for cleansing; reach out to God for it, and then press on to attain the standard God has set before you.
6. Being unable to resist temptation.

Chapter 18: Characteristic Activities of Demons

1. Defenses; evil.
2. They are trying to find a way to gain entrance into our lives.
3. Physical, mental or spiritual.
4. Smoking, alcoholism, drug use, gluttony, talking or nail-biting.
5. Continuing personal frustration and deep unmet emotional needs.
6. To disrupt our communion with God.
7. Spiritual deception.
8. They are restless.

Chapter 19: Areas of Personality Affected by Demons

1. Emotions and attitudes, the mind, the tongue, sex, physical appetites.
2. A demon that enables other demons to enter into a person's personality.
3. Passive; aggressive.
4. Doubt, unbelief, confusion, forgetfulness, indecision, compromise, humanism and insanity.
5. The "strong man."
6. Self-indulgence.
7. Pride.

Chapter 20: Demons of Sickness and Infirmity

1. False. Not all sickness comes from demons. Some illnesses have a physical cause.
2. Lying; lost.
3. They must be willing to take an active stand against the demon.
4. Discernment is required.
5. Moment; place.
6. Depend daily on God; trust him for discernment and authority.

Chapter 21: Preparing for Deliverance

1. The sacrifice of Jesus on the cross.
2. High Priests; intervene.

3. Third or fourth.
4. Accept personal responsibility for what you have done; hate your sin the same way God does.
5. Emotion; decision.
6. Physical healing; deliverance from evil spirits.
7. Dignity, pride, failure to confess and repent of sin, unforgiveness, any association with the occult or false religions.

Chapter 22: A Prayer for Deliverance

1. Praise and thanks to God.
2. Make Jesus Lord over every area of your life.
3. No.

Chapter 23: How to Keep Your Deliverance

1. Think the Word of God; speak the Word of God; act the Word of God.
2. Undisciplined; demonic.
3. Continually singing praises to the Lord; thanking God unceasingly; being humbly submissive to one another.
4. We are separated from the world. We are cut off from the kingdom of Satan.
5. Girdle of truth, breastplate of righteousness, shoes of the preparation of the gospel of peace, shield of faith, helmet of salvation, sword of the Spirit, all prayer.
6. Obedience to the Lord.

Chapter 24: Why Some Are Not Delivered

1. Lack of repentance; lack of desperation; wrong motives; self-centeredness; failure to break with the occult; failure to sever soulish relationships; lack of release from a curse; failure to confess a specific sin; not "separated" by water baptism; part of a larger battle.
2. Repentance; valid.
3. Desire to continue in a life of selfish pleasure; desire to gain personal attention.
4. By severing that relationship.
5. The exchange that took place on the cross.
6. The Holy Spirit will reveal it to us.

Chapter 25: Helping Others Be Set Free

1. Be under authority; two are better than one; do not minister alone to a member of the opposite sex; use the cross and the sword of the Spirit.
2. To be spiritually protected.
3. A married couple.
4. Word; boldly; faith.
5. Repentance, forgiveness and renunciation.
6. False. Shouting at demons only wastes energy.

Chapter 26: After Deliverance ... ?

1. For each one of us to possess our God-given inheritance.
2. Deliverance from bondage; a life of holiness.

For Further Study

Deliverance and Demonology

With the ministry of Jesus as his pattern, enforced by personal experience, Derek Prince first exposes the nature and activity of demons, then explains the crucial steps to receiving deliverance and permanent freedom.

6001   How I Came to Grips with Demons

6002   How Jesus Dealt with Demons

6003   Nature and Activity of Demons

6004   How to Recognize and Expel Demons

6005   Cult and Occult: Satan's Snares Disclosed

6006   Seven Ways to Keep Your Deliverance

DD1   (6 audios)

Basics of Deliverance

Drawing on 22 years of experience in the ministry of deliverance, Derek Prince imparts the basic truths that bring freedom.

| 4128 (audio) or v4128 (video) | How to Identify the Enemy |
| 4129 (audio) or v4129 (video) | How to Expel the Enemy |

How to Be Delivered

Deliverance from evil spirits is the one miracle that has no counterpart in the Old Testament. It is, therefore, the one distinctive sign that the Kingdom of God has come.

4398 (audio)
v4398 (video)

Blessing or Curse: You Can Choose!

Blessings and curses are two of the most powerful forces shaping your destiny – for good or for evil. Derek Prince reveals, from Scripture and personal experience, how to recognize a curse at work and how to pass from curse to blessing.

B56 (book)

Curses: Cause and Cure

Many people experience continual frustration in areas such as marriage, health or finances, yet never discern the underlying cause: *a curse*. This series reveals both cause and cure.

6011	Curses: Cause
6012	Curses: Cure, Part 1
6013	Curses: Cure, Part 2
CC1	(3 audios)

Protection from Deception

Navigating through the Minefield of Signs and Wonders. In the midst of confusion and deception, God's Word provides a clear path on which to walk in peace and safety.

4394	Let Us Honor God's Holy Spirit
4395	Earthly, Soulish, Demonic
4396	Four Safeguards
CDPD1	Protection from Deception (3 CDs)
B94	Protection from Deception (book)

Order books, CDs and DVDs from your local bookstore or visit our website: www.derekprince.com, where you can find the local DPM office for your region. Also visit our YouTube channel to deepen your understanding on spiritual warfare.

Index

tobacco, 40
torture, 202, 271
truth, 56, 188

U

unclean spirit, 22, 69, 150, 181
unforgivable sin, 272

W

witchcraft, 142, 203, 210, 220,
    223

women, 132, 174, 199, 390
word of knowledge, 219, 323,
    394
World Wide Web, 278

Z

Zambia, 116, 282

About the Author

DEREK PRINCE (1915–2003) WAS BORN IN INDIA OF British parents. He was educated as a scholar of Greek and Latin at Eton College and King's College, Cambridge, in England. Upon graduation, he held a fellowship (equivalent to a professorship) in Ancient and Modern Philosophy at King's College. Prince also studied Hebrew, Aramaic, and modern languages at Cambridge and the Hebrew University in Jerusalem. As a student, he was a philosopher and a self-proclaimed agnostic.

Bible Teacher

While serving in the British Medical Corps during World War II, Prince began to study the Bible as a philosophical work. Converted through a powerful encounter with Jesus Christ, he was baptized in the Holy Spirit a few days later. Out of this encounter, he formed two conclusions: first, that Jesus Christ is alive;

second, that the Bible is a true, relevant, up-to-date book. These conclusions altered the whole course of his life, which he then devoted to studying and teaching the Bible as the Word of God.

Discharged from the army in Jerusalem in 1945, he married Lydia Christensen, founder of a children's home there. Upon their marriage, he immediately became father to Lydia's eight adopted daughters – six Jewish, one Palestinian Arab, and one English. Together, the family saw the rebirth of the state of Israel in 1948.

In the late 1950s, they adopted another daughter while Prince was serving as principal of a teachers' training college in Kenya.

In 1963, the Princes immigrated to the United States and pastored a church in Seattle. In 1973, Prince became one of the founders of Intercessors for America. His book *Shaping History through Prayer and Fasting* has awakened Christians around the world to their responsibility to pray for their governments. Many consider underground translations of the book as instrumental in the fall of communist regimes in the USSR, East Germany, and Czechoslovakia.

Lydia Prince died in 1975, and Prince married Ruth Baker (a single mother to three adopted children) in 1978. He met his second wife, like his first wife, while she was serving the Lord in Jerusalem. Ruth died in December 1998 in Jerusalem, where they had lived since 1981.

Teaching, Preaching and Broadcasting

Until a few years before his own death in 2003 at the age of eighty-eight, Prince persisted in the ministry God had called him to as he traveled the world, imparting God's revealed truth, praying for the sick and afflicted, and sharing his prophetic insights into world events in the light of Scripture. Internationally recognized as a Bible scholar and spiritual patriarch, Derek Prince established a teaching ministry that spanned six continents and more than sixty years. He is the author of more than eighty books, six hundred audio teachings, and one hundred video teachings, many of which have been translated and published in more than one hundred languages. He pioneered teaching on such groundbreaking themes as generational curses, the biblical significance of Israel, and demonology. Prince's radio program, which began in 1979, has been translated into more than a dozen languages and continues to touch lives. Derek Prince's main gift of explaining the Bible and its teachings in a clear and simple way has helped build a foundation of faith in millions of lives. His nondenominational, nonsectarian approach has made his teaching equally relevant and helpful to people from all racial and religious backgrounds, and his messages are estimated to have reached more than half the globe.

Dpm Worldwide Ministry

In 2002, Derek Prince said, "It is my desire – and I believe the Lord's desire – that this ministry continue the work, which God began through me over sixty years ago, until Jesus returns."

Derek Prince Ministries continues to reach out to believers in over 140 countries with Derek's teaching, fulfilling the mandate to keep on "until Jesus returns." This is accomplished through the outreaches of more than forty-five Derek Prince offices around the world, including primary work in Australia, Canada, China, France, Germany, the Netherlands, New Zealand, Norway, Russia, South Africa, Switzerland, the United Kingdom, and the United States.

For current information about these and other worldwide locations, visit www.derekprince.com.

Derek Prince Ministries Offices Worldwide

DPM – Asia/Pacific
✉ admin@dpm.co.nz
🌐 www.dpm.co.nz

DPM – Australia
✉ enquiries@au.derekprince.com
🌐 www.derekprince.com.au

DPM – Canada
✉ enquiries.dpm@eastlink.ca
🌐 www.derekprince.org

DPM – France
✉ info@derekprince.fr
🌐 www.derekprince.fr

DPM – Germany
✉ ibl@ibl-dpm.net
🌐 www.ibl-dpm.net

DPM Indian Subcontinent
✉ secretary@derekprince.in
🌐 www.derekprince.in

DPM – Middle East
✉ contact@dpm.name
🌐 www.dpm.name

DPM – Netherlands
✉ info@derekprince.nl
🌐 www.derekprince.nl

DPM – Norway
✉ xpress@dpskandinavia.com
🌐 www.derekprince.no

Derek Prince Publications Pte. Ltd.
✉ dpmchina@singnet.com.sg
🌐 www.dpmchina.org (English)
    www.ygmweb.org (Chinese)

DPM – Russia/Caucasus
✉ dpmrussia@gmail.com
🌐 www.derekprince.ru

DPM – South Africa
✉ enquiries@derekprince.co.za
🌐 www.derekprince.co.za

DPM – Switzerland
✉ dpm-ch@ibl-dpm.net
🌐 www.ibl-dpm.net

DPM – UK
✉ enquiries@dpmuk.org
🌐 www.dpmuk.org

DPM – USA
✉ ContactUs@derekprince.org
🌐 www.derekprince.org

Lightning Source UK Ltd.
Milton Keynes UK
UKHW041327110322
399879UK00009BA/2154